T0150691

First published in Great Britain in 1999
by Collins & Brown Limited
London House
Great Eastern Wharf
Parkgate Road
London SW11 4NQ

and

Richard Dennis Publications
The Old Chapel
Shepton Beauchamp
Ilminster
TA19 0LE

Copyright © Collins & Brown Limited and Richard Dennis Publications 1999

Text copyright © Christopher Frayling and Royal College of Art 1999

The right of Christopher Frayling to be identified as the author of this work has been
asserted by him in accordance with the Copyright, Design and Patents Act, 1988.

All rights reserved. No part of this publication may be reproduced, stored in a retrieval
system, or transmitted in any form or by any means, electronic, mechanical,
photocopying, recording or otherwise, without the prior written permission of the
copyright owner.

1 3 5 7 9 8 6 4 2

British Library Cataloguing-in-Publication Data: A catalogue record for this book is
available from the British Library.

ISBN 1 85585 7251

Editor: Ulla Weinberg
Art Director: Tony Cobb
Designer: Anna Subirós with thanks to Paul Freeth and Frank Stebbing

Reproduction by Classic Scan Pte Ltd., Singapore
Produced by Phoenix Offset, Hong Kong
Printed in China

100 years at the Royal College of Art

ART AND DESIGN

CHRISTOPHER FRAYLING

RICHARD DENNIS
PUBLICATIONS

C&B
COLLINS & BROWN

CONTENTS

COMMUNICATIONS

THE FUTURE

FLIGHT OF THE PHOENIX

In February 1954, Robin Darwin – my predecessor as Rector of the Royal College of Art – gave a now-famous lecture at the Royal Society of Arts. Called 'The Dodo and The Phoenix', the lecture contrasted the Dodo of old-style art and design education with the Phoenix of the new. An extinct creature, gently mocked in *Alice in Wonderland*, had made way, through natural selection, for a fabulous bird which, according to Greek legend, burned itself to ashes and rose again with new life. Something dead had become a symbol of everlasting renewal. Darwin, a direct descendant of Charles Darwin, concluded:

'It will not escape the attention of keen ornithologists, and quite ordinary persons besides, that the Dodo is, or at any rate was, a real bird, whereas the Phoenix was never more than a fantasy of the imagination. It may well be that in my enthusiasm for the College as it has risen from its ashes, I ascribe an equally mythical importance to it. If

so, I hope I may be forgiven. But I do sincerely believe that just as the Dodo and Phoenix are not only different in species but in kind, so has the Royal College of Art changed in a like manner during the last few years ...'.

The Phoenix soon became the unofficial symbol of the RCA. Richard Guyatt was commissioned to design a Phoenix motif for the Senior Common Room crockery. 'It was Robin's fantasy,' he recently told me, 'he said he felt pictorially peckish.' Then came publications and menus and ceremonial robes and mosaics and eventually holograms and digital drawings: even the silver College 'yardstick', still used on Convocation Day, has a Dodo at one end and a Phoenix at the other.

Meanwhile, this bird of the imagination seemed to be becoming a symbol of national renewal as well, in the brave new world of post-war reconstruction. Sir Basil Spence, architect of the new Coventry Cathedral, called his book about its building *Phoenix at Coventry* and his pamphlet *Out of the Ashes*. It was Spence, incidentally, who, on seeing the stained glass work of two young RCA students in their College studio one day, was 'excited beyond measure' and immediately commissioned them to design the nave windows for his great project. About 30 years later, another Rector – Jocelyn Stevens – flamboyantly referred to the College under his style of management as 'finger-lickin' Phoenix' and to the Darwin era as the 'era of the Dodos'. So today's Phoenix had become, by some law of the species, tomorrow's Dodo.

The Bauhaus lasted 14 years. Other art and design schools have been centre stage for a while, then faded into the background. The RCA is over 150 years old, or over a century old if the clock is started in 1896 when it was granted permission to use the name – the longest continuous experiment in publicly funded art and design education anywhere in the world. This is the story of 100 years of flights of the Phoenix, of an institution which has almost by definition renewed itself over and over again. It is preceded by a Victorian prologue which outlines the thinking and practices of the College's earliest incarnations – the Government School of Design and the National Art Training School, from 1837 to 1896.

The sourcebook you are reading is the result of teamwork. I co-ordinated the project, wrote the introductions, conducted the interviews and edited the texts of the theme and chronological spreads. Claire Catterall and her researchers, Juliet Bingham, Hannah Ford and Alistair O'Neill – all graduates of the RCA – compiled and drafted the spreads, wrote the captions, and selected the illustrations; very complex and time-consuming processes. The illustrations show work completed and exhibited while the individuals concerned were still at the College or work completed during subsequent professional careers. Occasionally, work is attributed to a particular decade when in fact it was made earlier: this is because the work is a key reason why the individual was involved with the College in the later period. Every possible effort has been made to trace copyright holders, and to check dates and career details. The design was co-ordinated by Tony Cobb, Visiting Professor of Graphic Arts at the College; his vision, determination and flair turned the concept of this ambitious book into reality. The designer of the book is Anna Subirós – herself a successful recent graduate of Graphic Design at the RCA.

Two aspects of the College's long history could not be fully acknowledged in a book of this format. The first is the fact that because the RCA is postgraduate – the only entirely postgraduate university of art and design on the planet – it depends to an unusual extent on the teaching, commitment and talent of staff and students on a multitude of undergraduate courses; not just in Britain but all over the world. The ex-students covered by this book are graduates of the RCA: in almost all cases, they also took first degrees or diplomas before they arrived there.

Secondly, the work of a key School – the School of Humanities – which offers courses in the history, philosophy and criticism of art and design to all College students, and has done so in one form or another for the last half century, could not be illustrated in the same way as the work of the studios. And yet it has helped in many different ways to shape the culture and atmosphere of today's RCA. Three of the book's researchers graduated from the V&A/RCA joint course in the History of Design, one from the Visual Arts Administration course. So the teaching and research of the School of Humanities is at the heart of this book, too.

Grateful thanks are due to the researchers, the designers and all the many graduates of the College, plus the arts organizations who have helped make this sourcebook possible. No one has ever before attempted a project on this scale about a single educational establishment, and it depended to an unusual extent on a network of contacts and supporters far too numerous to mention by name here. Very special thanks are due to Michael Frye CBE, who generously agreed to sponsor the book in the hope that the result would inspire future generations of young artists, craftspeople and designers. I hope so, too. The great fashion designer Issey Miyake once referred to the students of the RCA as 'a nourishment to the world'. This sourcebook is dedicated to them all.

Christopher Frayling, Rector, RCA, May 1999

VICTORIAN PROLOGUE

'You are to be in all things regulated and governed by fact. We hope to have, before long, a board of fact composed of commissioners of fact, who will force the people to be a people of fact, and of nothing but fact. You must discard the word fancy altogether.'

Emissary from the Government School of Design in Charles Dickens' Hard Times, *1854*

The biting satire on the Government School of Design in Charles Dickens' *Hard Times* (written a couple of years after the Great Exhibition in 1851) is an accurate portrayal of the bureaucratic and restricting system of art and design education in the Victorian period. Founded in 1837, the Government School was a product of the British government's decision to make the training of designers for industry a national responsibility, for the first time ever. By the early 1850s, the School was determined to propagate, among many other things, the view that a pattern on a flat surface should not – by reason of its over-lushness or illusory qualities – destroy the beholders' sense of its flatness. This was, it was felt, one of the hard lessons of the 1851 Great Exhibition. Advanced students at the School were to be told, with the aid of pictorial placards and with a high Victorian sense of infallibility, about 'false principles', such as 'the direct imitation of nature' and 'true principles' such as the application of conventional (meaning linear and geometrical) patterns to flat surfaces.

Design was popularly viewed to be a kind of visual language which could be taught entirely through drawing: as a training in mechanical accuracy of hand and eye. If students spent several years learning and practising the grammar of that language, then one day they might be able to go out into the world and improve the quality of everyday products – which was the point of the exercise. According to the School's Art Superintendent, the painter and critic Richard Redgrave, design was 'an aid to perception and a language of explanation ... a means of treasuring facts and collecting stores of truths'. And so the course at the Government School of Design began with simple line exercises and geometrical shapes, progressed to drawing from flat examples, then 'from the round' and then from nature, and then went on to modelling with charcoal, before finally reaching 'composition in design'. In the middle stages, students were required to make endless copies of plaster casts, some of which are still to be seen in the Victoria and Albert Museum's Cast Court.

In response to the criticism that this system did not give the students any direct knowledge of manufacturing processes or any understanding of how to think in three dimensions, another member of the School's staff Ralph

Wornum – who taught a somewhat dull course on the principles of ornament, as well as being Keeper of the Casts – had recently replied that the purpose of the Government School of Design was 'not how to apply a design, but what to design. While the accomplished practice of an Art may be a matter of five years, the mere mechanical process of application is, in comparison, a mere matter of five hours.' Design was something one did to things and the School was there to 'supply a complete and systematic course of education in relation to every kind of decorative work'. Successful students would be in a good position to apply their skills to a variety of manufactures. Like a visual poultice, perhaps.

Henry Cole and the Journal of Design and Manufactures

The system at the School of Design was masterminded by the indefatigable Henry Cole, one of the very few senior civil servants involved in British art and design education to have had an art education himself. He had studied watercolour painting with David Cox, had commissioned the first-ever Christmas card, had designed a prize-winning tea service (under the pseudonym of Felix Summerly) which Minton's manufactured for the rest of the century, and had a flair for publicity and drawing attention to himself that was unusual for his time. He was a pugnacious, rotund and easily caricatured fellow who was often pictured with his inseparable Yorkshire terrier Jim. That Charles Dickens had him in mind when he described 'the Government Officer' in *Hard Times*, is revealed by the manuscript draft in which 'Cole' is listed among the cast of characters. In June 1854, Dickens wrote to Henry Cole to let him know that he was passing the summer 'in the society of your friend Mr Gradgrind':

'I often say to Mr Gradgrind, that there is reason and good intention in much that he does – in fact, in all that he does – but that he overdoes it. Perhaps by dint of his going his way and my going mine, we shall meet at last at some halfway house where there are flowers on the carpets, and a little standing-room for Queen Mab's chariot among the Steam Engines.'

Cole had first let his outspoken views be publicly known in 1849, through the medium of his monthly *Journal of Design and Manufactures* – the first-ever periodical to be devoted to design. The Government School of Design, in its overcrowded base at Somerset House in the Strand, had, he wrote, started off well when it opened for business on 1 June 1837. A Select Committee of the House of Commons on Arts and Manufactures had reported in August of the previous year that, 'from the highest branches of poetical design down to the lowest connection between design and manufacture, the arts have received little encouragement in this country'. One way of improving Britain's poor performance relative to her overseas competitors (especially France, Prussia and Bavaria), in exporting the products of industries dependent on design, was to institute a School which would purvey 'not mere theoretical instruction only but the direct practical application of the Arts to Manufactures ... '. In England, such art education as existed, other than the tutoring of well-healed young people by itinerant drawing masters, seemed to be the monopoly of the Royal Academy Schools and was directed entirely towards fine art. But even at this very early stage, Cole noted, by referring to the fine arts as 'the highest branches', the Select Committee had sowed the seeds of future discord by implying that the decorative arts somehow fell into the 'lowest' category.

337–1896

Early Dilemmas

The founders of the School had known exactly what they didn't want: they didn't want any drawing from the human figure, since this might encourage young students to become artists rather than ornamentists; and they didn't want the School to be part of mainstream education, which in any case was in its infancy, so it would come under the aegis of the Board of Trade. But beyond these two negatives, they were working in a complete vacuum. There was no elementary training system on which to build and so, as one of the founders put it, 'we have established a university before we have any grammar schools'. Between 1842 and 1852, 21 'branch schools' were created or adapted from older foundations – Manchester, Coventry, Birmingham, York, Newcastle, Sheffield and Nottingham were among the earliest – following another recommendation of the Select Committee. The national system of art and design education in fact pre-dated the national system of any other kind of education, an indication of how seriously the early Victorians took the link in their minds between 'design' and industrial performance.

And yet, despite the well-meaning efforts of teachers such as the Aberdonian painter William Dyce (whose *Drawing Book of the Government School* became a standard text), the sculptor Alfred Stevens (who was appointed, as he said, 'Professor of everything'), and the young Richard Redgrave ARA, the course simply would not settle down. The collection of objects for students to copy soon took over most of the available space, evening classes proved far more successful than the daytime ones, there was too much emphasis on the laborious copying of architectural details, and the staff were divided into two warring aesthetic camps, the Nordic-Gothic tendency and the classical Italianizers. Most of the hapless students were, or aimed to be, skilled artisans, since this was the group targeted by the Select Committee as the key to design improvement in manufacturers. Many were in their teens, and some had been released from their apprenticeships by manufacturers who were only half convinced that the School could do better than their own factory floors; these manufacturers also seemed much more interested in establishing Academy-style art schools in their localities as a way of enhancing municipal prestige. The artisinal students preferred evening classes, the others preferred daytime.

A student revolt in April 1845, said to be the first sit-in in the history of British higher education, not only led to the introduction of figure drawing, but encouraged the School's governing body to make the practice compulsory, 'it being found by practical experience that the accurate delineation of beautiful models of the human figure is a most efficient means of educating the hand and the eye'. The opposite, in other words, of what the founders had said with equal vehemence a mere eight years before.

By the time Henry Cole entered the fray, a consensus was emerging that the future stability of the School depended on much more clear thinking about 'the science and principles of design', and on the removal of the heaps of plaster casts and exemplars (there were 800 casts of architectural ornament alone) from the pressurized teaching spaces. This latter thought was indirectly to lead to the foundation of what is today the Victoria and Albert Museum.

Cole was merciless in the *Journal of Design and Manufactures*. One of his editorials thundered that the School had only succeeded in taking skilled artisans or apprentices from the backstreets of England's soot-black

10

industrial cities and turning them after three or four years into unemployable facsimiles of fifteenth-century Florentines who 'normally cover dog kennels with crochets and finials ... and fall back on the dreary expedient of copying scroll and shell work ... '.

The First Generation

Although Cole had described the teachers and administrators responsible for the ill-conceived programme as a bunch of 'dilettanti half-informed bunglers', he was being less than fair to some of the early former students. Two of them, George Wallis and G. F. Duncombe, became his own personal assistants in the organization of the Great Exhibition: Wallis later became Keeper of Art in the South Kensington Museum. Another ex-student, Francis Moody, was made Instructor in Decorative Art responsible for supervising the decoration of the Museum's permanent buildings with mosaic panels, stained glass and engraved cement, and the crowning of the Albert Hall with its classical frieze. Octavius Hudson had already designed the Honiton lace for Queen Victoria's wedding dress; Frederic Shields was to become well known as an illustrator and architectural ornamentist; Henry Hugh Armstead rose to become an eminent designer of metalwork and jewellery, as well as one of the sculptors of the Albert Memorial; C. P. Slocombe designed an iron and brass gas-lamp for Buckingham Palace; and Frederick Andrew designed the backs of countless Victorian playing cards. Even a well-known painter, Edward Poynter, somehow managed to emerge from the early years of the School.

But the star of the group, and the first man ever to be called an industrial designer, had been Christopher Dresser. Dresser first entered the School in 1847 at the age of 15 and five years later was awarded a scholarship: his prize designs on the final stages of his course included 'printed fabrics', 'applying the principles taught by the School to a chintz' and 'garment fabrics'. In 1852 he became a student-lecturer. Some of his visual aids – careful botanical drawings of the structure of plants, mounted on canvas – have survived, and they reveal that he was teaching 'art botany' not as a form of surface decoration (nature as pattern and flatness), but as structure, the relationship of solid and void: he encouraged students to progress beyond copying to an understanding of form and 'fitness of purpose'. In one of his later lectures (he was to teach at the School until 1868), he argued that 'drawing schools' had their place 'furnishing the Royal Academy with pupils', but the real and still urgent need was for: 'a Royal Academy of decorative or applied art, wherein the highest knowledge of design in all its branches as required by our various manufactures, be fully given. Let ornament be treated as a fine art ... '. For him, knowledge of design – 'the science and principles' everyone was looking for – involved a mixture of the grammar of ornament, art botany, the study of type-forms, the history of ornament in Western and Eastern cultures, plus 'all technical knowledge necessary'.

The Art Training School

Cole had won his battle by the beginning of 1852. A new department of the Board of Trade, soon to be named the Department of Science and Art, was created with one permanent official at its head, Cole himself, assisted by one artist, and a Royal Academician at that, Richard Redgrave. New and slightly more spacious premises were secured on two floors of Marlborough House in St James's, the *Journal of Design and Manufactures* ceased publication, and a less dilettante teaching team was assembled with a distinct bias towards aesthetic rationalism and economy of ornament: professors and lecturers included the architect and design theorist, Gottfried Semper; the author of the compendious *Grammar of Ornament,* Owen Jones; the scientific botanist and author of *The Symmetry of Vegetation,* John Lindley; and Christopher Dresser, all of whose ideas were later to have an acknowledged influence on the architectural thinking of Frank Lloyd Wright and beyond him on the digital design of today. The new regime was launched with maximum public exposure when staff and students were involved in the design of the Duke of Wellington's funeral carriage (1852) and of the post office's new hexagonal cast-iron pillar box (1856), the first to bear the initials 'VR'. And the School was successfully moved from Marlborough House (where there were by now 1,500 plaster casts lying buried in the cellars) to a new site in soggy Brompton which would eventually accommodate a new museum of decorative art linked to the School in what was to become leafy 'South Kensington'. So Charles Dickens was being less than fair when he wrote that the Government Officer was obsessed to the exclusion of everything else with a deadening 'system to force down the general throat like a bolus'. But what gave chapter two of *Hard Times* a particular punch was the behaviour of Cole and Redgrave in their first few years of office.

Having taken the Government School apart, in print, for being 'a mere Drawing School', Cole and Redgrave's first report declared that in future 'general elementary instruction in art' would be their main priority, with 'the improvement of manufactures' – through the media of museums and travelling exhibitions – a secondary consideration. Cole had, apparently, become convinced, and it must have seemed to the art establishment something akin to a Damascus Road experience, 'that state interference in any special technical teaching, founded upon the assumption of trade requirements, does not succeed'. The original concept for the School had, he added, probably been based on a clerical error: the French phrase *école de dessin* had been mistranslated as 'School of Design' when what it really meant was 'Drawing School'. So the School would in future focus on drawing and be unrepentant about it. The Department of Science and Art became the responsibility of a Privy Council Committee on Education, the School's name was changed to The Central Training School for Art (1853) and then The National Art Training School (1863). Its prime function was announced as being to 'train Art Masters and Mistresses' and provide the printed materials for the ever-expanding, and ever-more-complex, national network of art schools. When Henry Cole took over, there were seventeen such 'branch schools' with a total annual grant of £16,200; by the time he retired in 1873, there were nearly 150 regional schools with a total grant of £286, 252, plus 'five hundred night classes for artisans' so that in all 'one hundred and eighty thousand boys and girls are now learning elementary drawing'.

Certificates from the National Art Training School were a passport, the only passport, into this system, and so the emphasis in future would be on the teaching of drawing, colouring, the human figure, modelling, ornament and 'technical instruction'. South Kensington would become the Vatican from which exact and fundamental guidance and a methodically graded, 23-stage course for pupils of all ages would be propagated, and in time this 'South Kensington system' would be exported to 'the Empire', to Canada and the USA. To use a more secular image, Britain's art education was now run on a uniform gauge and South Kensington was the terminus: one of Cole's earlier crusades had, indeed, been on behalf of a uniform gauge for the railways.

This was Charles Dickens's rule by the 'commissioners of fact'. At the same time, Cole and Redgrave increased revenue to the School by agreeing to admit private fee-paying students 'without reference to preparation for any branch of manufacture'. The sons and daughters of gentlemen, as distinct from apprentices and skilled artisans, could now pick up an education in drawing and painting – an offer which proved so popular that throughout the 1850s and 1860s the majority of daytime students came under this category. One unfortunate side-effect was that the integration of art and design, of 'the highest branches' and manufacture, made way for rich students studying art during the day, and poorer students studying design in the evenings. But, side by side with these developments, the School would still make an effort to 'instruct students in designing and c., to be applied to the requirements of trade and manufactures' and, with this in mind, Cole devoted virtually the entire departmental 'technical' budget to the South Kensington School in the expectation that the best design students from 'the branches' would apply there. Technical classes and workshops, at first co-ordinated by Gottfried Semper, were offered in ornamental metalwork, porcelain painting, woven textiles, furniture construction, enamelling, architectural decoration, casting and moulding (men only), wood engraving and lithography (women only). After Semper's departure, one of their main functions seems to have been to provide decoration for the new buildings of South Kensington – while the

printmaking courses for female students supplied illustrations for the Museum's catalogues.

Celebrated Artists and Successful Designers

Successive annual reports noted three major fault-lines in the technical classes: they were too expensive, they focused on the luxury end of the industrial spectrum rather than its mass-production centre, and there were tensions between the teachers-in-training, who had an amateur attitude, and the specialized designers, who wanted more access to the facilities. In 1863, at least one of these difficulties was addressed with the introduction of national scholarships for 'advanced students who might give evidence [in the form of an elaborate hatched or stippled drawing from an ornamental cast] of a special aptitude in design, and who intended to become designers for industry'. Over the next 20 years, according to the official literature, 76 (out of 145) of these scholars were to work as designers after leaving the School, either in-house or freelance.

But there were to be some very spectacular counter-examples. Scholar Luke Fildes was advised to become a designer of ecclesiastical mosaics: instead he became one of the great narrative painters of his age, with works such as *Applicants for Admission to a Casual Ward* and *The Doctor*, which became a great popular image, through printed versions, of devotion to duty.

George Clausen won a prize for the decoration of a horse-tramcar, but was also to become a very well-known painter of colourful rustic scenes and rural types such as *Labourers after Dinner* and *The Girl at the Gate*.

Other former students who became celebrated artists included Hubert von Herkomer, whose *The Last Muster* was the most often exhibited painting of late Victorian

England; Elizabeth Thompson (later Lady Butler) of *The Roll Call* and *Scotland for Ever* fame, whose popular depictions of the heroic ordinary British soldier became the standard representation in the quarter century before the First World War; and Henry Woods whose paintings of Venetian street life were almost as popular as the social realist works of his brother-in-law Luke Fildes. Lady Butler wrote about the public impact of such paintings, which, when exhibited, had to be railed off to protect them from the crowds of viewers: printed versions, she added, became a common accessory to the cluttered Victorian interior and she was torn between 'gratitude for the appreciation of one's work by those who know, and the uncomfortable sense of an exaggerated popularity with the crowd'. Maybe her work had become a form of interior design after all.

Other scholars who did take up a design career included Owen Jones's assistant Maria Edwards; Wedgwood designers Rowland Morris and Thomas Allen; three members of William Morris' Firm in Queen Square; six designers and modellers (including Leon Solon) for Minton's; several stained glass specialists for churches and textile designers based in Halifax and Kidderminster; the chief medallist of the United States Mint at Philadelphia; the engraver to the Royal Mint; and Mr Harbutt of plasticine fame. They had shared studio space with students such as Kate Greenaway, whose prize-winning floral tile design of 1864 was bought by the School as a teaching aid, and who published her earliest fantasy book illustrations while still on her course; and Gertrude Jekyll, whose garden designs were inspired by colour theories she first heard about in School lectures, and whose student sketchbook – full of ornamental motifs from Owen Jones – has survived. Jekyll, too, had one of her works used as a

visual aid, when her comparative anatomy lecturer used a Jekyll drawing as a printed illustration in a textbook. Summarizing this period in a valedictory lecture he gave at Manchester School of Art in 1877, Henry Cole noted that, 'when we talk of a School of Art now, everybody understands that we really mean a School of Fine Art'. But the phrase 'School of Fine Art' had a very particular meaning in this context: it meant 'training workmen to produce works of art for the whole people'.

The French Influence

In 1875, the painter of large-scale classical tableaux, Edward Poynter, had taken over from Richard Redgrave. He had been the very first Slade Professor of Fine Art and had strong views about 'the study of the living model' as distinct from 'the study of the antique', views which he called 'the French system,' because of its resemblance to the atelier system of the École des Beaux-Arts. One of the ironies of art and design education at this time is that as French educators were coming to admire the British system more and more – because it was grounded in principles – the Department of Science and Art decided to turn to the French system of fine art education because it wasn't. From now on, as a tired George Wallis put it, 'pictorial art is everything – ornamental art practically nothing'. But the pictorial art was of an academic kind. One of the characters in Daphne du Maurier's novel *Trilby* was based on Poynter, and for him 'there was never a modern – moderns didn't exist': the Impressionists were a passing craze; history painting with a moral message was the real thing.

Several of the old teachers left in a hurry, to be replaced by Alphonse Legros who would run the etching class, and Aimé-Jules Dalou (a refugee from the Paris Commune and

Rodin's studio) who took over the modelling class. Both were practitioners of the atelier system. Edward Lantéri, who had been one of Dalou's pupils in France and who was to succeed him at South Kensington, later wrote that through his enthusiastic teaching and demonstrating, Dalou gave an extraordinary impetus to sculpture and modelling. The birth of 'The New Sculpture' movement in Britain started here, building on the foundations laid by Alfred Stevens. Of the sculptors who made significant contributions to it, no less than ten – including Alfred Drury, Francis Derwent Wood, Albert Toft, Florence Steele and Esther Moore – emerged from the Dalou/Lantéri class.

Designers Edwin Lutyens and Detmar Blow, who would become important architects of the Edwardian era, were their fellow students. Lutyens in his late teens was already steeped in the writings of the Arts and Crafts Movement, and had a boyish interest in the vernacular architecture of Surrey; he won a national bronze medal for seven drawings of a 'country house'. There is a hoary old legend that Edwin Lutyens and Gertrude Jekyll – one of the great landscape and architecture partnerships – met as students at the School. In fact they were nearly a quarter of a century apart (Jekyll arrived in 1861, Lutyens in 1885), but met two years after Lutyens completed his course. An architect who was at South Kensington at about the same time as Jekyll was Herbert Gribble, who went on to design the Brompton Oratory.

A painter who was there at the same time as Lutyens was Jack Yeats, who registered in 1887 at a stage in his career when he was adjusting from graphic art and illustration towards painting in watercolour and oils: he was attracted to the School as a way of getting away from design.

The Birth of the RCA

The last decade of the nineteenth century saw the School renamed as The Royal College of Art. It now had the right to award its own diplomas, which entitled the recipients to a specially designed hood and gown, and a qualification that 'ranked as a degree for educational purposes'. The decade also saw its restructuring under the belated influence of the Arts and Crafts Movement, and its transfer of responsibility to the Board of Education.

Why Queen Victoria graciously granted permission for the change of style and title at this particular time is not clear. Was it because one of her daughters Princess Louise had studied modelling and sculpture at the School in 1868 at the age of 20 (the first princess to be educated publicly) and been guest of honour on prize day in 1888? Was it to bring the School into line with the other royal colleges of the South Kensington campus ('royal' in the sense of owing their origin to the vision of Prince Albert)? Queen Victoria had written to Princess Louise warning her about artists who 'mix with all classes of society and are therefore most dangerous'; she had added that sculpture was 'unnatural' for a lady, although 'watercolours are always nice' – provided, of course, the Princess remained an amateur. So one implication of the change may not have appealed to Her Majesty personally.

Whatever the reasons, the change was accompanied by some important reforms and by the hope – expressed in *The Studio* magazine – that the School would at last 'live up to its new title'. An official report had concluded with exasperation, 'how in the name of common sense can students be taught what is required for a special craft without the materials for that craft?' How this Arts and Crafts philosophy would accommodate other meanings of 'Art' was still an open question.

INTRODUCTION

The art curator Ann Compton has baldly – and justly – contrasted these two Hyde Park Corner sculptures. The Jagger howitzer, she says, was more than just an example of uncompromising realism by a soldier-artist who had had personal experience of the horrors of war: it was also 'a violent gesture of rebellion against the aesthetic cliché embodied by its neighbour, the langorous nude David by Derwent Wood, which commemorates, with sickening irrelevance, the dead of the Machine Gun Corps'. So, one of the great pieces of public sculpture in the realist tradition to be produced this century stood side by side with a formulaic and empty exercise in historical revival. Both were unveiled in 1925. The former student had evidently outgrown his Professor.

When Jagger was a student and Derwent Wood a Professor, the College was still dominated by the Arts and Crafts philosophy. But by the time the Royal Artillery Memorial was unveiled, the atmosphere and the philosophy had changed.

The New Spirit

By the mid-20s, William Rothenstein had been Principal for five years and was personally running the Painting School (which he did again in 1930). He dropped the adjective 'decorative', shifted the emphasis away from teacher-training, stated in his prospectus that the aim of the RCA was 'to give advanced students a full opportunity to equip themselves for the practice of Art', and employed practising artists and designers (many of them part-time) as staff instead of the traditional career 'art masters'.

Rothenstein's approach was a controversial departure from the historical mission of the RCA, and it took time to settle. The students of the transition period sometimes found the experience frustrating. The Principal, for his

At Hyde Park Corner there are two memorials to the fallen in the First World War, both of which have associations with the RCA. One is a massive stone sculpture of a 9.2in howitzer gun, guarded by four bronze figures, on a pedestal covered with elaborate reliefs: a memorial to soldiers of the Royal Artillery. The other is a nude male figure with his right hand on his hip and his left hand clutching a long sword: a memorial to the 'glorious heroes of the Machine Gun Corps'. The howitzer was by Charles Sargeant Jagger, who studied sculpture and modelling under Edward Lantéri between 1907 and 1911, and who then saw active service at Gallipoli and in the trenches of the Western Front. The nude was by Francis Derwent Wood, who had been a National Scholar at the National Art Training School in the late 1880s, before becoming Lantéri's successor as Professor of Sculpture at the RCA between 1918 and 1924.

part, reflected that 'the new spirit [of the College] was trying ... God's work was no miracle to some students, who looked rather at Cézanne's and Picasso's'. Although Rothenstein had more direct control over the Painting School, it was the Sculpture School which was the more successful at keeping 'the new spirit' at bay. Under Derwent Wood, Ernest Cole (1924–26), Gilbert Ledward (1926–29) and Richard Garbe (1929–46), the School continued to emphasize modelling, enlarging and academic sculpture, and to try and ignore the rise of the avant-garde in London.

Rothenstein was succeeded as Principal by the Post-Impressionist painter Percy Jowett, and wrote, 'the College was unlikely to become industrialized'. Gilbert Spencer (younger brother of Stanley) remained Professor of Painting and Richard Garbe remained Professor of Sculpture. Malcolm Osborne continued to run the Engraving School which he had taken over as Professor in 1924. The School had grown out of the 'etching class' of the Arts and Crafts period, which Frank Short had directed from 1891 onwards. It had now become an environment where original prints were created, and where wood-engraving and lithography were offered as well – monochrome copies of the old masters (Turner was Short's favourite) had long since made way for more personal works in interwar colours.

The Rise of the Phoenix

Robin Darwin, who became Principal in 1948, was to contrast the post-war revival of the College ('the Phoenix') with the dark days of Rothenstein and Jowett ('the Dodo'). His first priority was to turn the RCA into an institution with its own Council of Management and its own administration, in order to cut loose from the Ministry. The Dodo reference offended earlier generations of students – it still does – and Darwin's self-confidence in uttering it was helped by the fact that he was well connected in the higher echelons of the British establishment. Gilbert Spencer was asked to leave, making way for Rodrigo Moynihan. Frank Dobson took over from Richard Garbe, who had retired in 1946. And Robert Austin headed what was shortly to be called Printmaking rather than Engraving, in the footsteps of his teacher Malcolm Osborne – the last remaining link with the days of Lethaby and the Arts and Crafts.

Darwin was well aware of the pre-war pressure to realign teaching at the College, and he had agreed with the Ministry of Education that 'to provide a training for the professional easel-painter' was emphatically not a priority. So it is paradoxical that the reforms of the Darwin era (1948–71) made the Fine Art areas a force to be reckoned with. Paradoxical, too, that a non-hierarchical division of subjects, with industrial and graphic design and painting effectively on a par with each other, should prove so stimulating to fine artists. Robin Darwin, a painter himself, proved an adept promoter of the College's distinctive contribution to painting, sculpture and printmaking at a time when many undergraduate art colleges were offering a broader, more diagnostic approach. If his public statements in the early years were mainly concerned with 'the training of the industrial designer', he equally emphasized (in private or internal documents at first) that studies in painting and sculpture were not merely continuing 'on sufferance or for the sake of tradition', but as an essential adjunct to studies in design. It was unthinkable, he wrote in successive annual reports, to have an institution devoted to teaching and research in design, in isolation from the plastic arts.

Where students were concerned, according to Derrick Greaves – who was at the RCA in the transitional years from 1948 to 1952 – the staff at the College fell into two categories: 'chatters' and 'teachers'. The teachers believed in 'instruction', in teaching by demonstration, and in sitting with students while correcting their life drawings; while the chatters preferred a more discursive approach.

The Beaux Arts Years

The early to mid-1950s at the College have been dubbed 'The Beaux Arts Years', because of the strong connections between the School and Helen Lessore's Beaux Arts Gallery, with its emphasis on up-and-coming figurative and realist painters. College artists who exhibited there included former students Jack Smith, Derrick Greaves, Edward Middleditch, John Bratby, Frank Auerbach and Leon Kossoff. Works by Francis Bacon, who was an unofficial artist-in-residence at the RCA at this time after his studio burned down, were also exhibited at the gallery. In his 'Dodo and Phoenix' lecture of February 1954, Robin Darwin revealed that 'all the pictures in Mr. Francis Bacon's recent exhibitions have been painted in our studios'. Lessore later concluded that her great contribution was 'having concentrated into a little knot ... the best art of its time and place'.

Carel Weight and Two-way Traffic

Carel Weight succeeded Moynihan in 1957. 'A lively Fine Art Department', he said 'sparks off ideas.' By the early 60s, his 'two-way traffic' was in full swing. The influential 'Young Contemporaries' exhibitions showed the work of the so-called Pop generation, heralded by the autobiographical paintings of Peter Blake, the literary

Symbolist paintings of R. B. Kitaj and important works by David Hockney, Peter Phillips, Allen Jones, Derek Boshier and Patrick Caulfield (who arrived a year later than the others). It has been written of these young contemporaries: 'Perhaps the traditional College connections with design influenced these particular students, perhaps also they picked up on a new feeling in the air and drew it into their work, adopting a career commitment which underlay all their actions.' Actually, they had less in common than it seemed. But neo-romantic painter Keith Vaughan wrote that at last he understood 'how the stranded dinosaur must have felt'.

Sculpture Revitalized

In the Sculpture School, Bernard Meadows – who had been Henry Moore's assistant – was appointed as Professor at exactly this time, to shake the subject up. New materials, new technologies, new approaches seemed to be happening elsewhere, and Meadows' brief was somehow to give the School the kind of creative energy which painting had recently enjoyed.

There was a move from figurative sculpture towards abstraction, and from formal teaching to 'students discovering their own aptitude, their own direction, their own individuality'. The modelling stands at last disappeared. Some found the transition difficult, but sculptors such as Tony Cragg, Nigel Hall, John Panting, Roland Piché, Bill Pye and Alison Wilding were among the first generations to work as professional sculptors in significant numbers after leaving College. The Meadows philosophy has been inherited and developed by Phillip King (Professor from 1980 to 1990) and Glynn Williams (the current Professor).

Revolution in Painting

By the late 60s, the College had been granted the status of a university institution, and, under Peter de Francia (Professor from 1972 to 1986), the Painting School was beginning seriously to reflect on whether the painters wanted the RCA to be 'with it', when a university's job was more usually to stand outside it. 'Under Darwin', de Francia told the press, 'we were geared up to produce stars. We're not in a period of stardom now.' He added, in his inaugural lecture 'Mandarins and Luddites', that the 'mandarins' of the art world included 'the important dealers, a horde of cultural entrepreneurs and the majority of critics', while the 'Luddites' included all those who were attacking the practice of painting – including conceptual artists. For de Francia, painting was something to be thought about. The art establishment was not happy, but was reassured with its thought that the Professor was passionate about the making of paintings. Work in mixed media (performance, video, installations) was banished to the upper floors of the Darwin Building at Kensington Gore. There was talk of 'cultural workers'.

The result was an almighty collision, with the College authorities asking the School in 1980 to 'infuse aesthetic standards and values for the designers', and both staff and students of Painting replying that Fine Art could not be applied to design in this way – studied for its aesthetic standards and then put to something called practical use. The concept was very out of date where both art and design were concerned.

Peter de Francia was succeeded by Paul Huxley in 1986, who in turn was succeeded by one of de Francia's former students Graham Crowley – the current Professor – in 1998. The painting course moved in its entirety from Exhibition Road to the Kensington Gore site at the time of the changeover from de Francia to Huxley, and the transition from custom-made Victorian premises – with huge windows and a mural room – to new, smaller and lower-ceilinged studios was difficult: closer to the work of design and communications, yes, but no modern studio could hope to replicate those great spaces which went back to the days of Henry Cole.

The Continuing Debate in Fine Art

In 1986, the Printmaking course finally moved from within the ambit of Graphic Design to the School of Fine Art. Printmaking had been considered part of 'design' ever since the Arts and Crafts era, if not before: equally it was, and is, the only department in the College with an unbroken chain, from Professor to former student to Professor, which goes right back to the 1890s. Even with the arrival of Chris Orr, as successor to the late Tim Mara in 1998. So the move to 'Fine Art' was an historic one, just as the debates of 1980 about painting and design were historic – part of a series of reconfigurations of a central dilemma: how to teach art in a design environment and design in an art environment. There are, of course, no cut-and-dried answers, but the questions have continued to be very productive. The key, always, has been to balance, or collide, the orthodoxy of the moment with the innovations of successive young contemporaries: to know when the scaffolding can be taken away; or whether the student needed scaffolding in the first place, before finding his or her own way. The celebrated collision between Gavin Turk and the College authorities in summer 1991 – when Turk simply displayed at his final show a blue plaque which stated that Gavin Turk, Sculptor, worked here – symbolized an age-old dilemma, only with a very 1990s twist.

DAVID HOCKNEY

'I applied from Bradford in 1957, and started at the RCA in September 1959. That was because I was one of the last people still doing National Service – as a conscientious objector, I worked in hospitals for two years. On the application I wrote "occupation desired on leaving – teaching", because I think that was what you did to get the grant. Also, most people assumed that that's what you'd have to do to earn a living. In those days, in England, there were very few painters not associated with an art school. Francis Bacon wasn't associated, but there weren't many others. There are more full-time professional artists now, aren't there? Actually, I've never done much teaching – I feel perhaps I should have.

I was utterly provincial; I remember my first ever visit to London was when I was 17 or 18. I was brought up during the war and just after, and people didn't travel much. We hardly knew anyone who'd been to London. And the RCA was the main art school there; that's what they suggested to you at Bradford Regional College of Arts and Crafts, as it used to be called. I went to art school when I was 16, and you took their advice really. The painters teaching at the RCA were Carel Weight, Ruskin Spear, Ceri Richards, Roger de Grey, Colin Hayes, Sandra Blow. Some of them had been there 20, 25 years.

The very first thing I did there was two drawings of a whole skeleton, half life-size, and Ron Kitaj bought one of them. I thought, "Well, here I am, this is London and they'll all be very good", and I didn't know really what I should do. I hadn't been in art school for two years, so I remember thinking, "There's a skeleton hung up, I'll just make a kind of academic drawing of it which will take me 2 to 3 weeks." It did, actually. "This is how I'll start, and then I'll have a look around

FINE ART

and see what to do," I thought. There were the shows of American painting at that time. I saw the Pollock show at the Whitechapel in about 1958. Not long after he died, actually. Very lively. It seemed to be the first big new art that was un-Picassoesque. You'd become aware that American painting was more exciting than Paris, you see. Remember, in Bradford, life-drawing dominated everything, four days a week. And suddenly you were in a much more sophisticated School where they weren't going to impose this on you. So, "What will you do?" Lively people had noticed these exhibitions. And you didn't want to seem old-fashioned. Remember, too, that art school training before that was dominated by Sickert, therefore French painting from Sickert's time. So it was a question of "I'll develop something else."

After the abstract phase – well, anything on a flat surface is an abstraction, of course it is – but Ron Kitaj, who was the most serious student around, and about four years older than me, talked to me about dealing with the visible world and my own interests. Homosexuality was a big subject then. Taboo? Well, remember, in art schools it was a bit of a different world, a bohemian atmosphere. You didn't think quite like the rest of them. I remember Quentin Crisp was a model there, the first openly homosexual person I ever met. He would get up and make some amusing comments on people's drawings. And I'll tell you what I did. There used to be a student arts newspaper, just typed, and I did a review for it. There was this graffiti on the lavatory walls in 21 Cromwell Road, and you were always reading them, and so I did a review as though it was a gallery. One of the drawings I always remember was called "The Vomiting Cobra", and the moment you mentioned it,

DAVID HOCKNEY

every male person knew what you were talking about. I called the review "The Latrine Gallery, SW7". An influence at that time was Dubuffet – French art was still quite big – and he drew in a graffiti-like way. And I used graffiti a lot, realizing these were messages on a wall, meant to be read.

For my "major task", between the second and third years, the subject I did was "The Birthday", because I'd gone to New York on my 24th birthday, 9th July 1961, and that was a very exciting thing for me. I'd only been abroad once before, to Paris. The painting had "Queens" written on it, after the suburb of New York. I don't suppose they'd call anything "a major task" today. In New York you saw another life. It was much more open than London. Big gay bars you didn't have here. I remember going into a bar, and a popular song was *Hats off to Larry* and all these kids lifted their hats off. Stunning stuff, I thought.

One or two students who had a bit more space used to work at home, but I never did because I never had enough. I only slept in my room in Earl's Court. And I'd arrive at Exhibition Road at seven to seven-thirty in the mornings, before Lyons had opened in South Kensington, and I used to make my own tea in there. Always Typhoo, my mother's favourite. Then Mrs Buckett would come round and serve a cup of tea at eleven o'clock in the morning and three o'clock in the afternoon. You had to sign in in the morning. Everybody was on a grant, therefore you had to comply with the rules. You were taking their money. And you just signed in; lots of students weren't serious about it, some were working all the time. For instance, to get all the Painting School together – there were about 90 students – a notice would have to be put up at least a week before to make sure they'd all see it. And once they put up a notice: "All the School will meet in Studio D – very important. Signed Roger de Grey." And nobody knew what it was about, even I didn't know. And I used to work till ten o'clock at night, and I must admit occasionally I'd go into Carel Weight's office and look at the mail. I was known as "our man in the staff-room". Because it was wide open. So I knew about certain things going on. But even I didn't know what that notice was about. The staff would walk around the studios, but if they saw you were working away, they tended to leave you alone. There were always people painting flowers in the top corridor, in the old art school way, and usually they'd spend more time talking to them. And Carel Weight always had little girlfriends, favourites, who painted little flowerpots. Slowly, you know.

I'll never forget Richard Hamilton, who was teaching in Interior Design – he did this unofficial crit one afternoon and he was very excited by what was going on: he saw straightaway, and the students recognized he saw what was evolving there. The way Carel Weight and Roger de Grey probably didn't. They didn't know quite what was going on with us. They threw out Allen Jones at the end of the first year, and a lot of students were told their situation would be reviewed. But I always got on quite well, because I would spend time drawing in the life rooms. I always assumed modern art was confusing them in a way, and that's why they introduced the new system of General Studies when I was there. They didn't have a policy or any clear idea how to deal with it, so they left it to the students. It was a very lively place, with some bright students, so I suppose it didn't matter, if it was working fine. You can have teachers who are very influential on you, who fight with you, or ones you fight against. Either can work, as long as there's something stimulating. Argument is stimulating, just as long as there's an argument, not authority saying "this must be this". Actually, they encouraged the argument, they really did, which is one reason why it was lively.

When they said they were giving me a gold medal, I did laugh at that. I didn't think life was about prizes, but in the end you have to be gracious. What you do is what counts. Painting is still not an academic subject; on the other hand you do need schools for it. But I went out and bought a gold lamé jacket. People thought I'd worn it every day, but I only ever wore it twice, believe it or not – once for that gold medal and once for some photographs Snowdon took. My mother thought it was an official jacket that you got for getting a medal. Remember all young artists – anybody who is doing anything – naturally want to attract attention. It's a perfectly natural thing. And I always say, "Well, the lively ones will do that, whether someone's complaining about it or not." I'd seen the jacket in the window of Cecil Gee's in Shaftesbury Avenue. Student clothes were dingy then, really. This was for a bandleader – but overtones of Elvis, don't you think?

Those years when you're at College are very formative. I went there when I was 22 and left at 25. Those three years make a big difference: you're going to move quite quickly really. Looking back, I thoroughly enjoyed it and realized I'd learnt a great deal, coming into contact with a wider range of people. At that time they began to be interested in the young, what they called "The Young Contemporaries". And with the paintings I did for those exhibitions, I became aware as an artist rather than as a student. The College was a very alive place, and in a way the staff didn't hinder that – in the end they encouraged it. And they did pick the students in the first place. So you realized they were quite aware. I mean, they can't have been just blind.'

20s PAINTING

Following the appointment of Walter Crane as Principal from 1898 to 1899, the Council of Art recommended that the recently named Royal College of Art should be divided into four Schools: Mural and Decorative Painting, Sculpture and Modelling, Architecture, and Design.

The main purpose of instruction at this time was to train students to teach in art schools. But, as Crane had hoped, the Painting School began to produce a series of highly individual artists. In the years preceding the First World War, these artists experimented with a variety of styles.

However, it was not until William Rothenstein was appointed Principal in 1920 that the RCA was transformed from an institution that produced design and art teachers, and the occasional inventive practitioner, into a fully-fledged art school. Rothenstein did this, in part, by employing professional artists and designers on a part-time basis – an innovation at the time. The appointment of Paul Nash, a key artist of the interwar years, to the Design School in 1924, was to help widen the parameters of teaching far beyond the 'Elementary Ornament and Design' course of his predecessor W. R. Lethaby.

Jack B. Yeats
(1871–1957)
Student 1887
The Combat, 1897

Frederick Etchells
(1886–1973)
Student 1908–11
The Hip Bath, c. 1911

Barnett Freedman
(1901–58)
Student 1922–25
Staff 1928–40
Bagpipe Player, 1929

Douglas Percy Bliss
(1900–84)
Student 1922–25
Self Portrait, 1923

Ceri Richards
(1903–71)
Student 1924–27
Staff 1956–61
Couple Dancing, c. 1953

Edward Burra
(1905–76)
Student 1923–24
Harlem, 1934

FINE ART

Gilbert Spencer
(1892–1979)
Student 1912–14
Staff 1930–32
Professor 1932–48
The Crucifixion, 1915

Percy Horton
(1897–1970)
Student 1922–24
Staff 1930–49
Unemployed Man, 1936

Edward Bawden
(1903–89)
Student 1922–25
Staff 1930–40, 1948–53
Cliffs & Waterfall, Carsaig, c. 1950

Vivian R. Pitchforth
(1895–1982)
Student 1922–25
Staff 1937–39
Old Stone Waller, 1925

Eric Ravilious
(1903–42)
Student 1922–25
Staff 1930–39
Edward Bawden Working in his Studio, c. 1930

Charles Cyril Mahoney
(1903–68)
Student 1922–26
Staff 1928–30, 1938–39, 1946–53
Mural of Figures in a Garden, c. 1947–53

Elisabeth Vellacott
(b. 1905)
Student 1925–29
Portrait of Althea Willoughby, 1929

Morris Kestelman
(1905–98)
Student 1926–29
Sussex Farm, 1929

Paul Nash
(1889–1946)
Staff 1922–25, 1938–39
The Shore, 1923

30s PAINTING

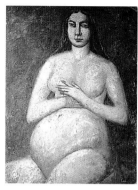

Cecil Collins
(1908–89)
Student 1927–31
Maternity, 1929

John Piper
(1903–92)
Student 1928–29
Visiting Staff
Collage, c. 1969

The awakening of Surrealism within British painting began to influence the student work produced within the Painting School. Taking their cue from the developing work of Paul Nash and Edward Burra, artists attempted to reconcile this foreign influence within a British context. The traditional landscape genre became the place where artists courted abstraction. Although the aesthetic objectives were still conservative, the works often made use of dislocated objects and unusual places to suggest a sense of unease. A distinctive feature was a politically progressive approach that acknowledged the climate of social unrest, but created images suggesting a retirement from reality.

In a somewhat different direction, the 'class of 22', which included Eric Ravilious and Edward Bawden, began to attract public attention with the large number of commissions they were undertaking as both designers and artists. This flexibility was in many ways stimulated by Nash who taught both painting and design. As Bawden was later to recount:

'Nash talked to us individually in the manner of two artists exchanging their personal experiences. There was no artificial barrier, no talking down

Evelyn Dunbar
(1906–60)
Student 1929–33
Landgirls going to bed, 1943

Thomas Samuel Haile
(1909–48)
Student 1931–35
Reclining Figures, 1935

Harry Thubron
(1915–85)
Student 1938–40
Setenit, 1976

Paul Nash
(1889–1946)
Staff 1924–25, 1938–39
Nocturnal Landscape, 1938

FINE ART

Kenneth Martin
(1905–84)
Student 1929–32
*Chance Order Change 13,
'Milton Park A', 1980*

Mary Martin
(1907–69)
Student 1929–32
*After Watteau: The Scale of
Love, c. 1929*

Ruskin Spear
(1911–90)
Student 1931–35
Staff 1948–75
Self Portrait, 1932

Robert Buhler
(1916–89)
Student 1936
Staff 1948–75
Dedham, Suffolk, 1959

John Nash
(1898–1977)
Staff 1934–40, 1948–58
The Cornfield, 1918

Sir William Rothenstein
(1872–1945)
Principal 1920–35
Self Portrait, c. 1930

as between God and man, teacher and the one who was being taught. Nash brought into the dingy mustiness of the room a draught of fresh air.'

The popularity of the works of the 'class of 22' owed much to their illustrational quality. Artists were greatly influenced by their training in wood engraving: woodcuts were the fashionable print medium of the interwar years.

The increasing attention focused on the RCA was the result of a concerted effort by Rothenstein to raise the profile of the whole school. Mural design, in particular, attracted attention, garnering prestigious public projects and bolstering the RCA's reputation. The Mural Room in the Exhibition Road building became the site for a major revival, especially in the 1930s. The Board of Education was impressed, but increasingly alarmed that the College was moving away from design. At a time of economic depression, the Board felt there were other national priorities.

40s PAINTING

The move to Ambleside following the outbreak of the First World War was to lend an idyllic air to the students' work: watercolour sketches and community projects flourished. *Picture Post* visited the site and reported: '... a throne, a model and a clutter of easels, paints and canvasses' littered the peacetime ballroom of a fashionable hotel, and that groups of young artists would go 'off into the mountains for several days at a time'.

After the war, the return to London proved problematic, as the Exhibition Road site was in chaos and the Queensgate sheds had been used as building huts. The lack of space and resources prompted the Board of Education to consider abandoning painting and sculpture at the RCA and even changing the school's name to the Royal College of Design.

But with the appointment of the flamboyant and well-connected Robin Darwin as Principal, this view was challenged and overturned; and the Board of Education lost its direct voice on RCA matters.

One of the first challenges Darwin faced was to make the College self-governing. He was instrumental in introducing the College's own board of management and control over admissions and examinations.

Albert Richards
(1919–45)
Student c. 1940
Building a Hutted Camp in Essex, 1942

Malcolm Hughes
(1920–97)
Student 1946–50
The Performers, 1950

Rodrigo Moynihan
(1910–90)
Professor 1948–57
The Teaching Staff of the Painting School, RCA, 1949–50, 1951

Sir Robin Darwin
(1910–74)
Principal 1948–67
Rector 1967–71
Portrait of Sir Hugh Casson, 1957

Colin Hayes
(b. 1919)
Staff 1949–84
Self portrait, 1982

Charles Cyril Mahoney
(1903–68)
Student 1922–26
Staff 1928–30, 1938–39, 1946–53
Wrotham Place from the Garden, c. 1952

Derek Hirst
(b. 1930)
Student 1948–51
Interior of a Kind, 1965–66

John Minton
(1917–57)
Student 1936–38
Staff 1948–57
Death of Nelson, 1952

The aftermath of the war brought an unusually diverse range of individuals into the College. Students were older – many of them had seen active service in the war and were given special grants (a new development) to retrain at the College. In addition, a wider range of social classes was represented. These changes were to prove crucial to the College's subsequent development.

However, in spite of the radical changes in the day-to-day life of the College, established ideas and techniques still persisted around painting, such as drawing with the paintbrush, using a coloured ground to unify composition, and using a limited palette. Much of this was stimulated through the tutors, and reflected a drab, austere environment.

Rodney Burn
(1899–1984)
Staff 1929–31, 1946–65
Two Standing Nudes, c. 1930

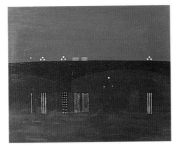

Kenneth Rowntree
(1915–97)
Staff 1949–58
Putney Bridge Night-piece, c. 1958

Robert Buhler
(1916–89)
Student 1936
Staff 1948–75
Barnett Freedman, 1947

Graham Sutherland
(1903–80)
Visiting Staff
Entrance to a Lane, 1939

PAINTING

Alistair Grant and *The Rebel*

1. GENESIS Scholarship to the Royal College of Art. Praised by Mr Darwin

2. RECOGNITION Designs tableau for the Chelsea Arts Ball. First painting exhibited at the Tea Centre

3. SUCCESS Discovers Banana Motif. One-man exhibition (on a banana motif) sells out. Praised by Sir John Rothenstein

4. TRIUMPH Commissioned to paint Lady Docker in gold leaf. Praised by Sir Alfred Munnings

5. DOWNFALL Expelled from the London Group. Paints Lady Munnings' dog. A.R.A

6. RUIN Televised sitting next to Sir Winston at Royal Academy banquet. R.A. Knighted.

Ronald Searle. The Rake's Progress: The Painter, published in Punch, 1954

Stills from The Rebel, 1961

When W. A. Whittaker, producer of a new comedy film about an artist, arrived at the RCA in 1959, his intention was to commission the worst student painter to make some truly awful pictures as props for the film. The film was to be called *The Rebel* and was to star Tony Hancock as a frustrated city clerk who finds salvation as a 'Sunday Painter', but who is then mistaken in Paris for an artistic genius.

The script, written by Ray Galton and Alan Simpson, demanded two sets of paintings: a 'serious' and 'painterly' set, and a set in 'Infantilist' style to be attributed in the film to Hancock. 'Infantilism' was a fictional artistic term of Galton and Simpson's making, meaning an unskilled painter with no formal training, whose work is mistaken as 'primitive' or 'naive'. Herein lies the comedy.

When Whittaker arrived at the Painting School, he was met by tutor Donald Hamilton-Fraser who recommended that he first went to Zwemmer's galleries to see the work of young tutor Alistair Grant which would certainly fulfil the criteria for the 'serious' set of paintings. On liking what he saw, Whittaker commissioned Grant to paint the 'Infantile' paintings as well.

PAINTING

Alistair Grant and *The Rebel*

The Rebel has gone on to achieve cult status as a British film about popular attitudes towards painting in the 50s – relying on Paris as a setting rather than say, New York. Lucien Freud claimed it was a 'pithy film about the contemporary art world', exposing the hypocrisy of its value systems. The art critic Peter Fuller claimed he was impressed by the film as a child and in his later career even used 'Infantilism' in his own critical vocabulary.

Much of the film's script was inspired by the press of the day, in particular the notoriety of the Painting School at the RCA. Galton and Simpson relied on Sunday papers and art magazines as source material for the 'art' elements of the storyline. A survey of the press the Painting School received, reveals interesting parallels.

A cartoon by Ronald Searle from *The Rake's Progress* series published in *Punch* is similar to scenes in the film. Although based on the famous series of paintings and later prints by William Hogarth, Searle transposed these to the life of a painting student at the College in the 50s. The painter's downfall within the cartoon happens when he enters the art world through

William Green, RCA Painting studio, 1958

Still from The Rebel, 1961

**Fred Buckett
Bob The Cat, 1945**

an institutional route (Robin Darwin makes a cameo appearance), and ends up a pompous figure of the establishment.

Fred Buckett, a janitor at Exhibition Road who was often sent to tidy the mess left by painters in the annexe attached to the museum, became well known as a 'Sunday painter' who hung his efforts in the corridors. An article in a *Picture Post* of 1953 shows him as very near in spirit and painterly style to Hancock in *The Rebel*.

Even the famous bicycle painting scene in the film was based on an article which appeared in *Life* magazine in 1958, and on the action paintings of student William Green.

Yet in spite of all this, within the film an institutional route to becoming an artist is never mentioned, nor is there any direct reference to the RCA. In many ways, the film reinforces the popular view of a painter as being born with his/her talent rather than learning it. Perhaps even sadder is the fact that after the shooting of the film, the 'Infantile' paintings were destroyed by Elstree Studios who considered them merely props. Today, they are much preferred to the 'painterly' ones.

50s PAINTING

Following the devastation of the Second World War, the staff of the Painting School, under the direction of Professor Rodrigo Moynihan, introduced changes in teaching practice in the wake of contemporary artistic trends, such as social realism and abstraction.

Rodrigo Moynihan, Ruskin Spear, John Minton and Robert Buhler were recruited by the Principal, Robin Darwin, from the staff at Central School of Art and Design. Their appointments brought a new style of teaching to the School that was informal, almost conversational in approach, in contrast to the earlier method of teaching by demonstration.

Championing the mural for the social cause of the Welfare State, many members of staff were commissioned by the Arts Council to produce work for the exhibition '60 Paintings for '51', part of the Festival of Britain. The exhibition also included Moynihan's monumental painting of the teaching staff at the Painting School.

In contrast to the brave new world that the Festival was meant to set into motion, British painting developed an interest in the drab, the ordinary and the everyday of post-war austerity. Critic David Sylvester, a lecturer at

Derrick Greaves
(b. 1927)
Student 1948–52
Domes of Venice, 1953–54

Edward Middleditch
(1923–87)
Student 1948–52
Portrait of a Woman, 1951

Bruce Lacey
(b. 1927)
Student 1951–54
Vultures, 1954

Alan Reynolds
(b. 1926)
Student 1952–53
The Village, Winter, 1952

Joe Tilson
(b. 1928)
Student 1952–55
Visiting Staff
A-Z Box of Friends & Family, 1963

Anthony Whishaw
(b. 1930)
Student 1952–55
Drawing (Landscape), 1983

34

FINE ART

Jack Smith
(b. 1928)
Student 1950–53
Still Life with Cherries, 1954–55

Peter Coker
(b. 1926)
Student 1950–54
Percy Jowett, 1954

John Bratby
(1928–92)
Student 1951–54
Staff 1957–58
Mural Studio at RCA, n.d.

Frank Auerbach
(b. 1931)
Student 1952–55
Untitled, 1955

John Barnicoat
(b. 1924)
Student 1952–55
Staff 1976–80
Two abstract compositions, 1955

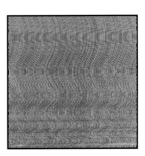

Bridget Riley
(b. 1931)
Student 1952–55
Fall, 1963

Jean Cooke
(b. 1927)
Student 1953–55
Staff 1964–74
Portrait of John Bratby, c. 1968

Peter Blake
(b. 1932)
Student 1953–56
Staff 1964–76
Children Reading (Comics), 1955

Leon Kossoff
(b. 1926)
Student 1953–56
City Building Site, 1953

50s PAINTING

Brian Fielding
(1933–87)
Student 1954–57
Antique Room, 1957

Malcolm Morley
(b. 1931)
Student 1954–57
SS France, 1974

the RCA at the same time as Francis Bacon was artist-in-residence, wrote in an exhibition review at this time:

'The post-war generation takes us back from the studio to the kitchen ... as part of an inventory which included every kind of food and drink, every kind of utensil and implement, the usual plain furniture, and even the baby's nappy on the line. Everything but the kitchen sink? The kitchen sink too ...'

At the Royal College the 'kitchen sink' gave early success to artists such as John Bratby and Jack Smith, but diverted attention from the work of Frank Auerbach and Leon Kossoff. The difference of age and experience between the young and older students became a source of friction. As Bratby wrote in a humorous article of 1952, entitled 'Frustrated Painters of a Generation':

'... the art schools ... suddenly became overcrowded with men who had seen death and sometimes caused it ... Barrack discipline, and austerity, and philistine army conversation, were replaced by the loosest scholastic freedom, the glamour of nude models ... instead of the sergeant-major there was the tired, sloppy art-teacher who lived in philosophically justified adultery ...'

Alan Green
(b. 1932)
Student 1955–58
Cerulean, 1986

Sonia Lawson
(b. 1934)
Student 1955–59
Homage to Molière and Watteau, 1981

Alistair Grant
(1925–97)
Student 1947–51
Staff 1955–86
Professor 1986–90
Purple Composition, n.d.

Leonard Rosoman
(b. 1913)
Staff 1956–76
Portrait of Lord Esher in a Studio at the RCA, 1978

FINE ART

Robyn Denny
(b. 1930)
Student 1954–57
Drawing, 1957

Richard Smith
(b. 1931)
Student 1954–57
First Fifth, 1962

Stuart Brisley
(b. 1933)
Student 1956–59
Head, 1957

Ruskin Spear
(1911–90)
Student 1931–35
Staff 1948–75
Portrait of Sir Robin Darwin, 1961

John Nash
(1898–1977)
Staff 1934–40, 1948–58
Fallen Tree, 1955

Francis Bacon
(1909–92)
Artist-in-Residence 1950–51
Man Turning on the Light, 1973/4

America became a cultural force in its promotion of abstract expressionism and in its aesthetic of plenty. By the mid-fifties this had opened the Painting School to student abstract painters. Probably unbeknown to them (and to their tutors), the Independent Group, which met at the ICA (Institute of Contemporary Arts), was already formulating a British popular aesthetic based on America's model of abundance.

By the time of Carel Weight's appointment as Professor in 1957, the Painting School had become the permissive yet prescriptive environment that would incubate the beginnings of British Pop. Weight's regime was not prescriptive – there was no longer any attempt to impose an academic style. But there were arguments between the generations when students interpreted their 'major projects' in too loose a way, or took their interdisciplinary contacts with other courses too far.

PAINTING

Pop & Ark

Pop in its broadest sense was germinated and cross-fertilized at the RCA from the mid-50s. Much of this was due to the interdisciplinary structure of teaching, as Carel Weight, Professor of Painting from 1957, noted:

'A lively Fine Art Department sparks off lively ideas. There is a strong two-way traffic. A lot of our students work in plastics, and the Textiles students gave an exhibition of their work recently that looked like an exhibition of paintings.'

Almost as important as the generation of visual ideas was the notoriety keenly cultivated by students and some staff that fuelled widespread exposure. Robyn Denny's 1959 shop-window mural for men's outfitters Austin Reed was an act of artistic entrepreneurship that heralded Swinging London and set the tone.

Ken Russell's 1962 television documentary *Pop goes the Easel* featuring Painting tutor Peter Blake and students Peter Phillips, Pauline Boty and Derek Boshier sharply presented a visual education that was as rigorous in lifestyle as it was in referencing popular culture.

Unlike the Independent Group, the cultural think-tank at the Institute of Contemporary Arts of the early 50s, that originated the Pop aesthetic from

Robyn Denny
Austin Reed Mural, 1959

the American realm of mass production, practitioners at the RCA added a witty use of their own visual heritage and a dash of emotion to their version of Pop. Inspiration was as likely to come from Portobello Market as it was from Tinseltown; particularly important was the visual mix – brash American imagery would be whimsically hand-rendered as if to assert cultural difference.

The student magazine *Ark* came to define the range of these influences and became emblematic of Pop's developing

relationship with the professional design industries. This was mirrored at the RCA in the rise in significance of the School of Graphic Design, which gave a new edge to the public 'look' of the College and its activities.

Such was the 'two-way traffic' that a small detail of some medals in a painting by David Hockney became the inspiration for final year work by Textiles student Zandra Rhodes, which in turn became a furnishing fabric for Heals. Rhodes then went on to become a fashion designer.

Peter Phillips
Sunday Times Magazine cover,
July 1964

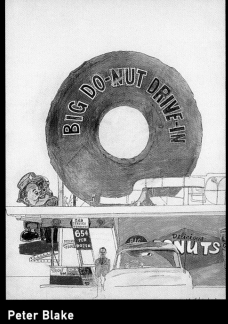

Peter Blake
Big Do-Nut Drive-In, 1963

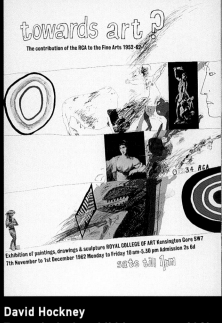

David Hockney
Towards Art?, exhibition poster, 1963

Pauline Boty
The Only Blond in the
Whole World
(Marilyn Monroe), 1964

60s PAINTING

Students in the late 1950s were the first to react in unison against the top-down education offered by the Painting School. Robin Darwin noted:

'The student of 1959 is less easy to teach because the chips on his shoulder, which in some cases are virtually professional epaulettes, make him less ready to learn; yet this refusal to take ideas on trust, though it may not be congenial to the tutor, may in the long run prove to be a valuable characteristic.'

One group in particular was quick to establish a self-mythologized status. Comprising R. B. Kitaj (who was the oldest of the group), Derek Boshier, Allen Jones, Patrick Caulfield, Peter Phillips and David Hockney, the group established itself as early as 1961 at the 'Young Contemporaries' exhibition. With Phillips as president of the organization committee and Jones as the secretary, they created a group identity aided by the critic Lawrence Alloway and in opposition to the students of the Slade School of Art.

In response, the Arts Council put on a touring show illustrating the contribution of the RCA to British art between 1952 and 1962, called 'Towards Art?'.

Bill Culbert
(b. 1935)
Student 1957–60
Kensington Gore, 1960

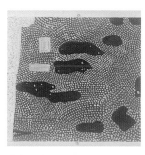

John Doughill
(b. 1934)
Student 1957–60
Staff 1977
Window 16/14, 1996

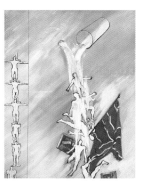

Derek Boshier
(b. 1937)
Student 1959–61
Drinka Pinta Milka, 1962

Pauline Boty
(1938–66)
Student 1959–62
It's a Man's World II, 1965–66

Patrick Caulfield
(b. 1936)
Student 1960–63
Christ at Emmaus, 1963

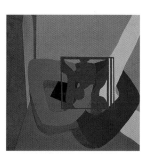

John Loker
(b. 1938)
Student 1960–63
Untitled, 1963

FINE ART

Adrian Berg
(b. 1929)
Student 1958–61
Staff 1987–89
*Gloucester Gate, Regent's Park,
June, 1982*

Allen Jones
(b. 1937)
Student 1959–60
Orange Skirt, 1964

R. B. Kitaj
(b. 1932)
Student 1959–61
Homage to Herman Melville 1960

Frank Bowling
(b. 1936)
Student 1959–62
Painting No. 2, 1962

David Hockney
(b. 1937)
Student 1959–62
Adhesiveness, 1960

Peter Phillips
(b. 1939)
Student 1959–62
Motorpsycho (Club Tiger), 1962

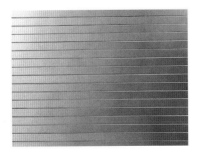

Michael Moon
(b. 1937)
Student 1960–63
Untitled, 1970

Victor Burgin
(b. 1941)
Student 1962–65
Untitled, 1965

Ian Dury
(b. 1942)
Student 1963–66
Nightboy, 1966

60s PAINTING

Bill Jacklin
(b. 1943)
Student 1964–67
The Invitation Card, 1962–64

John Bellany
(b. 1942)
Student 1965–68
Staff 1969–73
The Witch, 1968

The sense of conflict between staff and students fuelled a rebellious attitude among the young artists. Jones failed his interim assessment and was thrown out, Phillips received a warning and Hockney nearly failed on a technicality.

Their strongly-directed figuration can be traced in part to the influence of Peter Blake who was now teaching at the RCA and exhibiting widely. As Ian Dury, a student of Blake, recalled:

'... it took Mr Blake to show my generation of Essex layabouts how to convert our lifestyle and private obsessions into artistic energy. Easels were soon creaking with real culture. Art suddenly became a living thing. I once showed Peter a flash Harry collage of 100 pairs of naked bosoms snipped from *Jean*, *Nugget* and *Playboy* magazines and he correctly identified every tit either from memory or by print colour.'

In general, there was a concerted interest in style and in being style-conscious. This became apparent in the flatness of much of the glamorous imagery, and in the wide range of visual source material.

Matching the evolution of style with the speed of ideas, a pace was created that gave Carel Weight cause for concern:

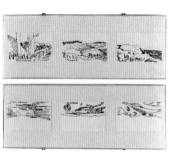

David Tremlett
(b. 1945)
Student 1966–69
The Cards, 1972

Keith Milow
(b. 1945)
Student 1967–68
1 2 3 4 5 6 ... B, 1970

Roger de Grey
(1918–95)
Staff 1954–73
Path in Wood, 1979

Merlyn Evans
(1910–73)
Student 1931–33
Staff 1964–73
Polynesian Fantasy, 1938

FINE ART

Graham Ovenden
(b. 1943)
Student 1965–68
Contemporary Girl, 1971

Brendan Neiland
(b. 1941)
Student 1966–69
Degree Show, 1969

Peter Blake
(b. 1932)
Student 1953–56
Staff 1964–76
Kamikaze, 1965

Sandra Blow
(b. 1925)
Staff 1960–75
Untitled Abstract, c. 1961

Mary Fedden
(b. 1915)
Staff 1958–64
Untitled, n.d.

Carel Weight
(1908–1997)
Staff 1947–57
Professor 1957–72
Country Lane, n.d.

'With all this going on ... the scene by about 1965 must have appeared chaotic to a student desperately looking around for new means of expression. It must have seemed as though everything had been done.'

The Pop generation had excited the media, and the subsequent generation found it difficult to establish a niche. Meanwhile, the Pop painters' careers continued to develop after they had left the College, sometimes in radically different directions.

At the same time, the Painting School began to develop a reputation for turning out a consistent stream of abstract painters. Although historically eclipsed by American Abstract Expressionism and the figuration of RCA Pop, abstraction was to become a key thread in the development of modern British painting.

PAINTING

David Hockney

At the RCA, David Hockney was allocated an Exhibition Road cubicle to use as a studio in 1959. Quickly realizing that it would be noticed by the regular stream of people who passed each day, Hockney staged an on-going exhibition of his paintings – and him painting them – which taught him the importance of an audience.

On enrolling in the Painting School, he threw himself into rigorous studies of the human figure to demonstrate his considerable skill. He then dabbled in abstraction for a while, but his disdain for the titling of such works as 'Compositions' led him to try something new. In an attempt to send up the vogue for employing overly descriptive titles, he found a way to attract even more attention:

'I assume people are always inquisitive and nosy, and if you see a little poem written in the corner of a painting it will force you to go up and look at it ... it's not just as Whistler would say an arrangement in browns, pinks and blacks.'

This curiosity extended to graffiti on the lavatory walls of Earl's Court underground station. Slogans such as 'Britain's future is in your hands' began to appear as ambiguous statements written in paint against

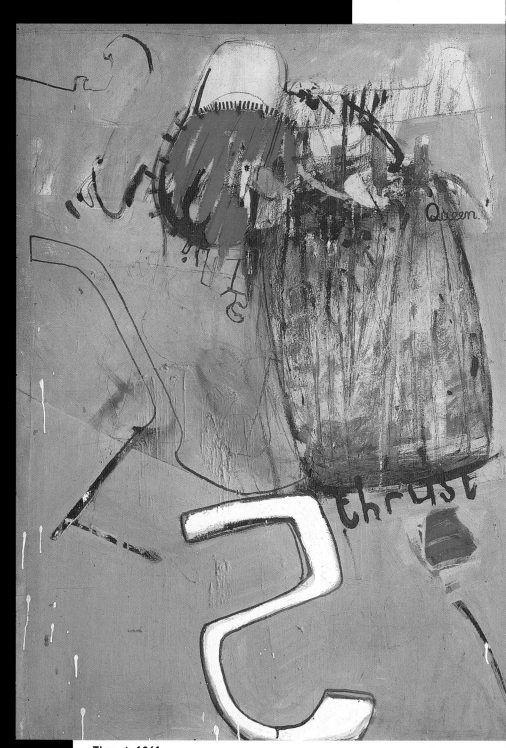

Thrust, 1961

I'm in the Mood for Love, 1961

Going to be Queen Tonight, 1960

We Two Boys Together Clinging, 1961

PAINTING

David Hockney

suggestive Dubuffet-like figures. His paintings began to develop a coyly private dimension – Walt Whitman's coded use of the alphabet matched to numbers became the vehicle for Hockney to paint his desires; words such as Queen and Doll Boy suggested a wish to express his sexuality in a manner more seductive than a figurative depiction could ever be.

A newspaper headline that had caught Hockney's eye 'Two Boys Cling to Cliff All Night' made him first think that this referred to Cliff Richard, but actually it referred to a cliff. The double-take was to inspire the painting *We Two Boys Together Clinging* (1961). Such everyday objects in his studio became transformed into props. A Typhoo Tea packet became a formal device to imbue depth in a depiction of a seated figure, the back of a playing card a basis for abstraction.

After winning £100 for a print designed in the Graphics School, Hockney set off for America in the summer of 1961. His personal experiences of the art world and the gay world there were the inspiration for his great series of prints *The Rake's Progress*. The medium was chosen because of the closeness between the etched line and the

The Diploma, 1962

The Rake's Progress: Bedlam, 1961–63

printed word, and the images reveal a moral tale, close to Hogarth's, that warns of the loss of individuality to external pressures.

The reluctance of the RCA to grant Hockney his diploma resulted in him delivering *Life Painting for a Diploma* in which a male nude from *Physique Pictorial* was coupled with a perfectly executed drawing from his first days at the RCA. The painting represents an artistic development that was matched by the emergence of a provocative and uninhibited character.

70s PAINTING

With the exhaustion of Pop by the 1970s, a new attitude towards the discipline of painting was ushered in by the appointment of Professor Peter de Francia. In his inaugural lecture he promised 'an alternative to the idea of the artist seen as a kind of two-man circus horse made up of Lucky Jim at one end and Neanderthal Man at the other'.

Openly opposing the fashionable successes the School had become famous for, de Francia rigorously defended the intellectual importance of European figurative painting and the social conscience of the artist in ways which extended well beyond the scope of the British art establishment. De Francia's ideal was to produce painters who were intellectually well-equipped cultural workers. This sometimes created tensions within the College.

Challenged on one side by radical developments in artistic practice and on the other by the Conceptualists' attack on traditional media (which de Francia called 'Luddism'), and a lack of confidence from the art market, 'the new spirit of painting' developed quietly but firmly.

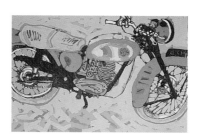

Kevin Sinnott
(b. 1947)
Student 1971–77
Degree Show, 1974

Graham Crowley
(b. 1950)
Student 1972–75
Professor 1998–present
Degree Show, 1975

Peter Griffin
(b. 1947)
Student 1974–77
Degree Show, 1977

Andrzej Jackowski
(b. 1947)
Student 1974–77
Earth Stepper with Running Hare, 1987

Donald Hamilton Fraser
(b. 1929)
Staff 1957–83
Still Life with Fish, 1975

Patrick Heron
(1920–1999)
Visiting Staff
Complicated Green and Violet March, 1972

Yehuda Safran
(b. 1944)
Student 1973–75
Staff 1976–91
A Painting, 1989

Stephen Farthing
(b. 1950)
Student 1973–76
Staff 1978–85
Flat Pack, Rothmans, 1975

Eileen Cooper
(b. 1953)
Student 1974–77
*Taking Root and Falling
Leaves, 1984–85*

Michael Heindorff
(b. 1949)
Student 1975–77
Staff 1980–present
Cave Dance, 1987

Julia Peyton Jones
(b. 1952)
Student 1975–78
No. XXI Conspectus, 1978

John Barnicoat
(b. 1924)
Student 1952–55
Staff 1976–80
Painting, 1985-86

Howard Hodgkin
(b. 1932)
Staff 1974–76
*A Henry Moore at the Bottom
of the Garden, 1975–77*

Peter de Francia
(b. 1921)
Professor 1972–86
Family in an Interior, 1978

Roberto Matta
(b. 1911)
Artist in Residence 1975–80
Je m'espionne, 1974

80s PAINTING

The orthodoxy of British Modernism had been questioned by artists in the 1970s by the use of unusual materials and strategies. In the 1980s it was further challenged by a forceful return to figurative painting. The tradition established by the 'London School', comprising artists such as Bacon, Auerbach and Freud, continued to develop to international acclaim. A spate of important London exhibitions prompted American interest in buying a very particular kind of British work.

These factors contributed to a return to the practice of painting in the 1980s. The Painting School was well equipped to respond, producing a range of artists keen to establish themselves in the newly discovered lineage of figuration. Peter de Francia called aspects of the fashionable new spirit 'fast-food figuration'.

Although stylistically diverse, the content-laden imagery of many of the paintings of this period had a skewed, almost naïve realism that was underpinned by a strong sense of narrative: the subject-matter was often based on real-life experience espousing a personal mythology and executed in an oversized format.

Philip A. Davies
(b. 1953)
Student 1978–81
Degree Show, 1981

Jim Mooney
(b. 1955)
Student 1978–81
Staff 1989–present
Invisible Cities, 1987

Denzil Forrester
(b. 1956)
Student 1980–83
Untitled, 1983

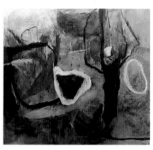

Madeleine Strindberg
(b. 1955)
Student 1982–85
Aftermath, 1985

Paul Huxley
(b. 1938)
Staff 1976–86
Professor 1986–98
Surrogate, 1982

Ken Kiff
(b. 1935)
Visiting Staff
Talking to a Psychoanalyst: Night Sky no. 13, 1973–79

Lucy Jones
(b. 1955)
Student 1979–82
Three Trees South Bank, 1987

Thérèse Oulton
(b. 1953)
Student 1980–83
Redux, 1983

Jake Tilson
(b. 1958)
Student 1980–83
The High Street, SW11, 1983

Rachel Budd
(b. 1960)
Student 1983–86
Degree Show, 1986

Christopher Cook
(b. 1959)
Student 1983–86
Degree Show, 1986

Ansel Krut
(b. 1959)
Student 1983–86
Degree Show, 1986

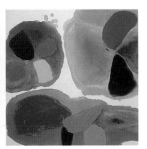

Gillian Ayres
(b. 1930)
Visiting Staff
Lure, 1963

Paula Rego
(b. 1935)
Visiting Staff
Prey, 1986

Lisa Milroy
(b. 1959)
Staff 1995–96
Shoes, 1986

90s PAINTING

In the 90s, a definition of new British painting has largely been engulfed by the term 'Young British Art'. Although primarily cultivated at Goldsmiths College and recognized by an entrepreneurial spirit and a derelict pose, 'Young British Artists' have also emerged, albeit rather more slowly, from the Painting School.

The climate for these graduating artists has largely been controlled by the collector Charles Saatchi. In the mid-80s, he had started to acquire a large and eclectic range of British art. By the beginning of the 90s he was buying it young and in bulk, and by 1997 with his 'Sensation!' show at the Royal Academy, he had set the seal.

In the case of painting from the RCA, the prevailing theme of self-narration has in many ways replaced the positing of identity as a central issue. In addition, the marked trend towards the depiction of the human figure in the urban landscape is symptomatic to the deflection of identity and the assertion of unease.

Dinos Chapman
(b. 1962)
Student 1988–90
Two Horizontal Planes, 1990

Dexter Dalwood
(b. 1960)
Student 1988–90
The Night Attendant, 1990

Chantal Joffe
(b. 1969)
Student 1992–94
Odalisque, 1994

Tim Stoner
(b. 1970)
Student 1992–94
Ocean to Ocean, 1994

Dawn Mellor
(b. 1970)
Student 1994–96
Pigtails and Blue Ribbons, 1996

Kate Donachie
(b. 1970)
Student 1995–97
False Eyelashes, 1997
Andy Davey's degree show

FINE ART

John Greenwood
(b. 1959)
Student 1988–90
Mr. Reasonable, 1990

Tracey Emin
(b. 1963)
Student 1987–89
Family of Women, 1989

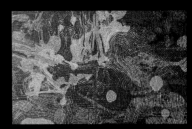

Chris Ofili
(b. 1968)
Student 1991–93
Missing You, 1993

Alex Veness
(b. 1965)
Student 1992–94
Cycles, 1994

Kate Belton
(b. 1972)
Student 1994–96
Interim, 1996

Philip Jones
(b. 1971)
Student 1994–96
Eurydice's Bathroom, 1996

Rita Donagh
(b. 1939)
Tutor 1989–94
*Cell Block (Maze Prison,
Co. Antrim), 1989*

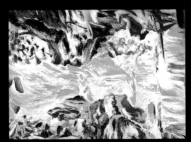

Michael Heindorff
(b. 1949)
Student 1975-77
Tutor 1980-present
Heraclitean Landscape, 1990

Peter Doig
(b. 1959)
Visiting Staff
Concrete Cabin II, 1993

PAINTING

Tracey Emin

Tracey Emin is one of the few recent British artists to have gained mainstream recognition. This feat is largely due to an infamous drunken performance on British television during the Turner Prize Awards in 1997. The performance was interesting not because she 'had breached acceptable standards' (the Broadcasting Standards Commission), but because it could be perfectly reconciled within her artistic body of work.

Emin makes art from personal revelation, translating emotion directly into tangible representations. Her best known work *Everyone I Have Ever Slept With 1963–1995* is a tent appliquéd and embroidered with the names of every person she has slept next to in her life. The piece received sensationalist press for the title's claim, when in reality the work merely played with the euphemism of the word 'sleep' and revealed a far deeper intimacy.

Tracey Emin graduated from the Painting School in 1993 and, as is customary, donated one of her paintings to the RCA Collection. Having second thoughts about the choice, she replaced the painting with another which had a handwritten note of apology pasted onto the back

Everyone I Have Ever Slept With 1963–1995

PAINTING

Tracey Emin

Friendship, (verso), 1989

> Really Sorry
> But I love my
> to much to Part with
> (I culd have sold this one)
> It's a good picture too th
> Thank you TRACEY

of the canvas. The note is indicative of the self-confessional statements she would later adopt as her visual style. Emin herself has said that she is better represented in the collection by the reverse side of the picture.

The work is particularly rare because Emin destroyed all her paintings after a period of crisis, and began 'to start with myself but end up with the universe'. Initially this took the form of an offer for people to 'invest in her creative potential' for £10, sold at The Shop, a temporary but influential outlet in East London run by Emin and Sarah Lucas. By opening The Tracey Emin Museum in a minicab office in Waterloo in 1995, Emin made a grand statement that could easily have been accused of narcissism. Instead, the museum has become symbolic of how her work is essentially about contact, shared experience and a two-way dialogue.

Raised and educated in Margate on the south coast of England, Emin places strong reference in her work on what she cites as the 'windswept, forlorn and forgotten'. Her use of

Friendship, (recto), 1989

Neon Love Poem 1993–96
'I Need Art Like I Need God', South
London Gallery, 1997

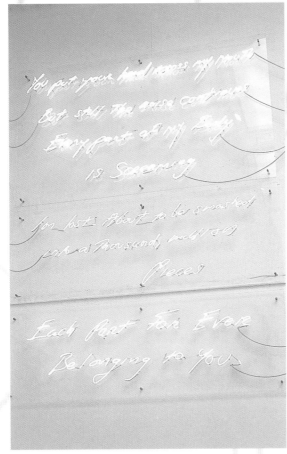

neon as a material has strong associations with the neon along 'The Golden Mile', while much of her viewpoint is constructed from the seaside town's expansive horizon coupled with its limitations. The escapism that the cheap pleasures of such places promise has become central to the mixture of hedonism and despair communicated by much of her work.

Perhaps most of all, it is her ability to transcend everyday circumstance that marks her strength. The video piece *Why I Never Became a Dancer* (1995) is an account of when Emin entered the local finals of the 1978 British Disco Dance Championships and was shouted off-stage by a group of men she had previously slept with. The video ends with Emin giving a dedication: 'Shane, Eddie, Tony, Richard, Doug, this one's for you!' while dancing alone to Sylvester's hit *You Make Me Feel, Mighty Real*. Her work symbolizes a change in the social role of the artist in the late 1990s, and certainly merited inclusion in the 'Sensation!' exhibition at the Royal Academy in 1997.

Outside Myself (Monument Valley), 1994

PRE-WAR SCULPTURE

The specialist School of Sculpture and Modelling was founded in 1899, offering vocational training for teachers and architectural sculptors. The emphasis placed on modelling, enlarging and academic sculpture equipped students with the necessary skills for a number of public projects in London, including numerous war memorials to commemorate the First World War.

In the early 1920s there was a renewed interest in carving, led by British sculptors inspired by what was then called 'primitive art'. This approach was encouraged at the RCA by technical assistant Barry Hart who taught carving to students Henry Moore and Barbara Hepworth. Much disliked at the time by the public and opponents of the Modernist programme, the style provoked extreme reactions. Ex-student Charles Sargeant Jagger wrote in *The Studio*:

'I have often watched the pathetic spectacle of the passer-by gazing in bewilderment ... at some strange shape in stone. I have watched him glance furtively right and left lest his bewilderment should be detected by the self-elected intellectual snobs who find these monstrosities an open opportunity for loudly demonstrating their assumed intellectual superiority.'

Alfred Drury
(1859–1944)
Student
*Sculptural Panel, main entrance,
Victoria and Albert Museum, 1906*

Albert Toft
(1862–1949)
Student
*Hall of Memory Memorial,
Birmingham, n.d.*

Charles Sargeant Jagger
(1885–1924)
Student 1907–11
Artillery Monument, 1925

Charles Wheeler
(1892–1972)
Student 1912–17
Mother and Child, 1926

Henry Moore
(1898–1986)
Student 1921–24
Staff 1924–31
Mask, 1928

James Woodford
(unknown)
Student 1920–22
*Bronze Doors (detail),
Norwich, n.d.*

FINE ART

Francis Derwent Wood
(1871–1926)
Student 1889–90
Professor 1918–24
Machine Gun Corps Memorial, 1925

Gilbert Ledward
(1888–1960)
Student 1907
Professor 1927–29
Monolith, 1936

Edward Lantéri
(1848–1917)
Staff 1874–80
Professor 1880–1917
The Sacristan, 1917

Barbara Hepworth
(1903–75)
Student 1921–24
Torso, 1928

Ernest Cole
(unknown)
Professor 1924–26
Sculpture, County Hall, London, n.d.

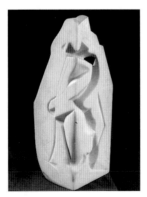

Merlyn Evans
(1910–1973)
Student 1931–33
Sculpture, 1932–33

With the exception of the 'Leeds Group' of sculptors headed by Moore and Hepworth, the Sculpture School largely ignored the direction of the interwar avant garde. Teaching methods remained unchanged and resistant to modernism. However, the belief in 'truth to materials' and a dedication to carving rather than modelling were considered progressive by many students. The programme also contrasted with the monumental and ecclesiastical opportunities still offered by public and private commissions.

The Sculpture School suffered when the RCA was relocated to Ambleside in the summer of 1940 after the outbreak of the Second World War, because heavy machinery had to be left behind. However, this did encourage a makeshift interdisciplinary approach, as students moved freely between disciplines without any official barriers, in what was called the 'potato loft university'.

SCULPTURE

Barbara Hepworth and Henry Moore

Henry Moore
Marble Head of the Virgin
(after a relief by Domenico
Roselli), 1922
Direct carving was not
practised at the College;
instead a pointing machine
was used to produce finished
work from casts modelled by
the students. Moore
deliberately peppered this
work with tiny holes to give
the impression that it had
been carved by machine rather
than by hand.
Henry Moore Foundation

Henry Moore arrived at the Royal
College of Art in 1921, a 23-year-old
veteran of the First World War. His
first few months were an exhilarating
experience, though this had as much
to do with living in London and
visiting museums in South Kensington
and Bloomsbury as with the teaching
he received. The Sculpture School at
the time was run by Derwent Wood, a
scholarly and academic sculptor, while
the mandatory course in architecture
was taught by Beresford Pite, an
ageing architect whose sentiments lay
firmly with the late nineteenth-
century Arts and Crafts movement.
Neither seemed to have much to
offer the young Moore.

Barbara Hepworth also
arrived in 1921, at the
unusually young age of 18.
Both Hepworth and
Moore had studied at
the Leeds School of Art,
and with two other
Leeds alumni,
Raymond Coxon and
Edna Ginesi, they
formed 'the Leeds
group', renowned in
the College for their
'lively and confident'

Henry Moore
Head of a Girl, clay, 1923
Moore's taste for 'primitive' art
was in direct conflict with the
academic teaching at the
College, and he worked on his
own carvings only at weekends
and during vacations.

Barbara Hepworth
Large and Small Form,
white alabaster, 1934

Barbara Hepworth
Doves, Parian marble, 1927
Hepworth did no direct carving
until she left the RCA. Her
interest in the technique
developed when she and her
first husband, John Skeaping,
were studying in Rome.

SCULPTURE

Barbara Hepworth and Henry Moore

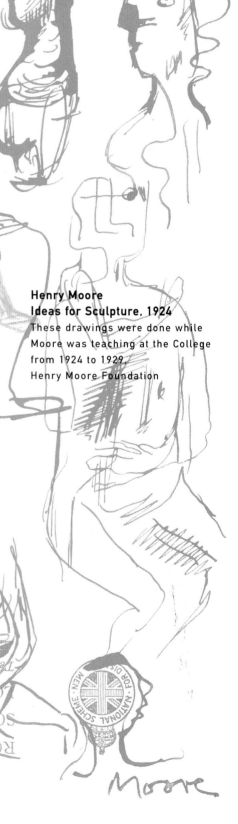

way, with the men always marching in step. Although Moore confessed to being 'a bit sweet on her' while they were studying together at Leeds, by the time they reached London he saw Barbara Hepworth rather 'as a kind of young sister'.

Hepworth has stated that she, too, felt a sense of 'united purpose' with Henry Moore in their enthusiasm for what was then known as 'direct carving' as practised by Eric Gill and Jacob Epstein. This was not taught at the College, and the two young sculptors drew their inspiration instead from the 'primitive' African, Japanese and Mexican art to be found in the British Museum, the pre-Renaissance art at the V&A, and the works illustrated in the pages of the magazine *Cahiers d'Art*.

But both Moore and Hepworth eventually recognized the value of an academic grounding and were keen to master all the conventional academic techniques taught at the College. Moore, in particular, was fortunate in having Leon Underwood as his drawing tutor. Underwood was also a sculptor and 'set out to teach the science of drawing, of expressing solid form on a flat surface – not ... the art-school imitation of styles in drawing'.

Moore also knew the technical assistant Barry Hart (a trained stonemason) well enough to persuade him to allow direct carving in the studio, rather than the then standard practice of preparing a model and using a pointing machine to transfer and enlarge it.

Hepworth only occasionally experimented with direct carving and seemed more open to the idea of benefiting from conventional academic teaching. Apart from anything else, she could not afford to lose her scholarship. However, there is no doubt that Hepworth, too, was profoundly influenced by what was seen as the more abstract work exhibited at the British Museum. Henry Moore's final report from Derwent Wood judged that 'his drawings are excellent, but his design might show improvement. He appears to be somewhat limited in his interest of tradition in Sculpture'. Principal William Rothenstein was much more enthusiastic: he offered the young Moore a senior teaching post the moment he completed his diploma. This was, the sculptor later wrote, excellent preparation 'for meeting the widespread philistine atmosphere which prevailed in England up to 1940 towards the so-called Modern Art'.

Henry Moore
Ideas for Sculpture, 1924
These drawings were done while Moore was teaching at the College from 1924 to 1929.
Henry Moore Foundation

62

FINE ART

Barbara Hepworth Mother and Child, grey Cumberland alabaster, 1934
During the 1930s Hepworth's work became bolder and more abstract. With Moore, she became a leading member of the British avant-garde. Both Moore and Hepworth were interested in the theme of 'Mother and Child'. This example was influenced by her meeting with Hans Arp.

Barbara Hepworth Infant, Burmese wood, 1929

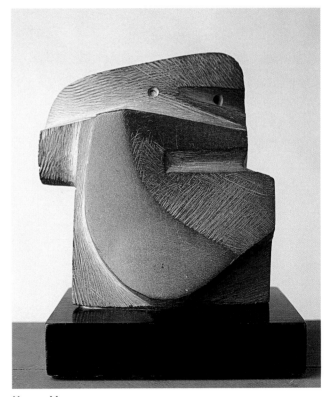

Henry Moore Carving in African Stone, 1935
Moore first met Jacob Epstein around 1925. Epstein encouraged Moore's passion for ethnic art and inspired him with courage in the face of public opposition to his work.

63

50s SCULPTURE

The changes ushered in by Robin Darwin, who was appointed Principal in 1948, were soon appreciated by students of the Sculpture School under the direction of Frank Dobson. One of the first to encourage a culture of fellow-practitioners, Dobson often invited students to comment on his own work, which they did with aplomb.

The period was marked by the Festival of Britain in 1951 which cemented a relationship between the British public and modern British sculpture, opening up further possibilities for public art. Much of the sculpture of the day, although still figurative, began to convey anxiety as a post-war condition, with neuroses expressed through texture and tortured form. This was heightened by the introduction of cut and forged metal as a material.

By contrast, the appointment of John Skeaping in 1953 produced a greater emphasis on carving, away from the decorative tradition. In 1955 a studio was lent to Jacob Epstein for the construction of two large-scale sculptures. These works were to invigorate carving as a technique for students, who repaid the compliment by publishing a small book on Epstein's work in progress.

Franta Belsky
(b. 1921)
Student 1941–42, 1948–50
Joyride, bronze, 1957–58

Geoffrey Clarke
(b. 1924)
Stained glass student 1948–52
Figure, 1950

Ralph Brown
(b. 1928)
Student 1952–56
Staff 1958–72
The Queen, 1963

Hubert Dalwood
(1924–76)
Visiting Staff
Mirage II, 1966

Christopher Ironside
(1913–92)
Staff 1953–63
*Tapestry, Dovecot Studio,
with Robin Ironside, 1959*

Frank Dobson
(1886–1963)
Professor 1946–53
Ham Hill Torso, 1928

FINE ART

Robert Carruthers
(b. 1925)
Student 1950–53
Torso. pre-1960

Sydney Harpley
(1927–92)
Student 1953–56
Girl on a Swing. 1974

The retrospectives of both Epstein and Moore at the Tate underlined the strength of British sculpture in this period, both at home and abroad. In 1957, an Arts Council open-air, regional exhibition entitled 'Contemporary British Sculpture' attracted more than 215,000 people, demonstrating its new popularity as an art form.

Overseas, with support from the British Council, modern sculpture became associated with the nation's culture for the first time.

More permanent was the integration of sculpture into the planning and building of Britain's new towns, often appearing as a symbol of optimism for the newly housed community.

Edward Folkard
(b. 1911)
Staff 1948–50
Onlookers. 1956

G. Heinrich Clusman Henghes
(1906–75)
Staff 1949–53
The Dancers. 1950

John Skeaping
(1901–80)
Professor 1953–60
Head of a girl. c. 1958

Jacob Epstein
(1880–1959)
Artist in Residence 1950–51
Madonna and Child. 1951

60s SCULPTURE

The 1960s can be considered one of the most inventive and unorthodox periods in British sculpture. During this time sculpture received much public attention, enhancing its reputation abroad. New materials and technologies supported a shift from figuration to abstraction, and from carving to construction.

Bernard Meadows was appointed Professor in 1960 to shake up the School of Sculpture. He helped to widen the horizons of the students to the outside professional world, by teaching them to learn for and among themselves, by increasing the number of visiting practitioners and by insisting on high technical standards.

The experimentation was aided by the lack of a professional tradition in British modernist sculpture. Colour began to be used as an element in itself, as a reaction against expressive textural surfaces; fibreglass, polyurethane and plastic began to be welded in reaction against 'truth to materials'. Even the sculptural base was abolished in favour of integration with the piece as a whole.

Much of the approach was influenced by abstract painting – many sculptors respected its fundamental qualities, considered both serious and daring. Pop also played a part,

David Hall
(b. 1937)
Student 1960–64
Nine, 1967

Roland Piché
(b. 1938)
Student 1960–64
Sunset & Deposition, 1964

Nigel Hall
(b. 1943)
Student 1964–67
Untitled, 1964

John Maine
(b. 1942)
Student 1964–67
Prism, 1977

Dame Elisabeth Frink
(1930–93)
Visiting Staff
Winged Beast, 1962

Bernard Meadows
(b. 1915)
Professor 1960–80
Black Crab, 1953

FINE ART

David Horn
(b. 1937)
Student 1960–64
*Suddenly There Are Flowers
Everywhere, 1964*

William Pye
(b. 1938)
Student 1962–65
Confluence, 1992

John Panting
(b. 1930)
Student 1964–67
Untitled, 1967

Keith Milow
(b. 1945)
Student 1967–68
Cross, 1979–80

Robert Clatworthy
(b. 1928)
Staff 1961–68
Bull, 1957

Kenneth Draper
(b. 1944)
Student 1965–68
Ascend, 1968

delivering a playfulness in colour and form that was to transform sculpture beyond the public's recognition.

The trend for 'suggestive forms' caused the decline of figurative sculpture. Meadows and other sculptors abandoned human elements, shrinking and distorting them to unrecognizable ends. For many, representation had simply disappeared.

The spirit of experimentation permeating the School at this time was partly due to the freedom Meadows was given by Robin Darwin to run the School. Many of the rigid traditions the School had spent so very long upholding were circumvented in the name of innovation. When the modelling stands from the Queensgate huts were abandoned, the connection with the arts and crafts tradition of sculpture was finally severed.

70s SCULPTURE

The early years of the 1970s were dominated by interest in Conceptual and Performance art. The enquiries of the previous decade had dissolved into unconventional assemblages of material and media – innovation had almost become orthodoxy.

Within this climate, sculpture at the RCA was divided between the making of 'objects' or 'assemblages' in Bernard Meadows' School of Sculpture, and the rise of 'environmental media' under Peter Kardia, an initiative that was to produce a string of important artists.

For most, this was the decade of a new-found belief in 'truth of process' rather than 'truth to materials'; analysis of the process was favoured over the finished piece.

Innovation consisted of a series of reactions against the dominant form – objects became so reduced that some feared an exhaustion of form. With the establishing of Conceptual art, the 'deobjectification' of sculpture became a possibility. Many sculptors addressed this possibility by challenging the system by which their sculptures were classified.

Kardia made his students aware of decision-making in the creative process, fostering an individuality which resisted stylistic categorization.

Richard Wentworth
(b. 1947)
Student 1966–70
Siege, 1983–4

Martin Naylor
(b. 1944)
Student 1966–70
Important Mischief, 1971

Terry Powell
(b. 1944)
Student 1970–73
Staff 1977–98
Degree Show , 1973

Alison Wilding
(b. 1948)
Student 1970–73
Echo, 1995

Alan Boyd Webb
(b. 1957)
Student 1972–5
Nostrum, 1989

Tony Cragg
(b. 1949)
Student 1973–77
Stack, 1977

FINE ART

Carl Plackman
(b. 1943)
Student 1966–70
Degree Show, 1970

John Cobb
(b. 1946)
Student 1970–73
The Chair, 1973

Brian Catling
(b. 1948)
Student 1971–74
Degree Show, 1974

Jim Pearson
(b. 1948)
Student 1972–5
Degree Show, 1975

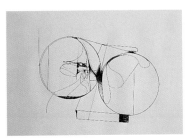

Bryan Kneale
(b. 1930)
Staff 1964–95
Pelican, 1987

David Nash
(b. 1945)
Visiting Staff
Wall Sheaves, 1993

Many graduates from this period brought a personal dimension to their work – a private layer of meaning of individual, unrevealed significance. This usually involved a sculptural arrangement of found objects which, when combined with the title of the piece, often conjured up a kind of visual poetry. The illogical arrangement of objects often communicated a sense of frustration. In many ways the visual tension became equal to the expressed tension, a feature that was to unite much of the sculptural output from the RCA.

Friendships were forged between practitioners of sculpture and students of environmental media, and later many of them were represented at the Lisson Gallery, London. By the 1980s, in contrast to painting's celebrated but unresolved return to figuration, these sculptors were establishing an international reputation.

80s SCULPTURE

During the 1980s, British art became highly rated internationally. The continuing presence of sculptors at the British Pavilion of the Venice Biennale confirmed a central position for sculptural enquiry in the visual arts.

Under the professorship of Philip King between 1980 and 1990, there was a dramatic rise in the number of female students studying sculpture. In addition, the critical success of students from non-Western cultures served as a challenge to the art establishment of the 1980s.

Much of the work of the period demonstrated an imaginative resourcefulness: discarded mass-produced objects or non-hierarchical materials were employed to striking effect. The ordinariness of the surface often concealed an underlying depth. Also important was the unashamed use of narrative.

A keenly developed interest in the marketable qualities of the work, among other things, gave a slightly traditional flavour to much of the output of this period. This was also a time when student work was beginning to be well documented by the media.

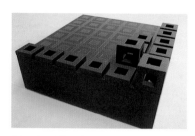

Charles Mendoza
(b. 1953)
Student 1977–80
Degree Show, 1980

Eric Bainbridge
(b. 1955)
Student 1978–81
Degree Show, 1981

Brian McCann
(b. 1952)
Student 1981–83
Bend Over Backwards, 1983

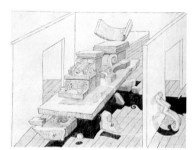

Edward Allington
(b. 1951)
Student 1982–85
Seated in Darkness, 1987

Nicola Hicks
(b. 1960)
Student 1982–85
Job's Ally, 1985

Sokari Douglas Camp
(b. 1958)
Student 1983–86
Degree Show, 1986

David Mach
(b. 1956)
Student 1979–82
Silent Running, 1982

Dhruva Mistry
(b. 1957)
Student 1981–83
Degree Show, 1983

Denise de Cordova
(b. 1957)
Student 1981–83
Degree Show, 1983

Christopher Summerfield
(b. 1955)
Student 1981–84
Degree Show, 1982

Edward H. Kirkham
(b. 1947)
Student 1981–84
*The erosion that leaves nothing
but a few furrows of past life, 1982*

John Atkin
(b. 1959)
Student 1982–85
Textiles Staff 1996–present
*Single File & Study for Single
File, 1997*

Kathy Prendergast
(b. 1958)
Student 1983–86
Stack, 1989

Bethan Huws
(b. 1961)
Student 1986–88
Degree Show, 1988

Charles Hadcock
(b. 1965)
Student 1987–89
Justica Vacat, 1989

90s SCULPTURE

The year 1991 was to prove a historic time for the School of Sculpture. This was the year when the School left the wood and iron huts it had occupied since 1911, and moved to a disused factory building in Battersea. The new building facilitated the technological updating of the course. In many ways it also effected a change in the nature of the work produced, giving it an industrial edge, for example.

In the same year, Glynn Williams was appointed Professor. The spirit of the new work has been generally grand, epically proportioned yet of humble materials. In keeping with the irony of much Young British art of this period, it has developed a kind of minimalism inspired by the patterns of the everyday. Other marked trends include an interest in domestic *angst* expressed through constructed objects.

A symbolic moment occurred in 1991 when Gavin Turk failed his final examination. His blue plaque has since been treated as a memorial to the collision between the demands of a postgraduate course and the cultivation of personal notoriety. Turk's career was launched.

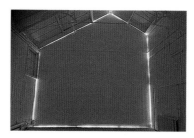

Tania Kovats
(b. 1966)
Student 1988–90
Degree Show, 1990

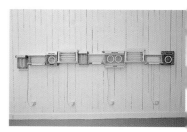

Jake Chapman
(b. 1966)
Student 1988–90
Degree Show, 1990

Ben Panting
(b. 1964)
Student 1989–91
Honi soit qui mal y pense, 1991

Katherine Dowson
(b. 1962)
Student 1989–92
Degree Show, 1992

Susan Stockwell
(b. 1962)
Student 1991–93
Paper Installation, 1993

Louise Evans
(b. 1963)
Student 1991–93
Untitled, 1993

Alex Hartley
(b. 1963)
Student 1988–90
Degree Show, 1990

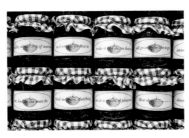

Rachel Evans
(b. 1965)
Student 1988–90
Harvest (detail), 1990

Gavin Turk
(b. 1967)
Student 1989–91
Degree Show (detail), 1991

Emma Rushton
(b. 1965)
Student 1990–92
English Clergy 92 (detail), 1992

Hadrian Pigott
(b. 1961)
Student 1990–93
Degree Show, 1993

Naomi Dines
(b. 1968)
Student 1991–93
Held (detail), 1993

Tim Noble
(b. 1966)
Student 1992–94
Concrete Boots, 1994

Geraldine Marks
(b. 1956)
Student 1994–96
Ooo–er!!!, 1996

Glynn Williams
(b. 1939)
Professor 1990–present
Stone Bridge No. 1, 1988

The Department of Light Transmission and Projection encompassed two strands of practice: work in plastic and glass, and work concerned with the behaviour of the spectator and the influence of the environment on this behaviour. From the latter sphere emerged the Department of Environmental Media, which became an autonomous subject under Peter Kardia in 1976, continuing until its closure ten years later.

The emphasis of the course lay in the development of mixed-media and time-based work. Due to the specialized needs of mixed-media artists, who often fall between the confines of 'sculpture' or 'film', the Department encouraged speculation on the overlap between the differing media, providing facilities which included video equipment and audio-visual technology. Drawing upon the history of performance, video, film and installation, much of the students' work dealt with language and perception, gender and sexuality, ethnicity and history, authorship and spectatorship.

Although a range of mixed-media work evolved from the Department, video work in all its forms emerged as a central practice, and in the 90s it has become one of the leading art forms of the decade.

David Hall
(b. 1937)
Student 1960–64
Stooky Bill TV, 1990

Richard Deacon
(b. 1949)
Student 1974–77
Art For Other People No. 5 (For those who have eyes), 1982

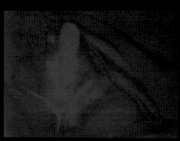

Nina Danino
(b. 1955)
Student 1978–81
'Now I am yours', 1993

Patrick Keiller
(b. 1950)
Student 1979–81
The End, 1986

Katherine Meynell
(b. 1954)
Student 1981–83
Hannah's Song, 1987

Mike Stubbs
(b. 1958)
Student 1981–83
Gift, 1997

Lis Rhodes
(b. 1942)
Student 1975–78
Visiting Staff
Running Light, 1997

Ian Bourn
(b. 1953)
Student 1976–79
Sick as a Dog, 1989

John Tappenden
(b. 1953)
Student 1976–79
Dawn Chorus, 1988

Catherine Elwes
(b. 1952)
Student 1980–82
Autumn, 1991

Judith Goddard
(b. 1956)
Student 1981–83
The Garden of Earthly Delights, 1991

Steve Littman
(b. 1957)
Student 1981–83
I Really, 1983

Keith Piper
(b. 1960)
Student 1984–86
Go West Young Man, 1997

Simon Robertshaw
(b. 1960)
Student 1984–86
One of those things you see … , 1986

Stuart Marshall
(1949–93)
Staff 1977–86
Pedagogue, 1988

Raymond Moore
(1920–87)
Student 1947–50
Allonby, 1977

Denis Postle
(b. 1936)
Student 1957–60
*'Ark came at 4', Ark 24,
Autumn 1959*

It was not until 1956 that a photography facility was tentatively introduced to the College. It provided short courses for students specializing in other disciplines, especially design. Robin Darwin stated his position on the role of photography a few years later:

'We are not so much concerned with photography as a creative medium in its own right ... but with it as an essential adjunct to professional practice in many fields of industrial design today. Only when allied to another discipline, [does] photography have a proper function in life.'

Darwin was reflecting contemporary British artistic opinion on photography as a largely functional medium, best allied to the fashion, advertizing and magazine industries.

The facility was part of the School of Graphic Arts, and graphic design students produced some of the earliest photographic work to emerge from the College. Much of their work was given exposure through the RCA's own student magazine, *Ark*. The style of the magazine after 1956, when it changed to A4 portrait, was shaped by the photographic skills of such designers as Denis Postle, Terry Green, Allan Marshall and Steve Hiett.

Terry Green
(b. 1938)
Student 1960–63
*Advertisement for Ark 24,
Autumn 1959*

Victor Burgin
(b. 1941)
Student 1962–65
*What does possession mean
to you?, 1976*

Albert Watson
(b. 1942)
Student 1966–69
Alfred Hitchcock, 1973

Denis Waugh
(b. 1941)
Student 1969–70
Untitled, c. 1970

FINE ART

Allan Marshall
(b. 1938)
Student 1958–61
Cover of Ark 28, Spring 1961

David Hockney
(b. 1937)
Student 1959–62
Ian washing his hair, 1983

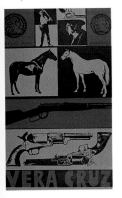

Laurence Cutting
(b. 1939)
Student 1962–65
Vera Cruz, 1964

Steve Hiett
(b. 1940)
Student 1962–65
'Teenage Netherworld', Ark 36, 1964

Ken Griffiths
(b. 1945)
Student 1969–71
Untitled, c. 1971

Sue Wilks
(b. 1948)
Student 1969–72
Untitled, c. 1972

Graduates from the Painting School, as well as graphic designers, used photography as a means of expression in remarkably different ways. Work ranged from Raymond Moore's transcendental, melancholic landscapes to David Hockney's later Polaroid montages (disparaging as he was about the medium) and Victor Burgin's image and text pieces presenting a critique of consumerism, the imagery of the mass media and state apparatuses.

Only in 1968 did the Photography Department finally accept its own specialist students – the first two were Henry Moore's daughter, Mary, and a Fulbright scholar, Richard Rogers. The department continued, however, to have a special relationship with Graphic Design. Robin Darwin and colleagues had finally accepted that photography could indeed be 'a creative medium in its own right'.

70s PHOTOGRAPHY

The first Professor of the Photography Department was John Hedgecoe, author of several best-selling photography guides. With the support of Professor Michael Langford, Hedgecoe laid emphasis on commercial, advertizing and documentary photography. However, the 1970s also saw the development of the official support structure for 'independent' photography in Britain.

This decade produced a range of styles. Graham Smith presented an insider's knowledge of life in the north of England through his realist documentary work; Sue Packer's photographs had a strong sociological dimension. Important commercial photographers to emerge from the Department included Rolph Gobits who produced stylish advertizing work, and Keith Collie and Jo Gaffney who were regularly commissioned by *Vogue*. In addition, the increasingly popular colour supplement (using many ex-*Ark* photographers) provided an important vehicle.

Verdi Yahooda, whose work draws on feminist art of the 1960s, and Boyd Webb, who produces photographed, stage-set tableaux, went on to achieve recognition within the British art world.

Peter Lavery
(b. 1948)
Student 1970–72
Untitled, 1972

Keith Collie
(b. 1948)
Student 1971–73
Untitled, 1973

Graham Smith
(b. 1947)
Student 1971–73
Untitled, 1973

Boyd Webb
(b. 1947)
Student 1972–75
Untitled (tethered ray), 1981

Sandor Bodo
(b. 1953)
Student 1976–78
Untitled, 1978

Yve Lomax
(b. 1952)
Student 1977–79
Sometime(s), 1995/6

FINE ART

Jo Gaffney
(b. 1948)
Student 1971–73
Untitled, 1973

Rolph Gobits
(b. 1947)
Student 1971–73
Untitled, 1973

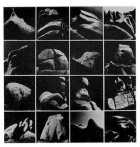

Suzie Maeder
(b. 1948)
Student 1971–73
Untitled, 1973

Bob Carlos Clarke
(b. 1950)
Student 1973–75
Building with Batgirl, 1975

Barry Lewis
(b. 1948)
Student 1974–76
Untitled, 1976

Verdi Yahooda
(b. 1952)
Student 1975–77
Untitled, 1977

Sue Packer
(b. 1954)
Student 1977–79
Untitled, 1989

Bill Brandt
(1904–83)
Visiting Staff
Lambeth Walk, 1948

John Hedgecoe
(b. 1933)
Staff 1966–75
Professor 1975–94
Mary Quant, n.d.

PHOTOGRAPHY

Boyd Webb and Calum Colvin

Calum Colvin
Sloth, 1993
From the series The Seven Deadly Sins and The Four Last Things

Boyd Webb
Glorious Morning, 1986

Boyd Webb and Calum Colvin have developed their practice as 'constructor-photographers' since the mid-70s and the mid-80s respectively. Both construct elaborate sets incorporating a wide range of domestic debris. Webb uses carpet, linoleum, rubber or tarpaulin, while Colvin arranges charity shop debris: broken record players, comics, action men, tacky lampshades and 1970s furniture. Both artists share an interest in the presentation of dystopias, and both have developed their ideas at the same time as a wider shift in RCA photography work away from commercial images for magazines and advertisements towards gallery pieces.

Webb trained as a sculptor but by the mid-70s had turned to photography. The previous decade had encouraged a questioning of the traditional art object and the adoption of photography, film and video to document activities, ephemeral objects and performances. However, Webb uses the

PHOTOGRAPHY

Boyd Webb and Calum Colvin

'object' in its own right. His imagery has a DIY quality within which he creates a fictional world, playing on the absurdity of his manufactured sets. Referencing classical Western mythology, Webb's *Nemesis* (1983) shows the actions of a subterranean being wreaking havoc on the earth's surface. Although still strongly anthropocentric, Webb began to create fictional worlds, using themes of the earth, the sea and outer space. His works also reflected an interest in political and environmental concerns, such as the threat of pollution or some other global catastrophe. By the late 80s, human actors had been replaced by inflatable plastic animals, and the fictional quality of the works became even more pronounced, for example in *Chromosome* (1989).

Colvin's postmodern work combines a number of techniques, including photography, montage, the stage set and painted scenery. He draws on the tradition of assemblage, in addition to Georges Rousse's use of spatial ambiguity and George Segal's

Boyd Webb
Nemesis, 1983

symbolic tableaux. Colvin developed the technique of painting onto specifically constructed three-dimensional sets, which, when photographed from a certain angle, create the illusion of two-dimensional space. Classical or Christian iconography feature in Colvin's symbolic dramas, such as *The Death of Venus* (1986). Colvin sets his work within an epic universe, anamorphosing gods or 'masters', scaling them down and ironizing them using counter-perspective. He presents scenarios of omnipotent male fantasy in which notions of heroism and male sexuality are undermined, along with the superhuman characters of Western tradition. Colvin's works from 1985 build in textual references, either through the origins of the work (a myth or proper name) or through an open page, a comic strip or a caption within the actual set. In *Narcissus* (1987), a nude (reminiscent of an Ingres drawing) is painted across a table. Colvin's interest in the theme of the gaze and self-reflection is reiterated, and a book on sexual anomalies lies open on the table. Colvin seems to revel in mixing high art and kitsch, and in more recent work this has been enhanced by the use of electronic and computer technology.

80s PHOTOGRAPHY

Throughout the 1980s, a wide diversity of approaches to photographic work, and differing ideologies, were brought to bear both within the College and in the wider international context. Sunil Gupta has continued to express notions of diaspora, cultural exchange and colonialism as an artist, writer and curator: he included the work of Joy Gregory and Yve Lomax in the first Johannesburg Biennale in 1995. The work of Calum Colvin reveals a fascination with constructed imagery in which fabrication and make-believe, fiction and performance, improvisation and authorship predominate. His constructed mythologies contrast with the imagery of his fellow student David Hiscock, whose distressed surfaces hint at the metaphysical world and present a disenchanted view of contemporary culture. However, the work of both artists marks a shift within the Department towards photography for exhibition.

In 1984, graduate Maureen Paley opened Interim Art, a significant contemporary gallery that promotes the work of young artists, such as David Rayson and Hannah Starkey.

Maureen Paley
(b. 1953)
Student 1978–80
Homework, 1979

Sunil Gupta
(b. 1953)
Student 1981–83
Untitled, 1986
from the Exiles series

David Hiscock
(b. 1956)
Student 1983–85
Staff 1990–present
Towards Aceldama, 1989

Mary Robert
(b. 1951)
Student 1983–85
Staff 1993–present
Sibel, 1994
From Transexuals Istanbul
series, 1989–98

Tim Daly
(b. 1964)
Student 1987–89
Untitled, 1989

Michael Langford
(b. 1933)
Staff 1967–94
Course Director 1994–97
Untitled, c. 1975

Anita Corbin
(b. 1958)
Student 1981–83
Untitled, n.d.

Nick Adler
(b. 1957)
Student 1982–84
Untitled, n.d.

Calum Colvin
(b. 1961)
Student 1983–85
Visiting Staff
Death of Venus, 1985

Andy Wiener
(b. 1959)
Student 1984–86
Untitled, n.d.

Joy Gregory
(b. 1959)
Student 1984–86
The Blue Room, 1985

Joelle Dépont
(b. 1951)
Student 1986–88
Le combat, n.d.

Dick Swayne
(b. 1936)
Staff 1981–98
Untitled, c. 1982

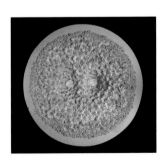

Helen Chadwick
(1953–1996)
Visiting Staff
Staff 1994–96
Wreath to Pleasure No. 6, 1993

Gus Wylie
(b. 1935)
Student 1957–61
Staff 1987–92
Untitled, 1981

90s PHOTOGRAPHY

While sculpture dominated the British art scene during the 1980s, the main feature of the 1990s has been a proliferation of photography, video and digital technologies, which have had a major impact on contemporary art. In 1994, reflecting the increasing acceptance of gallery photography, the College regrouped the course into the newly formed School of Fine Art. Its broad remit is reflected in the work of graduates and tutors in the 1990s. The work ranges from Platon Antoniou's work in fashion and portraiture, to the 'community' photography of Tom Hunter and Frauke Eigen's powerful responses to the histories of Germany and Bosnia as sites of conflict. Exile and gender politics inform the work of Jananne Al Ani, who has drawn on her Arab/Irish descent. A broadening of the concept of landscape photography can be seen in Daro Montag's work, which uses a technique whereby micro-organisms in the earth etch directly onto the film. Digital technology has enabled Paul Smith to use the device of the *doppelgänger* to explore male fantasies and military stories.

Melanie Manchot
(b. 1966)
Student 1990–92
Untitled, 1992

Nick Waplington
(b. 1965)
Student 1990–92
Circles of Civilisation, 1992

Frauke Eigen
(b. 1969)
Student 1993–95
Untitled, 1995

Jananne Al-Ani
(b. 1966)
Student 1995–97
Digital Fellow 1997–98
Untitled, 1997

Peter Kennard
(b. 1949)
Student 1977–80
Staff 1994–present
Germany Shakes, 1989–90

Paul Kilsby
(b. 1953)
Student 1990–95
Staff 1997–present
After Pietro da Cortona IV, 1994

Platon Antoniou
(b. 1968)
Student 1990–92
Fashion: Philip Treacy, 1992

Robert Davies
(b. 1964)
Student 1991–93
Eye No. 2 (female), 1993

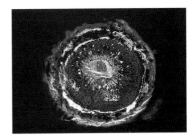

Daro Montag
(b. 1959)
Student 1992–94
Fruit of the Sun, 1994

Paul Smith
(b. 1969)
Student 1995–97
Untitled, 1997

Hannah Starkey
(b. 1971)
Student 1995–97
Untitled, 1997

Tom Hunter
(b. 1965)
Student 1995–97
The Art of Squatting, 1997

John Stezaker
(b. 1949)
**Humanities Staff
1991–present**
Third Person, 1990

Anna Fox
(b. 1961)
Staff 1996–present
Afterwards, 1991

Olivier Richon
(b. 1956)
Director 1997–present
A Real Allegory, 1997

20s PRINTMAKING

Frank Short became Director of the 'Etching Class' in 1891, overseeing what were then seen as the craft activities of etching and engraving. The class then became the School of Engraving. In the early 1920s, William Rothenstein encouraged the introduction of lithography to the Department and, concurrently, wood-engraving and book illustration became important activities.

Douglas Percy Bliss, Edward Bawden, Helen Binyon and Eric Ravilious tutored by Paul Nash in the School of Design, were encouraged by him to practise book illustration, wood-engraving, lino-cutting and watercolour painting. During the 1920s Bliss published *Border Ballads*, illustrated with wood-engravings, and Bawden worked with Curwen Press. Bawden's earliest lithographic works were for London Underground posters in 1925. Binyon went on in the late 1930s to work as an illustrator for the Penguin Illustrated Classics series. Ravilious first made his reputation as a wood-engraver, illustrating a number of books in the 1930s. In addition, all of them contributed to the RCA student magazines *Gallimaufry* and *Mandrake*.

Alfred Anderson
(1884–1966)
Under Frank Short
The National Gallery, 1926

Malcolm Osborne
(1880–1963)
Student 1904 and 1912
Professor 1924–48
The Tredrose Salonica, 1926

Enid Marx
(1902–98)
Student 1922–25
Pattern paper, n.d.

Douglas Percy Bliss
(1900–84)
Student 1922–25
Sunt Lachrymae rerum, c. 1927

Stanley Badmin
(1906–89)
Student 1925–28
Wareham, 1934

James Boswell
(1906–71)
Student 1925–29
Empire Builders, 1935

FINE ART

Job Nixon
(1891–1938)
Student 1911–15
Staff c. 1924–27
The Arno, n.d.

Robert S. Austin
(1895–1973)
Student 1919–22
Professor 1947–55
Portrait of the Artist, 1930

Barnett Freedman
(1901–58)
Student 1922–25
Staff 1928–40
Pattern paper, n.d.

Edward Bawden
(1903–89)
Student 1922–26
Staff 1930–40, 1948–53
The GPO's underground mail train in London, c. 1935

Helen Binyon
(1904–79)
Student 1922–26
Nicolite, n.d.

Eric Ravilious
(1903–42)
Student 1922–25
Staff 1930–38
Dr Faustus conjuring Mephistophilis, Curwen Press, 1929

Evelyn Gibbs
(1905–91)
Student 1926–29
Umbria, 1931

John Piper
(1903–92)
Student 1928–29
Visiting Staff
Chapel of St. George, Kemptown from 'Brighton Aquatints', 1939

Sir Frank Short
(1857–45)
Staff 1891–1912
Professor 1913–24
When the weary moon was in the wave, n.d.

30s–40s PRINTMAKING

The most significant stimulus to British printmaking in the 1930s and 1940s was the poster. Becoming more widespread in the 1920s, posters were sometimes called 'the people's art gallery' in the interwar years. Especially popular were the promotions for corporations such as Shell and organizations such as London Transport. At the same time lithography became respectable in art circles through the original poster print; artists associated with the RCA in the 1920s, including Bawden, Nash, Ravilious and Freedman, made significant contributions. However, the printmaking industry was severely hampered by the depression of the 1930s, and was only fully to recover in the mid-to-late 1950s.

Enid Marx, although affiliated to the Painting School, created a diverse range of work during the 1930s, including woodcut designs for bookcovers, pattern papers and woven materials. Merlyn Evans taught drawing and engraving, and after the war practised intaglio printmaking: he became in the later 1940s and 1950s the most highly regarded etcher in Britain, through the size and ambition of his plates.

During the 1930s, numerous official enquiries into the orientation of the

Leonard Brammer
(b. 1906)
Student 1926–31
Canal Scene, 1929

Leslie Evans
(unknown)
Student 1928–32
Untitled, 1931

Robert Dent
(b. 1909)
Student 1931–35
Church at Goldcliffe, n.d.

Edwin La Dell
(1914–70)
Student 1935–38
Staff 1948–54
Director 1955–70
Bandsmen, c. 1953

Harry Ecclestone
(b. 1923)
Student 1947–50
Little Venice from Calendarium Londinese, 1968

John Roberts
(b. 1923)
Student 1947–50
Clown, 1950

FINE ART

Ernest F. Powell
(unknown)
Student 1928–31
Untitled, n.d.

Merlyn Evans
(1910–73)
Student 1931–33
Staff 1964–73
The Chess Players, 1949

Erik Smith
(b. 1914)
Student 1944–47
Morning, 1940

Bernard Cheese
(b. 1925)
Student 1947–50
Shakespeare's Kings, 1964.
From Shakespeare Lithographs
series, 1964

James Sellars
(b. 1927)
Student 1948–52
Symbolic Soldier, 1953

Malcolm Osborne
(1880–63)
Student 1904 and 1912
Professor 1924–47
Portrait of Sir Frank Short, n.d.

College had noted that its fundamental purpose to unite 'art and industry' (a fashionable phrase during the depression) had been partly met through the connections of staff and ex-students with the design of lithographic posters for public hoardings. In this sense, printmaking was far ahead of product design where professional networks were concerned. This aspect of the practice was then known as 'commercial art', occupying a very different world to the artists' books and fine prints sold through galleries. However, thanks to the pressure of specialist groups, lithography crossed the boundary between the two worlds. Jack Beddington, then in charge of Shell's publicity, was to become a member of the Council in the post-war period.

During the years of the Second World War, calligraphy, engraving, life-drawing and textile design continued to flourish in the confined spaces of the College's temporary home in Ambleside.

50s PRINTMAKING

By the mid-1950s, print publishing in Britain had revived, largely through the efforts of Robert Erskin who successfully united the roles of publisher and retailer through his St. George Gallery. Print publishing began to flourish again with the foundation of the Curwen and Kelpra printing studios, Editions Alecto and, later, the Petersburg Press.

Within the College, when Robert Austin retired as Professor of Engraving, the professorship ceased to exist. As part of Robin Darwin's restructuring, Edwin la Dell took over the School of Engraving, which was now known as the Department of Printmaking, and located within the School of Graphic Design headed by Professor Richard Guyatt: artists and designers would work together.

La Dell began emphasizing lithography (until then etching, aquatint and engraving had predominated), and he invited artists such as John Piper, Graham Sutherland, Keith Vaughan, Ceri Richards and William Scott to work in the Department. Significant colour lithographic works began to emerge, and La Dell organized important publishing projects such as the Coronation Series of 1953, Wapping to Windsor and the Shakespeare series.

Philip Reeves
(b. 1931)
Student 1951–54
Fragment 3, c. 1983

Brian Perrin
(b. 1932)
Student 1951–54
Macbeth – Birnham Wood to High Dunsinane. Shakespeare Lithographs series, 1964

Edward Ardizzone
(1900–79)
Staff 1953–61
Birthday telegram issued by the GPO, 1967

Julian Trevelyan
(1910–88)
Staff 1954–64
Villa Joyosc, 1982

Anthony Gross
(1905–84)
Visiting Staff
A Midsummer Night's Dream – Bottom and the Fairies, 1964. From Shakespeare Lithographs series, 1964

John Piper
(1903–92)
Student 1928–29
Visiting Staff
Hampton Court, 1953

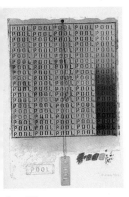

Joe Tilson
(b. 1928)
Student 1952–55
Visiting Staff
Pool Mantra, 1976

John Brunsdon
(b. 1933)
Student 1955–58
Street Scene, Putney, 1959

Robert S. Austin
(1895–1973)
Student 1919–22
Professor 1947–55
State Trumpeters, 1953

Edwin La Dell
(1914–70)
Student 1935–38
Staff 1948–54
Director 1955–70
Shakespeare's Birthplace, 1964.
From Shakespeare Lithographs
series, 1964

Ceri Richards
(1903–71)
Student 1924–27
Staff 1956–61
Costers Dancing, 1953

Michael Ayrton
(1921–75)
Visiting Staff
Falconer, 1957

William Scott
(1913–89)
Visiting Staff
Composition, 1982

Graham Sutherland
(1903–80)
Visiting Staff
Go out into the Country, London
Transport, 1938

Keith Vaughan
(1912–78)
Visiting Staff
A Season in Hell, Arthur Rimbaud
Cover, 1949

60s PRINTMAKING

In 1960, Richard Guyatt noted that inherent in the reorganization of the College was the tenet that 'the fine arts are the inspiration of the applied arts'. This cross-over of disciplines created an atmosphere of possibility and experimentation within the College, that was spurred on by the economic boom years of the 60s.

Screenprinting was in vogue, and print publishers were racing to meet the demand for prints of every kind. During the early 1960s, Alistair Grant introduced silkscreen printing to the Department. Adopting the photographic imagery of Pop, screenprinting was ideally suited to the clean edges and flat, dense colour of hard-edge abstraction.

Eduardo Paolozzi created his first major screenprint *Metalization of a Dream*, while R. B. Kitaj adopted the medium as a vehicle for his fragmented compositions. The Kelpra Studio was to have an immense impact, along with the publishing work of Editions Alecto. One of the earliest successes from Editions Alecto was David Hockney's series of etchings of *The Rake's Progress* in which Hogarth's rake becomes an art student in New York.

Roy Grayson
(b. 1936)
Student 1958–61
Untitled, 1960

Allen Jones
(b. 1937)
Student 1959–60
No. 2 from the series Life Class, 1968

David Hockney
(b. 1937)
Student 1959–62
A Rake's Progress: Plate No. 2A.
The Gospel Singing, 1961–63

Norman Ackroyd
(b. 1938)
Student 1961–64
Malignant Topography, 1964

Jean Maddison
(b. 1945)
Student 1966–69
A Cube of Sand, 1969

John Hoyland
(b. 1934)
Visiting Staff
Tiger's Pupil, 1983

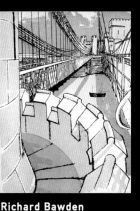

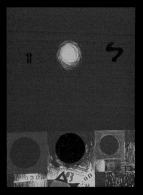

Richard Bawden
(b. 1936)
Student 1959–61
Telford's Bridge, Conway, 1965

R. B. Kitaj
(b. 1932)
Student 1959–61
The cultural value of fear, distrust and hypochondria, 1966

Alf Dunn
(b. 1937)
Student 1959–62
Staff 1969–95
Untitled, 1961

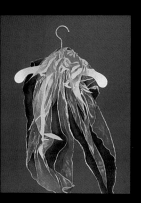

Brian Love
(b. 1942)
Student 1963–66
Coat Hanger, 1966

Christopher Orr
(b. 1943)
Student 1964–67
Staff 1974–98
Professor 1998–present

Anthony Biss
(1942– c. 1969)
Student 1964–67
Try and Say Something Good, 1967

70s PRINTMAKING

In 1970, Alistair Grant was appointed to take over the Department following Edwin La Dell's death. His belief that printmakers should be artists as well as printmakers enabled students to diversify into painting and sculpture. Looking back in 1987 over the past two decades as Professor of Printmaking, he wrote:

'I have been at pains to encourage Edwin La Dell's original conception of the Department being used as a workshop by practising artists; but schools cannot be a very fertile ground for students if teachers do not practise what they preach, and it is on this basis that all members of staff are appointed.'

Alf Dunn, an ex-RCA student, took over from Edward Ardizzone as Senior Tutor and established his reputation as a kinetic sculptor, and painter, alongside his practice as a printmaker.

Jeffrey Edwards
(b. 1945)
Student 1967–70
A Question of Taste, 1982

Michael Richecoeur
(b. 1946)
Student 1968–71
Fine Day, 1969

Chris Plowman
(b. 1952)
Student 1973–76
Untitled, 1976

Tim Mara
(1948–97)
Student 1974–76
Professor 1990–97
Alan's Room, 1974

Stephen McNulty
(b. 1950)
Student 1977–79
Untitled, 1979

Shelagh Sartin
(b. 1953)
Student 1977–79
Untitled, 1979

Anthony Davies
(b. 1947)
Student 1972–73
Peter Grimes, 1981/2

Joan Key
(b. 1948)
Student 1971–74
Mars and Venus after Poussin,
Dawn, 1988

John Brisland
(b. 1947)
Student 1973–76
The Family, 1976

Dick Jewell
(b. 1951)
Student 1975–78
Found photo, 1977

Susie Allen
(b. 1949)
Student 1976–79
Branded, 1982

Timo Lehtonen
(b. 1953)
Student 1977–79
Untitled, 1979

Elaine Shemilt
(b. 1950)
Student 1976–79
Untitled, 1979

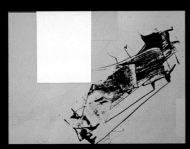

Alf Dunn
(b. 1937)
Student 1959–62
Staff 1969–95
Correction, 1982

Paul Huxley
(b. 1938)
Painting Tutor 1976–86
Professor 1986–90
Modus Vivendi, 1983

80s PRINTMAKING

Responding to government cuts in the funding of art education, and rising costs, Alistair Grant set up the Printmaking Department's Appeal Fund in the early 1980s. This fund not only gave financial support to printmaking students, it also provided a new impetus to the print publishing tradition which had grown within the Department since the 1950s, and in turn provided an excellent method of promoting the College's work.

Significant artists gained exposure in various portfolios published during this decade, including *35 Artists Printmaking* (1982) and *Artist's Choice* (1988). The Barbican hosted a major retrospective exhibition celebrating the work of, amongst others, Peter Blake, Derek Boshier, Anthony Davies, Jeffrey Edwards, Terry Frost, John Hewitt, David Hockney and Zandra Rhodes. A popular image was the diploma certificate which Hockney had printed and defaced, in 1962, showing a hapless student bumping his head on the Royal Coat of Arms – supported, or perhaps pushed, by the Rector. Another retrospective coincided with Grant's retirement.

John Hewitt
(b. 1955)
Student 1978–80
Staff 1995–present
Ah-Ha-Ha-Ha-Har!, 1985

Stephen Mumberson
(b. 1955)
Student 1979–81
Street Person 2, 1981

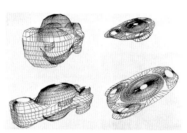

William Latham
(b. 1961)
Student 1982–85
Untitled, 1985

Peter Nevin
(b. 1952)
Student 1983–85
Untitled, 1985

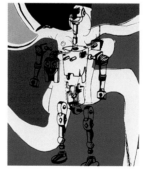

Simon Ringe
(b. 1965)
Student 1988–90
Sketchbook Ideas, 1989

Terry Frost
(b. 1915)
Visiting Staff
Newlyn Rhythm, 1982

FINE ART

Lol Sargent
(b. 1959)
Student 1981–83
Staff 1989–present
Untitled, 1983

Juliette Goddard
(b. 1959)
Student 1982–84
Untitled, 1984

Michael Wootton
(b. 1957)
Student 1982–84
Untitled, 1984

Peter Dover
(b. 1954)
Student 1986–88
Sunflower, 1988

Ann Nicolle
(b. 1959)
Student 1986–88
Untitled, 1988

Oscar Romp
(b. 1963)
Student 1988–89
Smoking and Dancing, 1989

Helen Chadwick
(1953–96)
Visiting Staff
Staff 1994–96
Coitus, 1993

Richard Wentworth
(b. 1947)
Visiting Staff
Boy with Shadow, 1982

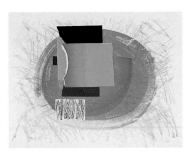

Alistair Grant
(b. 1925)
Student 1947–51
Staff 1955–86
Professor 1986–90
Boule de Sucre, 1982

90s PRINTMAKING

Tim Mara's appointment as Professor in 1990 brought significant changes to the facilities of the Department. Mara encouraged a wide spectrum of approaches to the creation of prints. His enthusiasm for new technologies led to the use of the computer, the internet and laser and ink jet printing side-by-side with traditional methods. In his inaugural lecture he said:

'I see Printmaking as a major means of expression within Fine Art, without stylistic constraints towards content or medium, and through which technique and process are completely integrated into the artist's work.'

The work of graduating students in the 1990s reflected a diversity of subject matter as well as technique. Work ranged from Faisal Ammar Abdu'allah's etchings of young black men exploring identity and ethnicity in Britain today to Katia Liebmann's use of photography in her Gotham series, which draws on the iconography of the superhero.

After Mara's untimely death, Chris Orr became Professor. His inaugural lecture was entitled 'From God to Gates via Gutenberg'.

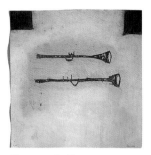

Duncan Bullen
(b. 1962)
Student 1989–91
Two Times, 1991

Max Davison
(b. 1965)
Student 1989–91
Puur, 1991

Rosalind Kunath
(b. 1946)
Student 1991–93
The Oracles, 1993

Faisal Ammar Abdu'allah
(b. 1969)
Student 1991–93
Aqil, 1993

Katia Liebmann
(b. 1965)
Student 1995–97
Gotham, 1997

Rebecca Davies
(b. 1973)
Student 1996–98
Bearing All, 1998

Adam Dant
(b. 1967)
Student 1990–92
Endree, 1992

Mark Hampson
(b. 1968)
Student 1990–92
Staff 1997–present
'Shipwrecked' he suggested.
'Maroon(ed)' I replied., 1992

Sioban Piercy
(b. 1957)
Student 1990–92
The Angels' Insecurities, 1992

John Miller
(b. 1962)
Student 1991–93
Cognitive Pugilism, 1993

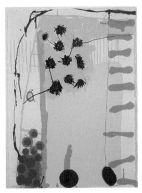

Amanda Clarke
(b. 1968)
Student 1993–95
Ladder, 1995

Daphne Prevoo
(b. 1970)
Student 1994–96
Cramped series: Hands, 1996

Leigh Clarke
(b. 1973)
Student 1996–98
Bright Town Revisited, 1998

James Hutchinson
(b. 1968)
Student 1996–98
Golden Days (Bay view), 1998

Tim Mara
(1948–97)
Student 1973–76
Professor 1990–97
Wire Glass and Carrier Bag, 1996

DESIGN

INTRODUCTION

Walter Crane, a leading figure of the Arts and Crafts movement, became Principal of the RCA in 1898. His intention was to orient the College away from teacher-training (the institution had just dropped the word 'training' from its title) towards the study and practice of design: 'I do not believe in any cast iron system of education', he wrote in *The Claims of Decorative Art*, 'from any point of view. It must be varied according to the individual ... There is nothing absolute in art. Art is not science.' He went on to argue that the distinctions between 'fine' and 'decorative' art were not helpful, believing them to be more to do with social status than the practices themselves.

Crane did not last long as Principal, but his ideas, example and enthusiasm decisively influenced the future direction of the College. According to his organizing concept of design education at the College, students in

their first year studied architecture – theory and practice – under the tutorship of architect Beresford Pite, calligraphy with Edward Johnston, and design games (outline, shapes, colour) with William Richard Lethaby. They could then choose from among four specialized studio areas: decorative and mural painting, sculpture and modelling, architecture, and design (meaning craft) – the heirs of Gottfried Semper's technical classes.

These curriculum developments were also the direct ancestors of the Bauhaus, and of basic design. But they weren't quite as radical as they may seem today. Lethaby, the very first Professor of Ornament and Design in Britain, said that the following words should be inscribed – in the finest quality lettering, of course – over the College's front door: 'No art that is one person deep can be very good art'. The important thing was to belong to a tradition of designing and making, and to work from within that tradition: it was a question of quality, not quantity, with a strong ethical dimension. Early graduates – enameller and teacher Alexander Fisher; silversmiths Omar Ramsden, Alwyn C. E. Carr, Nelson Ethelred Dawson and E. B. Wilson; textile designer Lyndsay P. Butterfield; ceramic designer Gordon Forsyth; stained glass designer Margaret Chilton; and calligraphers and letterers Dorothy Mahoney, Violet Hawkes and Irene Wellington – seemed to thrive in this new atmosphere, and on the looser structure which had immediately preceded it.

Education to Art

Thirty-five years later, when he was being considered for the post of Principal, the critic and poet Herbert Read would draw the important distinction between 'education to art' and 'education through art' – meaning the education of the professional artist on the one hand, and the bringing out of various conceptual and manual skills through the medium of art on the other. Throughout the nineteenth century, the School had attempted to achieve both. From now on, it would begin to concentrate on education to art. One question was whether the new emphasis on the crafts would have any impact on the world of heavy industry or be content simply to criticize it. Would the RCA turn into the Royal Cottage of Art? Only time would tell.

The catalogue published by the Board of Education in 1908 shows prize-winning exhibits that were produced in the schools of Architecture and Design in the decade since the RCA had been renamed. There were careful drawings of a restored mausoleum at Halicarnassus; 12 examples of William Morris-style wallpaper; plus rows of William de Morgan-style plates, displayed on the shelves of a wooden dresser, and an altar installation covered with examples of ecclesiastical metalwork. *The Studio* magazine noted among all this 'a prevailing spirit of sincerity and courage' as well as 'achievements of real interest and merit': at last there was evidence of 'a generally practical outlook'.

Out of this Arts and Crafts debate came some significant contributions to design. For example, while Edward Johnston was delivering his monkish lectures on lettering to all the first years, in his own practice he was busy deriving his hugely influential sans-serif block alphabet from classical Roman capitals for the London Underground Railway. Typically, he regarded this all-time design classic as a distraction from his real work and 'a concession to Mammon'.

New Blood and New Ideas

When William Rothenstein became Principal in 1920, he stated publicly that the role of the RCA was emphatically not 'to limit itself to the education of designers and teachers and industrial craftsmen, while Schools elsewhere would provide training for students of fine art ... Each has lessons of value to learn from the other.' So, out with the 'somewhat doctrinaire pedantry of a pseudo-medieval character' which had dominated the Edwardian period, and in with the ambition to produce artists across the whole spectrum of visual disciplines. After the Principal had himself made portrait drawings of the rich and famous, he liked to encourage them to give informal talks to the students in temporary huts – situated between Exhibition Road and Queensgate – which had been given to the College by the Office of Works in 1911 to relieve severe overcrowding. These sitters included Lawrence of Arabia, who impressed the Fine Art students mightily, even though they couldn't hear a word he said. Rothenstein was taking up, in a hit and miss way, the Board of Education's advice to him that 'new blood and new ideas should at once be infused into the staff of the College'. The Board had meant by this that 'new blood' should bring the institution back into the orbit of 'design for industry'.

Rothenstein had other ideas. The RCA, he said, should be 'a centre which serves, not so much to give vocational training, as to give each student, whether he intends to be a simple designer of cotton fabrics or an ambitious painter or sculptor, the best possible general education through the arts.' His distinction between 'simple' (for designers) and 'ambitious' (for the fine artists) was duly noted by the Board. An early suggestion that sculptor Jacob Epstein should become a 'new blood' appointment was greeted with the appalled official response: 'for a Professor we would want not only a genius but also character.' Eric Gill turned down a job offer with the enigmatic words, 'may I whisper it, I think there are far too many women about.' Less controversial appointments included William Staite Murray (for ceramics), Reco Capey (for textiles), Martin Travers (for stained glass), and Paul and John Nash (for general design tuition).

Rothenstein firmly believed that, instead of spending their final year preparing to become teachers, the students should exhibit or become involved in public works. He planned a series of projects in London, including murals for St Stephen's Hall, India House, the Council Chamber in County Hall, employment offices in the Docklands, and Morley College, a commission sponsored by the art dealer Sir Joseph Duveen. The well-produced student magazines *Gallimaufry* (1925) and *Mandrake* (1926) involved many young designers including Enid Marx and Cecilia Dunbar Kilburn, who was later to become a partner in the innovative Dunbar-Hay shop – 15 Albermarle Street – an outlet for design and applied art work by ex-students 'which in the ordinary way might be difficult to market'.

Design tutor Paul Nash, meanwhile, curated the exhibition 'Room and Book' at Zwemmers in April 1932 which brought together work by his colleagues in both the fine and applied arts, in an attempt to 'exemplify the modern movement in England': Edward Bawden wallpaper, Henry Moore wall lights, Staite Murray pots, Enid Marx textiles and quotations from Le Corbusier's *Vers une Architecture,* translated by Frederick Etchells. For a brief historical moment, the distinctions seemed to be dissolving. Henry Moore sculptures were exhibited against Nash's or Marx's fabrics – a much better accompaniment, wrote one critic, than the usual figurative work by contemporary artists. William Staite Murray wrote of pottery as 'the connecting link between Sculpture and Painting', and he would offer Zen-style tutorials

which consisted of long silences punctuated by cryptic one-liners such as 'God is clay'. Herbert Read called Murray's students 'canvas-free artists'. Enid Marx was to look back on the interwar years as a time when 'all the arts flowered in such profusion', as she moved from painting to hand block-printed textiles to book jackets to seat covers for the London Underground; all the while promoting modernism in preference to 'the washed-out William Morris stuff'. Reco Capey, who was Chief Instructor in Design and eventually became the College's Industrial Liaison Officer, tried hard to harness this visual energy to the needs of mass-production: though he once observed that 'Murray couldn't have anything to do with design, because he was anti-industry'.

Growth and Change under Darwin

Capey's view that much of the work of the College might be becoming too rarified was shared by the Board of Education. An official report of 1936 stated: 'notwithstanding the prestige which it has achieved in various directions, it is impossible to feel that all is well with the Royal College.' The old distinctions were about to return with a vengeance, under the impact of economic recession. 'The attraction of the Fine Arts', the Hambledon Report concluded, 'should not again be allowed to divert the College from its primary function.' The studios should be re-equipped for 'art industries', courses should be made much more specialized, and the professionalization of the Fine Art areas should be matched by an equivalent professionalization of industrial design, commercial art and dress design. The Board of Education still seemed to be promoting the Victorian notion that art was something 'applied to industry' rather than part of a broad visual culture shared by many disciplines. The Board called for a functional approach, as Britain emerged from the slump. As ever, the College's closeness to government control – which went right back to 1837, and which was no longer shared by many regional Schools responsible to local authorities – meant that political anxieties made themselves felt more keenly and directly in South Kensington than anywhere else in the system.

Nevertheless, Rothenstein was succeeded as Principal not by Herbert Read or Walter Gropius – both of whom were seriously considered for the post – but by a minor Post-Impressionist painter, and the move to Ambleside in the Second World War both postponed and radicalized the Board of Education's plans. Meanwhile, many of the talented post-war design professors of the RCA, who implemented Robin Darwin's restructuring programme of 'narrow and concentrated fields' rather than 'a general course', first met during the war in the camouflage directorate. Partly as a result, there was a clubby, tweedy atmosphere at the College in the early Darwin years from 1947 onwards, with many public pronouncements about how designers should have 'amused and well-tempered minds' and how rigid specialization and connections with industry at the right level could elevate them from the servants' hall to the high table where they belonged. Darwin was determined to get away from the pre-war Arts and Crafts atmosphere of 'ornamental vases, hand-beaten christening mugs and suchlike things'.

There followed a series of symbolic gestures: the staff attendance book was discarded, the Phoenix became the new corporate image, war was declared on the Ministry of Education, and the qualification 'Designer of the RCA' was introduced for graduates who had spent 'nine months continuously in a factory'. There was also a series of very public commissions for staff, students and ex-students: the Lion and Unicorn Pavilion at the Festival of Britain (in which the lion's solidity and strength was contrasted with the unicorn's imagination and eccentricity – a fair summary of the whole Darwin project), the interior of the Time-Life Building in New Bond Street, and the 'Royal College' stained glass windows in Coventry Cathedral. The subdivision of 'general design' into Wood, Metals and Plastics (later Furniture and Industrial Design Engineering), Ceramics (from the 60s Ceramics and Glass), Silversmithing and Jewellery, Fashion Design, Textile Design, and Stained Glass – all of them presented in College publications under the general heading of 'Industrial Design' – coincided with the rise of the professional consultant designer, as distinct from the in-house employee, and the College, backed by the new Council of Industrial Design (later the Design Council), came to have a decisive influence on the new design landscape in the UK. In the professorial inaugural lectures at the beginning of the decade, collected under the title *Anatomy of Design*, the consensus was that 'good design is design in the creation of which true art has played a part'.

As early as 1952, an exhibition at the Imperial Institute called 'Art for the Factory' showed work by silversmithing students David Mellor, Robert Welch and Gerald Benney, textile students Pat Albeck and Audrey Levy, ceramics students Hazel Thumpston and Peter Cave, and furniture students Alan Irvine, Ron Carter and Robert Heritage. It was billed as 'the first-ever College show entirely devoted to industrial design' and the *Pottery Gazette* eagerly looked forward to 'a steady supply of trained designers of both sexes' who would work in Stoke-on-Trent after graduating from Robert Baker's course, a course which now explicitly opposed the fashion for studio pottery.

When the Design Centre Awards were introduced in 1957, they were widely seen – in historian Fiona MacCarthy's words – as 'an accolade for Royal College of Art training': members of the late 1930s generation, such as textile designers Lucienne Day and her husband the furniture designer Robin Day, were also honoured, a fact which Darwin 'in all fairness' was obliged to note.

When the optimistic 50s were over, Misha Black, the College's first Professor of Industrial Design (Engineering) wrote that young designers might well start to react against the white heat of industry and turn on the one hand to 'the socially useful' and on the other to 'the crafts' where they could sign their names: 'the atmosphere in professional offices and schools of industrial design is thick with ominous question-marks.' Black, supported by Frank Height, taught many notable designers at this time including Nick Butler, Roy Gray, Peter Isherwood and Ken Sadler, and introduced two key developments into the College: Design Research (with its pioneering 'optimal hospital bed' project, under Bruce Archer and Kenneth Agnew); and the Automotive Design Unit (later the Vehicle Design Department), heavily supported by the car industry.

RCA Design and 60s London

Fashion and Graphics played a large part in 'swinging London', which was treated by the new colour supplements as virtually synonymous with the RCA.

In Fashion Design, under Janey Ironside and Joanne Brogden, the era of white gloves and elongated rolled umbrellas made way for high street and ready-to-wear outfits. Independent retail – Pauline Fordham at Palisades on Carnaby Street, James Wedge at Countdown on Kings Road, Ossie Clark at Quorum – became fashion's

equivalent to the consultant designer, while Bill Gibb was described as 'fashion's David Hockney'. Art, craft and design all seemed to be merging in the buzzword 'commercial'. Zandra Rhodes adapted a medal motif from a Hockney student painting for her graduation show textile work, which was later bought by Heal's; Derek Boshier designed the lettering for Palisades boutique; and some furniture students experimented with throwaway paper pieces which resembled sculpture.

Meanwhile, the invention of the rebellious 'art student' was proceeding apace, and Robin Darwin, nearing the end of his career, wrote ruefully that, 'I personally say every night the opening words of the *Nunc Dimittis* – Lord, now letteth thou thy servant depart in peace.' From the mid-60s onwards, he seemed less concerned with the day-to-day realities of industry than with preparing the RCA ('his work of art', as one ex-student called it) to take on university status, which it finally did, amid much ceremonial, in 1967. And he saw that the heroic period was over.

The Birth of Modern Crafts

Misha Black had predicted a 'turn to the crafts' (to quote Walter Gropius' first Bauhaus manifesto of 1919), away from both design for industry and the rise of conceptual art. Not a 'return to the crafts', the Arts and Crafts version, but a 'turn' which would bring the applied arts into a contemporary idiom. It gathered momentum during the early 70s, in David Queensberry's Ceramics and Glass Department (with the sculptors Hans Coper and Eduardo Paolozzi as tutors), in Robert Goodden's Jewellery Department (from 1973 run by ex-students Gerald Benney and Philip Popham), and in David Pye's Furniture Department. Crafts no longer had to be functional,

traditional and made of natural materials: they could be non-functional, urban, up-to-date and made with synthetic materials in all colours of the rainbow; they could also be feminist and often were. And they were no longer expected to provide a solace in a rapidly changing world: instead, they could now provide a challenge, sometimes by means of an ironic statement about traditional notions of 'the crafts', sometimes by touching at their outer edges the worlds of fine art and design. The very word 'crafts' fell out of favour as an accurate description in the mid-80s, to make way for 'applied arts'. Staff and students at the RCA were at the centre of these developments, supported by a re-energized Crafts Council, style magazines and new galleries such as Contemporary Applied Arts. Under David Hamilton and Martin Smith of Ceramics and Glass, David Watkins and Michael Rowe of Metalwork and Jewellery, and Floris van den Broecke of Furniture, the 'turn to the crafts' of the early 70s – synthesized in major survey exhibitions such as 'The Craftsman's Art' (1973) and 'The Maker's Eye' (1981) – moved on to a new repertoire of visual languages and materials, and an emphasis on 'making' rather than 'craftsmanship'.

Redefining Design

Where design was concerned, the 70s saw an international 'Design for Need' conference, the rise of systematic design research in various forms, and Rector Lionel Esher observing that, 'since the brave days of the Festival of Britain, when the College was reborn, some of the industries on which we have hitherto depended have been through a period of traumatic decline'. It was time for the College to redefine itself as a postgraduate university. In the early 80s, this redefinition centred on the concept of 'an institute of advanced studies' supported by what were then known as the new technologies. By the middle of the decade, it had shifted towards 'design for profit' (in Mrs Thatcher's phrase) and the politicians' call for a 'design-led industrial revival' coupled with an emphasis on consumerism.

The student summer show of 1981, the same year as the Memphis design group was formed in Milan, was in retrospect a very important turning-point. At the heart of the show, which has been described as 'the origins of postmodernism in industrial design', was Daniel Weil's *Homage to Marcel Duchamp*, involving radios with exposed circuit-boards in PVC bags and the sounds of birdsong. Here was design as metaphor in the post-black box era; a rejection of 'good design' and of a stable notion of function; the primacy of image over object and idea over form; form follows fiction. At precisely the same time, Ron Arad was experimenting at One Off in Covent Garden with recycled rubbish (a Rover car seat, scaffolding and damaged breezeblocks). Was he a maker or was he a designer? 'I invented my profession,' he replied. Architect Nigel Coates was about to start his visual researches into cityscapes which celebrated information overload, the polar opposite of modernist planning. The discipline of industrial design branched out towards imagery and cultural theory on the one hand, and the fusion of design values and engineering principles on the other: both were radical educational developments. In 1981, the examiners had not known quite what to make of Weil's installation: should he be awarded a Master of Design or a Master of Art? It was, and is, a good question.

JAMES DYSON

'I went to the College from 1966 to 1970, and I cheated because, for a couple of years, they were running an experimental scheme by which you could get in straight from school, or having just done a Foundation Course. So three of us went into the Furniture School, about three more into Interior Design and three into Industrial Design. I had been at Gresham's School, and then did one year at the Byam Shaw with Bridget Riley teaching us, and we were taught very well how to draw, which I always think is the foundation of everything. What was missing was that I hadn't been to a traditional art school and had yet to discover there were other things you could do besides paint and draw. I had no idea about design. My headmaster wrote this very strange letter to me, saying he was very pleased I wasn't going to university because I'd be far better off without a degree round my neck, which rather demonstrates the attitude in public schools towards a career in art and design!

So I ended up in Furniture, but thank goodness they grouped us with the Interior Design and Industrial Design people – we formed a sort of three department class. They were trying to cram a DipAD course into one year instead of three, which indeed they did to a certain extent, and at the end of the first year we were awarded a Bachelor's equivalent, and at the end of our fourth we got an MDes(RCA). So I was really jolly lucky. I joined Furniture with Richard Wentworth and Charles Dillon, but Richard went to the Sculpture School, and I transferred over to Interior Design. I never really felt part of the Furniture course: it was very woody in those days, all secret lapped dovetails and that sort of thing. It didn't quite grab me. We did have Ron Carter, though, who was a wonderful teacher of dovetails. He used to do a demonstration in front of about 30 students with his hand shaking, but he

DESIGN

produced this joint which just clicked together beautifully. Interior Design I found much more fascinating, though, dealing in these very large three-dimensional spaces.

Two years into the Interiors course, I discovered Buckminster Fuller. Everyone else used to fall asleep in Tony Hunt's lectures on structures, but I found them riveting. And I had no inclination at all before this to be an engineer. I mean, I hated maths at school and hadn't got physics. Suddenly I became enthralled by structures, why they fall down and how you calculate stresses and so on – a very odd move for me. At first I saw it in the context of architecture, and Buckminster Fuller was a hero; so was everyone else who did space frame structures. This was before the time that Norman Foster and others started using them; in fact, the only example in England was an aluminium structure at the Rotork factory in Bath, which was a very design-conscious company. I was doing a project for Joan Littlewood at Stratford East, in my second year in Interior Design. I'd already done some rather silly things with her at the City of London Festival, Tower Precinct, and she started talking about a new type of open-air children's theatre she planned to build next to the Theatre Royal. So I designed this mushroom-shaped homage to Buckminster Fuller, which Tony Hunt engineered for me, and then I went down to Bath to see the founder-chairman of Rotork, Jeremy Fry, to ask him for some money. He didn't give me any money, but was quite interested in the project; then he asked me to do one or two small design jobs, which I did, and then the Seatruck, the landing-craft which I spent the rest of my second year doing, though it was really an engineering product design job. The Cassons did get a bit worried at one point – they had Jeremy Fry to lunch, and he had to reassure them. And then, at the end of my second year, they built a prototype

JAMES DYSON

of the boat, started testing it and, since it was evidently working, I then more or less decided that at the end of my College time I'd go and manage that business – the sales, the design and the manufacture. Jeremy Fry was quite happy to wait to the end of my final year. During that year I developed a water-wheel that skidded at high speed across the water and drove a vehicle, theoretically a jeep.

So my final project in the Interior Design Department was this strange engineering development. Plus my boat. And they gave me a degree. That was the good thing about the 60s, there weren't really any rules. I was offered various jobs but I really wanted to get into commerce myself for some reason. God knows why, it's a mad thing to do. I think I had this idea then that I still have, that I wanted to be a manufacturer completely controlling my product. I really couldn't bear the idea of someone else making it and making a hash of it. Or someone else selling it and misrepresenting it. Or someone else changing my design. Or being a consultant in an office where someone comes along and asks you to do something. So I was already a bit of a control freak, even when I was at the College. At heart, I really wanted to be a Brunel or a Buckminster Fuller. And I had sort of made my own course at the College to start achieving that.

I was a pretty studious student, and I used the Royal College to the hilt. There were some seminal moments for me. We were doing a project in the first term of the first year, designing a four-room exhibition on the theme of "The Four Seasons". And we all got into free-form full flow. And I'll always remember Bernard Myers, a rather dapper tutor with a bow-tie, coming up to me and saying, "One thing about design is that it has always got to have a purpose: there has to be a reason." So I felt suitably chastened by this extraordinary piece of advice. He said it quite angrily to me, obviously annoyed by what I'd done. And I was tremendously impressed. At the same time, they were doing the QE2 in the Department, which looked frightfully glamorous, and we could see what was going on there. The staff were John Miller, Margaret Dent and Tony Hunt, who was key for me.

In a curious way I wasn't attracted by Industrial Design. I went into the studio and in fact worked there for part of my very first year. But I didn't really connect with the concept of styling and still don't, to be truthful. I didn't see the meat in it. And the College's engineering course with Imperial College was very much a thing of the future. No, what riveted me was the concept of these huge buildings with engineering structures. No one was lecturing me about Bucky Fuller, though. The person who introduced me to this idea was another Interior Design student, Anton

Furst, who used to sit in a room on his own designing a holographic theatre with a Fuller Dome on it.

We were busy working through the holidays, too, and also we were all living on grants and running clapped-out old cars and things like that. So I supplied wine to the College Union – I was a sort of wine dealer. It was the start of the wine era, and a friend of mine was importing wine, bottling it and selling it to restaurants unlabelled. I would fill a van with cases of this unmarked stuff and supply it to quite a lot of the tutors as well as the Union. It took no time at all. A couple of cases to Bernard Myers, a couple to Hugh Casson, that sort of thing.

The most important things I got out of the College, apart from Bernard ticking me off, were things you take for granted throughout the rest of your life. Meeting professional designers or architects, even though not from professions I'd necessarily chosen to follow; seeing that they are surviving and watching how they operate; the fact that the thing they care most about is the design and function of what they're doing. Getting that from live practitioners is terribly important. Another thing you take for granted during your time at the College is the excitement you feel every time you walk into the building. When you've done that dreadful tube journey, and then you walk into the building, it is always uplifting. There's a huge vibrancy at the College now, as there was in the 60s. The RCA had just become very famous immediately after the Hockney era, and the Darwin Building was quite new. There was always this great moment at about five to one when the fashion students arrived in their little green bus, wearing wonderful clothes. There was the excitement of going round the Dip. show and watching the films in the theatre. All these elements you tend to forget. Just taking it all in, absorbing it, every day. I spent four years at the RCA, so it provided my entire design training. It taught me the importance of making things well, of making prototypes to prove ideas in action, and above all it gave me the confidence to dream.'

PRE-WAR DESIGN

In 1920, the painter William Rothenstein was appointed Principal of the RCA.

Rothenstein aimed to provide students with a sophisticated, all-round education in art and design, believing that good design could only emerge from a complete understanding of the arts. At the time, most industries preferred to train their own designers 'in house' – allowing them little creative licence or recognition. However, some began to encourage outside designers to 'apply their art' to industrial production. Rothenstein's views on art education stimulated students of both fine art and design to contribute to the needs of various industries while encouraging a closer relationship between the two.

In the Design School, students came under the influence of tutor Paul Nash, the modernist painter, who had been appointed to teach part-time. Nash encouraged his students to practise watercolour painting, book illustration, wood-engraving and textile design and helped them develop an interdisciplinary approach. 'The artist', he wrote, 'should invade the house as a designer.'

Alexander Fisher
(1864–1936)
Student 1884–86
'Bhanavar the Beautiful', enamelled panel, c. 1910

Nelson Dawson
(1859–1942)
Student 1891
Enamel and silver buckle, c. 1905

John Adams
(1882–1953)
Student 1908–13
Staff 1912–14
Vase for Poole Pottery, c. 1930

Dora Batty
(unknown)
Student 1913–17
Nursery Rhyme tiles for Poole Pottery, c. 1930

Victor Skellern
(1908–66)
Student 1930–34
Mug design for Wedgwood, 1940

Robin Day
(b. 1915)
Student 1935–39
Table radio for Pye, 1965

DESIGN

Gordon Forsyth
(1879–1953)
Student 1897–1901
Lustre vase for Pilkington's, 1912

Charles Vyse
(1882–1971)
Student 1905–10
Cat, c. 1930

Truda Adams/Carter
(1890–1958)
Student 1908–13
Vase for Poole Pottery, c. 1930

A. B. Read
(1899–1973)
Student 1919–23
Earthenware vases for Poole Pottery, c. 1955

Edward Bawden
(1903–1989)
Student 1922–25
Staff 1930–40, 1948–53
Tiles for Poole Pottery, c. 1930

Eric Ravilious
(1903–42)
Student 1922–25
Staff 1930–39
'Garden' plate for Wedgwood, c. 1939

Arnold Machin
(1911–99)
Student 1936–40
Figures for Wedgwood, c. 1940

Paul Nash
(1889–1946)
Staff 1922–25, 1938–39
'Gay' tea-set for Foley's China, 1934

Reco Capey
(1895–1961)
Student 1919–22
Staff 1925–53
Packaging for Yardley's, 1930

INDUSTRIAL DESIGN

Reco Capey: the neglected pioneer

The name of Reco Capey is not a familiar one in the design history books, yet he was clearly an important figure in British design and design education during his professional life. He was among the first 20 designers to be elected a Royal Designer for Industry by the Royal Society of Arts in 1937, and the first to be awarded this distinction for 'General Design'.

Reco Capey was the first professional industrial designer to be appointed to teach at the RCA. From 1924 to 1935 he was Chief Instructor in Design, and after three further years as a visiting lecturer, he became the College's first Industrial Liaison Officer, setting up placements for students within industry. In many ways, Capey was among the first British designers who truly understood the nature of 'industrial design', and was one of the earliest designers to promote the idea that design could be of value to every aspect of industry, from point-of-sale to the product itself.

Reco Capey, c. 1930

Reco Capey
Cigarette box, ebony, sycamore and carved amber, 1935

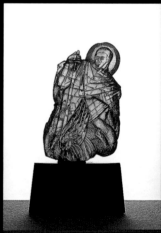

Reco Capey
St Michael, carved amber figure, 1929

DESIGN

View of Lucienne Day's degree show, 1940

Astrid Sampe, block-printed linen, student work, 1936

Façade of 32/33 Old Bond Street, previously Yardley's headquarters, refurbished by architects Hawkins and Brown in 1993. The stone frieze was recast from Capey's original design.

Born in Smallthorn in the Potteries in 1895 to a family of French descent, Capey worked briefly at Doulton's factory in Burslem before attending the RCA in 1919. As a student he learned the difficult craft of lacquer and proved himself a gifted carver. In 1924 he was invited to set up the new Textiles department. Among his students were Astrid Sampe and (later) Lucienne Day, both of whom were to become successful textile designers in the post-war years. He told Sampe, 'Never be afraid to experiment', advice she took to heart in reviving the post-war Swedish textile industry.

From 1928 he was appointed art director for Yardley's cosmetics, a post he held until his retirement in 1958. His work for Yardley's shows him as a pioneer of 'corporate identity', introducing a house style which extended from the design of the catalogues and packaging to the styling of the showroom interiors and the decoration of Yardley's headquarters in Bond Street.

40s–50s INDUSTRIAL

Robin Darwin's arrival at the RCA in 1948 heralded a new era for the College. In his first six years as principal, Darwin implemented reforms which transformed the College into an institution which resembles today's RCA. Abolishing the general and all-encompassing discipline of Design, he created entirely separate schools which provided rigidly specialized facilities and training. The schools of Fine Art were now to sit cheek by jowl with the schools of Fashion and Textiles, Graphic Design, Ceramics, Silversmithing and Jewellery.

There was no Department of Industrial Design during these early years; instead specialized units were presented under that umbrella term. This was a deliberate shift away from the pre-war practice of offering a broad and non-specific training which had often led students to a career in the teaching profession. Darwin's vision was of a system that inspired rather than simply fed industry. Creative excellence was seen as indispensable to post-war reconstruction, and the emerging 'profession' of designer was at last given due credit and recognition.

Norman Makinson
(b. 1921)
Student 1946–49
'Festival of Britain' mug for Wedgwood, 1951

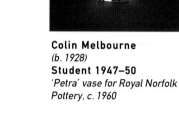

Colin Melbourne
(b. 1928)
Student 1947–50
'Petra' vase for Royal Norfolk Pottery, c. 1960

Tom Arnold
(b. 1928)
Student 1949–52
'Homemaker' (with Enid Seeney) for Ridgway Potteries, 1955

Frank Height
(b. 1921)
Student 1949–52
Staff 1959–74
Professor 1975–86
'Triplite' yarn fault detector, 1974

Robert Minkin
(b. 1928)
Student 1952–55
Plate for Wedgwood, c. 1950s

Robert Welch
(b. 1929)
Student 1952–55
Visiting Staff
'Oriana' stainless steel jugs for Old Hall, 1958

Peter Cave
(b. 1923)
Student 1948–51
Plate, c. 1950

Hazel Thumpston
(b. 1925)
Student 1948–51
'Thistledown' teapot for Foley Pottery, c. 1955

Peter Wall
(b. 1923)
Student 1948–51
'Big Top' nursery plate for Wedgwood, c. 1959

Geoffrey Baxter
(b. 1922)
Student 1950–54
'Banjo' textured glass vase for James Powell & Sons, 1966

Robert Jefferson
(b. 1929)
Student 1951–54
'Compact' and 'Contour' teapots for Poole Pottery, 1965 and c. 1969

David Mellor
(b. 1930)
Student 1950–54
Visiting Staff
'Pride' silver cutlery, 1955

Neal French and David White
(b. 1933, b. 1934)
Students 1955–58, 1956–59
'Royal College Shape' for W. T. Copeland, 1958

Naum Slutzky
(unknown)
Staff 1950–57
Chromium-plated steel teapot, Bauhaus, c. 1924

Robert Goodden
(b. 1909)
Professor 1948
Silver electric kettle for the Queen, from a design by Prince Philip, 1956

60s INDUSTRIAL DESIGN

The 1960s saw Industrial Design become a discipline in its own right. Introduced in 1959 as the Department of Industrial Design (Engineering) under the eminent industrial designer and architect Misha Black, the course was the earliest in the country to recognize that engineering was an important part of the design process. For the first time, students began to design scientific instruments, electronic equipment, industrial machinery and vehicles.

At the same time, interest in the process and definition of 'design' led to the setting up of a design research centre within the School. Because industrial design was a relatively new addition to the visual landscape of Britain, Black felt it important to explain publicly the process, in order to support the growth and recognition of the profession. Under the leadership of Bruce Archer, the Design Research Unit remained within the School for six years before becoming an entirely separate department with Archer as its professor. Its flagship project was the 'optimal hospital bed'.

Gillian Pemberton
(b. 1936)
Student 1957–60
'Chevron' oven-to-tableware for Denby, 1964

Kenneth Agnew
(b. 1933)
Student 1959–61
Staff 1961–78
King's Fund Hospital bed, 1966 (designed with research team)

Grahame Clarke
(b. 1942)
Student 1962–65
Staff 1970–89
Bone china cup, saucer and plate, 1965

Nick Butler
(b. 1942)
Student 1963–66
Visiting Professor
Telephone for British Telecom, BIB Design Consultants, 1986

Nick Holland
(b. 1946)
Student 1964–69
Digger, student work, 1965

Ross Kinneir
(b. 1947)
Student 1965–70
'Handihaler' for Boehringer Ingelheim, 1996

DESIGN

Roy Gray
(b. 1937)
Student 1957–61
Typewriter, Degree Show, 1961

David Brickwood
(b. 1939)
Student 1958–62
Window furniture for Gardiner & Sons, 1963

Stephen Bartlett
(b. 1942)
Student 1960–64
Gas water heater, Degree Show, 1964

Martin Hunt
(b. 1942)
Student 1963–66
Staff 1969–present
Contrast oven-to-tableware for Hornsea, 1975

Peter Isherwood
(b. 1940)
Student 1963–66
Staff 1979–83
Drill, Degree Show, 1966

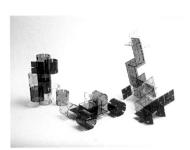

Patrick Rylands
(b. 1942)
Student 1963–66
'Playplax' for Trendon, 1965

L. Bruce Archer
(b. 1922)
Staff 1961–88
'What is good design?', in Design magazine, 1960

David Queensberry
(b. 1929)
Professor 1959–83
Fine tableware for Midwinter, 1963

Misha Black
(1910–77)
Professor 1959–75
'Anatomy of Design' exhibition at Britain Can Make It, 1946

70s INDUSTRIAL DESIGN

By the 70s, economic recession had led to a reassessment of the role of design in society. The certainties of the 50s and 60s gave way to an understanding of the need for design to respond to wider global issues – ecological, environmental and human. Young designers were attracted by 'the socially useful' and began to question the dominance of mass-production industry. The reaction against formal design methodologies was especially apparent, with the realization that rational and scientific knowledge plays only a part in the design process.

Bruce Archer, as Professor of Design Research, continued to champion the cause of design methodologies until his research department was disbanded in 1987. His department, however, was to have less direct impact on studio design teaching at the College as it moved more and more into theoretical enquiry. Although increasingly out of favour at the time, the development of design systems came to be recognized in retrospect as a very important step towards the development of computer-aided design.

Clive Garrard
(b. 1946)
Student 1967–70
Modular scale for WT Avery, 1983

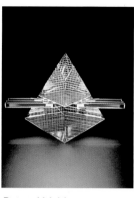

Peter Aldridge
(b. 1947)
Student 1968–71
Staff 1972–78, 1993–96
Glass project for Corning, n.d.

Geoff Hollington
(b. 1949)
Student 1971–74
Prototype videophone for Panasonic, 1990

John Stoddard
(b. 1948)
Student 1971–74
Staff 1987–88
'1+1' office furniture system (with Philip Davies), IDEO, for Steelcase Strafor, c. 1995

Howard Biddle
(b. 1949)
Student 1976–78
Stapler for Rexel, Cambridge Design Consultants, 1999

Paul Atkinson
(b. 1952)
Student 1977–80
Experimental fibre-optic clock for Rotaflex, 1986

James Dyson
(b. 1947)
Student 1966–71
'Dyson' vacuum cleaner, 1993

Nick Marchant
(b. 1947)
Student 1970–73
Radial saw, 1972

Roy Fischer and David Hodge
(b.1949, b. 1948)
Students 1971–74
*'Easygrow' adjustable
wheelchair, 1974*

Nick Leon and Ming Leung
(b.1952, b. 1948)
Students 1973–75
Filing machine, 1974

Robin Levein
(b. 1952)
Student 1973–76
*Personal headset telephone,
prototype, for Queensberry
Hunt, 1990*

Richard Seymour and Dick Powell
(b.1953, b. 1951)
Students 1974–77, 1973–76
Tefal SA Freeline kettle, 1986

Ralph Ball
(b. 1951)
Student 1977–80
Staff 1985–present
'Golden Delicious' light, 1997

Nick Oakley
(b. 1954)
Student 1977–80
Digital watches and calculators, 1980

Frank Height
(b. 1921)
Student 1949–52
Staff 1959–74
Professor 1975–86
Modular Desk System, 1971

INDUSTRIAL DESIGN

James Dyson and Dual Cyclone Technology

Seatruck, 1970
A flat-bottomed high-speed boat, designed by Dyson as a student. It was developed with the engineer and inventor Jeremy Fry and went on to earn sales of $750 million in more than 50 countries.

The story of James Dyson and Dual Cyclone Technology is a study in courage and determination. Every aspect of the Dyson story holds significant lessons for a new generation of British entrepreneurs and product developers.

James Dyson studied furniture and interior design at the RCA from 1966 to 1970. His interest in problem-solving, innovation and engineering was apparent even then, when, as a student, he developed the Seatruck – a flat-bottomed high-speed marine vehicle for use in the military, oil and construction industries. Other inventions followed, including the Ballbarrow. However, it wasn't until Dyson turned his attention to vacuum cleaners that he set himself on the path to becoming an international household name.

The cyclonic system first occurred to Dyson in 1979 when he saw 30-foot industrial cyclone chambers being used to clear the air in a spray-paint workshop.

Ballbarrow, 1974
Based on the traditional wheelbarrow, but with a ball replacing the front wheel for increased manoeuvrability. Within three years it had become market leader in the wheelbarrow sector.

G-Force, 1986
First produced in 1986 by the Japanese company Silver Reed. The G-Force was only available in Japan, where, despite costing £1,200, it became a cult object and was purchased by a number of museums.

DC01, 1993

The DC01, launched in 1993 at a price of £200, was the first model produced and manufactured by Dyson himself out of his own factory in Chippenham. By 1995 it had become market leader, outselling its rivals both at home and abroad.

Centrifugal force was being used to remove paint particles efficiently from the air, with no loss of suction or air flow. Dyson immediately saw the potential of applying such technology on a smaller, more domestic scale and mocked up his first cyclonic cleaner by customizing his own vacuum cleaner with the aid of cardboard and tape.

Five years and 5,127 prototypes later, Dyson perfected the Dual Cyclone system. The bag used inside the more traditional vacuum cleaner was replaced by two cyclone chambers. The result was a dramatic improvement in cleaning performance and efficiency, and the most significant development in cleaning technology since the invention of the vacuum cleaner in 1901.

At the end of the century, Dyson's own company has become a world-class, innovative production centre worth over £100 million, employing over 400 workers, including 17 RCA design graduates.

DC02, 1995

Models of the DC02 at various stages of development. The breadboard model is a working prototype and the blue foam model is visually correct.

A cylinder model, the DC02, appeared in 1995. With its revolutionary stair-hugging capability, it, too, became a market leader.

80s INDUSTRIAL DESIGN

The 80s marked an important shift in the direction of what now came to be known as 'product design' at the RCA. Established certainties about design were dismantled and the boundaries redefined as students began to question the meaning of designed objects as metaphors, and to explore new solutions which incorporated a wider understanding of the cultural implications of products. As the decade progressed, new possibilities were realized, as students were able to harness the latest advances in both materials and computer technology.

The birth of the postmodern – a rejection of 'good design' and of a stable notion of function in the era after the black box approach – coincided with this period of creative energy, and students were stimulated by, as well as stimulating, Italian design movements, such as Memphis. These radical developments were tempered by the engineering experience of Professor Frank Height, which meant that students were encouraged to understand the mechanics of mass production as well as commercial realities.

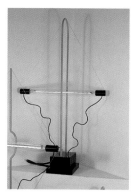

Uri Friedlander
(b. 1952)
Student 1979–81
Light, Degree Show, 1981

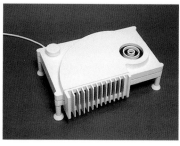

Winfried Scheuer
(b. 1952)
Student 1979–81
Staff 1994–98
Fan heater, Degree Show, 1981

Julian Brown
(b. 1955)
Student 1980–83
Visiting Staff
'Attila' can crusher for Rexite, Italy, 1997

Ross Lovegrove
(b. 1958)
Student 1980–83
Visiting Staff
'Pod' light for Luceplan, Italy, 1998

Paul Priestman
(b. 1961)
Student 1983–85
Staff 1987–91
Video conferencing camera, 1998

Andy Davey
(b. 1962)
Student 1983–86
Wind-up radio for Baygen, 1996

DESIGN

Gerard Taylor
(b. 1955)
Student 1978–81
*'Piccadilly' light for Memphis,
Italy, 1982*

Daniel Weil
(b. 1953)
Student 1978–81
Professor 1991–94
'Radio Bag', Degree show, 1981

Steven Peart
(b. 1958)
Student 1979–82
*'Animal' wetsuit for O'Neill,
USA, 1991*

Steve Kyffin
(b. 1959)
Student 1981–84
Visiting Staff
Director 1994–97
'Sextant', Degree Show, 1984

Jasper Morrison
(b. 1958)
Student 1982–85
Bottle rack, Magis, Italy, 1993

Ian Pearson
(b. 1960)
Student 1982–85
*Persona contraceptive device for
Unipath, 1996*

Tim Brown
(b. 1962)
Student 1985–87
Visiting Staff
*M500 Monitor for Ideo, NEC,
Japan, 1989*

Colin Burns
(b. 1963)
Student 1985–87
Visiting Staff
Degree Show, 1987

Tony Dunne
(b. 1964)
Student 1986–88
Staff 1991–present
'Faraday Chair', 1988

125

As the consumer boom of the 80s gave way to the more circumspect 90s, the teaching of design shifted. Design itself was to become a more intimate instrument, concerned with providing the tools for new approaches to the way we live our lives. Its aims now include the enrichment of simple everyday activities, the provision of emotional as well as physical comfort, a sense of cultural tradition and responsibility, and a greater respect for the limited resources of the planet.

Daniel Weil's appointment as Professor in 1991 was to have a significant impact on the teaching of design, as was the development of Computer Related Design under Professor Gillian Crampton Smith. Both have taught that design should be user-inspired and reflect richer conceptual possibilities. Another key development was the foundation of Industrial Design Engineering.

With the appointment of Ron Arad as Professor of Furniture and Industrial Design in 1997, the increasingly blurred division between the two disciplines has been seriously questioned, and the two areas brought together for the first time since the 50s.

Sebastian Bergne
(b. 1966)
Student 1988–90
Staff 1998–present
Lampshade 1, for Radius GmbH, Köln, 1990

David Constantine and Simon Gue
(b. 1960, b. 1963)
Students 1988–90
Wheelchair for Cambodia, 1993

Max Burton
(b. 1966)
Student 1991–93
'Hot Rocks' indoor barbecue prototype, Degree Show, 1993

Sam Hecht
(b. 1969)
Student 1991–93
'Whitebox' personal computer prototype 002 for NEC Technologies, Japan, 1996

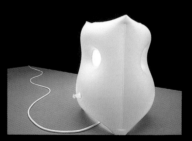

Nick Crosby
(b. 1971)
Student 1993–95
Table light for Inflate, 1996

Mark Garside
(b. 1969)
Student 1993–95
'Digital Grass' for Inflate, 1997

Guy Dyas
(b. 1968)
Student 1989–91
*'Vacman' vacuum cleaner, prototype,
Degree Show, 1991*

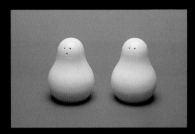

Shin Azumi
(b. 1965)
Student 1992–94
*'Snowman' salt and pepper
shakers, 1998*

Michael Anastassiades
(b. 1967)
Student 1991–93
Beaker-ansaphone, 1998

Peter Russell-Clark
(b. 1968)
Student 1991–93
Staff 1998–present
*'Therapeutic Alliance' video
endoscope, prototype, 1993*

Tord Boontje
(b. 1968)
Student 1992–94
*'Transglass' recycled glass vessels
(with Emma Woffenden), 1997*

Takeshi Ishiguro
(b. 1969)
Student 1992–94
*'Recasting Rice' salt and pepper
cellars, prototype, Degree Show, 1994*

Sixth Wu
(b. 1971)
Student 1993–95
*'Variety is the Spice of Life'
tableware, Degree Show, 1995*

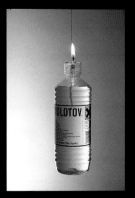

Georg Baldele
(b. 1968)
Student 1996–98
*'Molotov Cocktail' lamp,
Degree Show, 1998*

John Drane
(b. 1938)
Staff 1987–96
**Professor of Industrial Design
Engineering 1997–present**
Durabeam Torches for BIB, 1979

COMPUTER RELATED DESIGN

Digital dreams

Lorna Ross
Telephone Glove prototype, Interval Research, 1994
This glove was developed as part of a project to explore ways in which technology can be designed to enhance the relationship between product and user. It allows individuals to make private calls on their mobile phone without disturbing others, the user speaking discreetly into his or her hand.

As new technologies develop, so new fields of design emerge. The Computer Related Design (CRD) course was inaugurated in 1990 in response to the development of information technology. Under Professor Gillian Crampton-Smith, who studied philosophy and Fine Art at Cambridge before turning to graphic design, the new course set out to explore the possibilities the new technology could offer.

The course quickly became a pioneer in the field of interaction design. Emphasis was placed not on the technology itself, but rather on its uses. At its core was the belief that design should offer people products that are enjoyable to use. The emphasis of the teaching lay firmly in examining ways in which this new-fangled and in

many ways alienating technology could draw on a wider cultural perspective to develop imaginative and friendly tools for everyday life.

The course is structured around three different areas of design: software and virtual information space, including CD-ROMs and Internet sites; computer systems and electronic products; and intelligent environments – spaces and installations mediated by information and communications technology. In each area, avenues are explored which extended the boundaries of design, not only in the application of the new technology, but also in discovering ways in which it can be applied to effect change in people's behaviour – in ways of living, communicating and being.

Graduates are snapped up by companies who recognize the potential of this multidisciplinary, inventive approach to design. The American computer conglomerate Microsoft regularly employs CRD alumni, as do international design consultants IDEO, who currently employ 25 RCA graduates, and have employed over 50 in the last 25 years. Interval Research, Microsoft and IDEO, together with other international companies such as Apple Computers, Philips and Sony, also offer students work placements. The success of the course has already had repercussions on the international design stage: a dramatic example of the advantages of studying design in an art environment and art in a design environment.

Colin Burns
Kiss Communicator (with Duncan Kerr and Heather Martin), IDEO Europe, 1997.
A concept realization of a communication device for remotely located lovers.

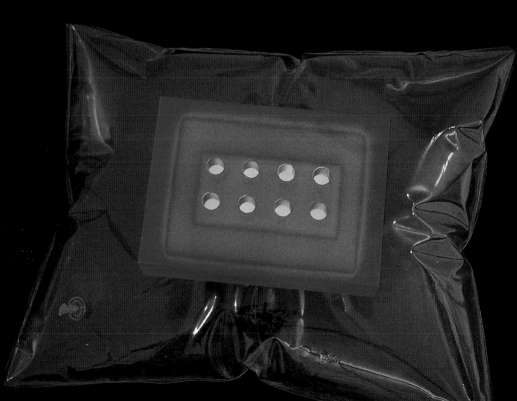

Tony Dunne
When Objects Dream, 1996
The pillow is an abstract radio that receives invisible electronic information, confronting the owner with the fact that we are inhabiting hertzian space, and that even our homes are being constantly invaded by the radiation of electronic information. It responds to local changes in the radio frequency environment within a 200m diameter of the home.

50s FURNITURE

The teaching at the RCA in the immediate post-war years reflected a close relationship with the Council of Industrial Design (CoID). Later known as the Design Council, the CoID was established in 1944 to promote a better understanding of the importance of design in British industry. Robin Darwin, together with others in senior positions at the College, had previously worked at the CoID, while the director of the CoID, Gordon Russell, served on the College's council. In addition, Gordon Russell's brother, Dick, was Professor of the Department of Woods, Metals and Plastics. The RCA worked as an essential buttress to the CoID, aiming to provide the type of specialized and professional instruction that would have a direct impact on the regeneration of industry.

Both tutors and students at the College shared the CoID's missionary zeal to introduce 'good design' to the nation. Based on the functional aesthetic of Modernism, 'good design' during the 1950s drew its inspiration from Scandinavian design. The look was 'simple but graceful', incorporating notions of traditional craft heritage and imbued with an explicit sense of integrity.

Robin Day
(b. 1915)
Student 1935–39
M5 stacking chair for Hille, 1962

Frank Guille
(b. 1926)
Student 1947–50
Staff 1960–86
Nursery bed for Prince Charles, 1951

Ron Carter
(b. 1926)
Student 1949–52
Staff 1955–74
Beech and mahogany chair, 1952

Alan Irvine
(b. 1926)
Student 1951–53
Museum bench for Gavina, Italy, 1980

Alan Tilbury
(b. 1935)
Student 1956–59
Staff 1975–94
Chaise longue, 1959

Ron Lenthall
(1917–82)
Technician 1956–82
View of Ron Lenthall memorial exhibition, RCA, 1982

DESIGN

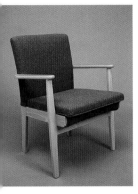

Robin Howland
(b. 1923)
Student 1947–50
'Langford' chair for Parker Knoll, 1954

Robert Heritage
(b. 1927)
Student 1948–51
Staff 1972–74
Professor 1974–77
Sideboard, 1954

Robin Wade
(b. 1929)
Student 1952–55
Bed-settee, 1955

Dick Young
(b. 1930)
Student 1954–58
Rosewood cabinet, 1958

David Pye
(1896–1993)
Staff 1948–63
Professor 1964–74
Rush-seated armchair, 1945

R. D. Russell
(1903–81)
Professor 1948–64
Welbeck sideboard, 1934, and Murphy A8 Radio, 1932

Furniture design had come under the umbrella of the Department of Woods, Metals and Plastics, but in 1955 it became a separate school. As part of their training, students were encouraged to take time out to visit Scandinavian countries. The students themselves viewed their travels as 'pilgrimages' to learn the basics of good design. Ron Carter went to work for the Danish company Fritz Hansen, while Alan Tilbury was apprenticed to Børge Mogenson, and Robin Howland to I. Christianson. After graduating, some students went to work for English firms, bringing the Scandinavian sensibility to the British high street – Robin Howland worked for Parker Knoll, Dick Young for G-plan and Frank Guille for Kandya. Other designers, such as Ron Carter and Alan Tilbury, set up their own workshops, which, like those of the Scandinavian makers, were on a smaller and more personal scale.

60s FURNITURE

During the 1960s, the RCA became the centre of British Pop art and design. This was partly due to the increasing interaction between different courses, which led to a convergence of the fine, graphic and applied arts, and to a more experimental and innovative approach to both fine art and design. The generation of students at the College in these years revolutionized the visual currency of the day, introducing youth, fun, sex and fashion to the high street. One of the RCA pop groups of the period coined the phrase 'Cool Britannia', but it was meant as a joke.

Students turned away from traditional notions of what constituted 'good design' to experiment with different materials, forms and uses in furniture design. Materials such as plastics, steel rod and paper were used, and young designers explored various avenues to make inexpensive mass-production furniture in kit form for self-assembly.

Geoffrey Harcourt
(b. 1935)
Student 1957–60
Chair for Artifort, 1967

Clive Bacon
(b. 1938)
Student 1958–61
Interlocking chairs, 1961

Desmond Ryan
(b. 1941)
Student 1961–65
Oak coffee table, 1964

Fred Scott
(b. 1942)
Student 1963–66
'Supporto' chair for Hille, 1979

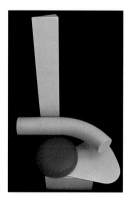

Jane Dillon
(b. 1943)
Student 1965–68
Staff 1994–present
Chair for Planular, Italy, 1970

Richard La Trobe Bateman
(b. 1938)
Student 1965–68
Oak table and chair, 1968

Roland Gibbard
(b. 1935)
Student 1958–62
Office chair and storage units, 1962

Peter Murdoch
(b. 1940)
Student 1961–64
Child's chair, c. 1960s

Peter Cornish
(b. 1941)
Student 1962–65
Coffee table in yew veneer, 1965

David Colwell
(b. 1944)
Student 1965–68
Acrylic chair, 1968

David Crump
(b. 1945)
Student 1965–68
Seat, 1968

Roger Dean
(b. 1944)
Student 1965–68
'Sea Urchin' chair, 1968

Christopher Sykes
(b. 1942)
Student 1966–68
Seat, 1968

Floris van den Broecke
(b. 1945)
Student 1966–69
Staff 1983–84
Professor 1985–97
Chaise longue, 1969

Sandy Webster
(b. 1945)
Student 1966–69
INCA museum showcase, 1984

70s FURNITURE

During the 1970s at the RCA, crafts (or 'the applied arts') emerged as the focal point for debate. At issue were the accepted distinctions between craft technique and industrial production, and between fine art and design. Breaking down these barriers provided a means of restoring individual skill and personal expression in the process of design and in the resulting product.

Furniture students under Professor David Pye, whose influential book *The Nature and Art of Workmanship* was published in 1968, were as much a part of the ongoing debate about the workmanship of risk and certainty as students from other design departments. Pye described the work of his department as 'taking pot-shots at the flock of duck-billed platitudes' which surrounded the subject. To the students, the main issues at stake were the role of furniture within material culture and in the history of design. This meant that furniture design was seen as less hermetic, and more concerned with the context in which the work was to function and be seen.

Jan Ekselius
(b. 1947)
Student 1967–70
Stacking stool, 1970

Colin Williams
(b. 1946)
Student 1967–70
Cabinet, 1970

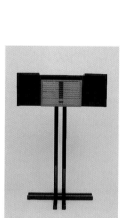

David Field
(b. 1946)
Student 1969–72
Staff 1979–97
'Numismatist's cabinet', 1972

Michael Gurney
(b. 1947)
Student 1969–72
Cabinet, 1972

Eric de Graff
(b. 1951)
Student 1973–76
Cross chair, 1980

Peter Wheeler
(b. 1947)
Student 1974–77
Staff 1994–98
Wardrobe, 1977

Malcolm Allum
(b. 1942)
Student 1967–70
Chess-set, 1970

Charles Dillon
(1945–81)
Student 1966–71
*'Jobber' chair (with Jane Dillon),
Casas, Barcelona, 1973*

Rupert Williamson
(b. 1945)
Student 1968–71
Dining chair, 1977

Fred Baier
(b. 1949)
Student 1972–75
Comfortable chair, 1984

Paul Haigh
(b. 1949)
Student 1972–75
Chair, 1975

Margaret Buck
(b. 1948)
Student 1973–76
Table and stools, 1976

John Coleman
(b. 1953)
Student 1976–79
Console, 1984

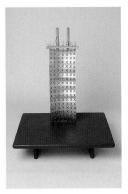

Lynne Wilson
(b. 1952)
Student 1976–79
Visiting Staff
Samurai chair, 1979

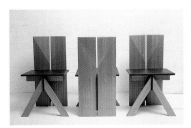

Paul Atkinson
(b. 1952)
Student 1977–80
Chairs, 1980

80s FURNITURE

The 80s signalled a move away from the intellectualizing of furniture design towards a quieter sensuality. Plain materials, bare woods and simple forms captured the new mood for unself-conscious, 'honest' furniture, and were as much an acknowledgement of production limitations as of a philosophical shift. The incorporation of found objects, ready-made components and common implements introduced an ironic 'human' element which lifted the rationalist aesthetic by adding charm and a gentle humour.

This movement – christened 'New Functionalism' by design journalists – was spearheaded by students Jasper Morrison, Konstantin Grcic and James Irvine under Professor Floris van den Broecke. These design students were to become among the most influential furniture designers of the late 20th century. Their work was about constraint and humility, rejecting unnecessary quirks and superfluous detail to concentrate on modular, minimal everyday furniture. As Morrison explained, the furniture designer now had to build 'his own factory, not with bricks but from the sprawling backstreets teeming with services and processes'.

Gerard Taylor
(b. 1955)
Student 1978–81
Desk, 1984

Paul Heritage
(b. 1956)
Student 1979–82
Reclining chair, 1982

Peter Christian
(b. 1958)
Student 1981–84
Chair, 1984

James Irvine
(b. 1958)
Student 1981–84
'Carugo' chair for Cappellini, 1993

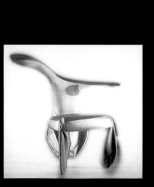

Mary Little
(b. 1958)
Student 1982–85
'Rudolph' chair, 1990

Jasper Morrison
(b. 1958)
Student 1982–85
Visiting Staff
Plywood chair for Vitra, 1989

Ross Lovegrove
(b. 1958)
Student 1980–83
F08 chair for Cappellini, Italy, 1992

John Small
(b. 1950)
Student 1980–83
'Knock-down' chair, 1983

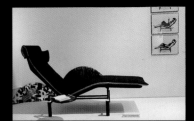

Paul Chamberlain
(b. 1958)
Student 1981–84
Chaise longue, 1984

Maxine Naylor
(b. 1957)
Student 1981–84
Staff 1987–88, 1995–98
Theo Light, 1994

Jiri Pelcl
(b. 1950)
Student 1983–84
Chair, 1984

Janette Carpenter-Donnelly
(b. 1959)
Student 1982–85
Chaise longue, 1985

Mark Robson
(b. 1965)
Student 1987–89
Fibreglass chair, 1989

Konstantine Grcic
(b. 1965)
Student 1988–90
Visiting Staff
'Tam tam' table for SCP, 1992

Alison Thomas
(b. 1965)
Student 1989–90
'Tutti-Frutti' stool, 1990

90s FURNITURE

During the 90s, the teaching of furniture design at the College built on the ideas of New Functionalism to direct work more specifically to the post-consumer boom era. With elegant designs that incorporated a simple charm, furniture was modular, flat-packing, folding and multi-functional. Designed for the 'urban nomad', this furniture provided solutions for contemporary ways of living. Another important consideration was the user's engagement with the piece – it was vital that he or she should delight in its use. There was a rejection of 'rehearsed solutions': the traditional distinctions between craft and design, one-offs and manufacture, seemed to have become irrelevant.

With Ron Arad's appointment as Professor of Furniture in 1997 (a year later he became Head of the new Department of Furniture and Industrial Design), the Department's international reputation as a hotbed of creative new talent was consolidated. Tutors brought in by Arad have included Jasper Morrison, Konstantin Grcic, Aldo Cibic and Michael Marriott.

Nazanin Kamali
(b. 1966)
Student 1989–91
'Magic Carpet' chaise longue, 1991

Simon Maidment
(b. 1993)
Student 1990–92
'Baby Tambour' chair, 1993

Luke Pearson and Tom Lloyd
(b. 1967, b. 1966)
Students 1991–93
'Homer' mobile office for Knoll International, 1998

Tord Boontje
(b. 1968)
Student 1992–94
'Rough and Ready' furniture, 1998

Greg James
(b. 1961)
Student 1993–95
Paper chair, 1995

Tom Hall
(b. 1970)
Student 1994–96
'Collector's Table', 1996

Jane Atfield
(b. 1965)
Student 1991–93
'RCP2' recycled plastic chair, 1993

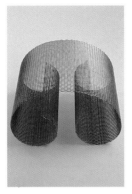

Christina Lamiquis
(b. 1965)
Student 1991–93
'Noodle' stool, 1993

Michael Marriott
(b. 1963)
Student 1991–93
Staff 1998–present
'Kit chair' 1993

Thomas Heatherwick
(b. 1970)
Student 1992–94
Gazebo (detail), Degree Show, 1994

Tomoko Azumi
(b. 1966)
Student 1993–95
'Table = Chest', 1995

Ineke Hans
(b. 1966)
Student 1993–95
'Goethe & Cervantes' storage, 1995

Alexander Hellum
(b. 1966)
Student 1994–96
Reclining chair, 1996

Roberto Feo
(b. 1964)
Student 1995–97
'Mind the Gap', El Ultimo Grito, 1998

Ron Arad
(b. 1951)
Professor 1997–present
'And the Rabbit Speaks' chairs, 1994

ARCHITECTURE &

Shaping the future: the post-war years

The School of Architecture had first been set up in 1901 following the turn-of-the-century reforms initiated by Walter Crane. Under Professor Beresford Pite, architecture was studied by all students within their all-round education in art and design.

In the post-war years, the architect Basil Ward was appointed to run the new School of Architecture, as part of the restructuring set in motion by Robin Darwin. The School still offered courses to all students in an attempt to make a grounding in the Modern Movement part of the College experience. In 1951, the Department of Interior Design was inaugurated by Hugh Casson as Professor and Margaret Casson as tutor. This became the School of Interior Design in 1952; the School of Architecture was disbanded a year later.

At first, the Department was temporarily housed in the aeronautical section of the Science Museum, which accommodated just three students, before moving to Cromwell Road. There were no undergraduate courses in interior design from which to recruit, so students came from all disciplines – painting, embroidery, textiles, jewellery, furniture and theatre design – as well as from other departments within the College itself. The course structure encouraged designers to develop their own paths and resulted in a rich mixture of results, from film to furniture. Gradually, other colleges established

Hugh Casson
The Elephant House, London Zoo, Casson Condor, 1965

Margaret Casson
Directors' Dining Room, Shell Centre, London, 1962

INTERIORS

H.T. Cadbury-Brown
Darwin Building, Royal College of Art, Cadbury-Brown, Casson and Goodden, 1962

Basil Ward
Houses at Wicklands Avenue, Saltdean,
Connell Ward and Lucas, 1934

interior design courses, many of which owed a debt to the model the Cassons had built.

Hugh Casson, Robert Goodden and H. T. Cadbury-Brown were the team responsible for designing and building the College's headquarters on Kensington Gore, now known as the Darwin Building. Completed in 1961, the building had a largely functional role. Cadbury-Brown wrote,

'As a place where art is in continual process of being made, the interior especially should be plain, and one of its principal functions should be to act as a background to art and not to assert itself as an "art thing", but outside it should be more positive in character ...'

By 1972, when the concept of interior design had become too strongly associated in the public mind with 'interior decoration', the name of the School had changed to Environmental Design. This allowed it to accommodate the increasing number of students working in a wide range of disciplines – such as Anton Furst with his holographic theatre. When John Miller became Professor in 1975, he was determined to reorient the course by bringing the more formal teaching of architecture into the programme. Within a few years he had radically changed the curriculum so that students could gain the equivalent of a professional qualification (Part II) in architecture. Students of interior design were also taught architecture. This was rather a controversial topic at the time, but Miller believed interior design students would benefit from a complete understanding of landscape and building. Miller brought in a number of internationally renowned architects as staff to support his changes, including Jeremy Dixon, John Outram and Leon Krier. At the end of the Miller years, the course was recognized by the Royal Institute of British Architects.

David Bentheim
(b. 1947)
Student 1971–74
'The Earth's Treasury', The Natural History Museum, London, 1998

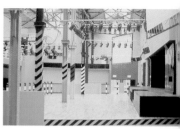

Ben Kelly
(b. 1949)
Student 1971–74 Staff 1994–95
Hacienda, Manchester, 1981

Julian Powell-Tuck
(b. 1952)
Student 1973–76 Staff 1991–96
Metropolis Studios, London, Powell-Tuck Connor & Orefelt, 1988

Ian Sharratt
(b. 1948)
Student 1973–76
Inland Revenue Centre, Nottingham, Michael Hopkins, 1995

Paul Keogh and Rachel Chidlow
(b. 1953, b. 1954)
Students 1977–79, 1977–80
Meeting House Square/Gaiety School of Acting, Temple Bar, Dublin, Paul Keogh Architects, 1996

Heidi Locher
(b. 1957)
Student 1978–80
New office/apartment building, Clerkenwell Green, Paxton and Locher Architects, 1996

INTERIORS DESIGN

Russell Bevington
(b. 1943)
Student 1972–75
*Staatsgalerie, Stuttgart, Germany,
with James Stirling, Michael Wilford
and Associates, 1984*

David Connor
(b. 1950)
Student 1973–76
Building for a Void, Seville, 1990

David Nelson
(b. 1951)
Student 1973–76
*New German Parliament, Reichstag,
Berlin, partner-in-charge for Foster
and Partners, 1999*

Malcolm Last
(b. 1953)
Student 1975–78
*Jack Dash House, Isle of Dogs, London,
Chassay + Last Architects, 1989*

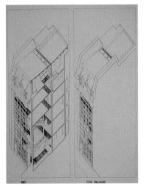

Tim Malloy
(b. 1951)
Student 1975–78
*Axonometric of roof and total
enclosure, Dean Street, Soho,
student project, 1978*

Eric Parry
(b. 1952)
Student 1976–78
*Foundress Court, Pembroke College,
Cambridge, 1998*

Su Rogers
(b. 1939)
Staff 1976–86
*Henry Moore Gallery, Royal College
of Art, 1986*

Kenneth Frampton
(b. 1930)
Staff 1964, 1975–77
*UDC Low-Rise High-Density Housing,
Marcus Garvey Park Village,
Brownsville, New York, USA, 1975*

John Miller
(b. 1930)
Staff 1962–64, 1971–75
Professor 1975–85
*The Queen's Building, University of
East Anglia, 1994*

80s ARCHITECTURE &

The 80s saw the demise of the 'white rationalist' modernist school of thought and the introduction of a more pluralist approach, influenced by early developments in post-modernism. In many ways, the College was both symptom and cause of the change, with students' work becoming increasingly experimental and exploratory. Degree shows were astonishing displays of lovingly crafted drawings, and models that expressed buildings and spaces rather than simply showing technical renderings. The new spirit was accelerated when Derek Walker became Professor in 1985, bringing with him such eminent members of the profession as James Gowan, David Chipperfield, Kit Allsopp and Michael Dickson. The close proximity of other disciplines – painting, fashion and film – added to the experience of being at the College, and gave graduates an individual approach and confidence that distinguished them from their contemporaries. Many graduates chose to set up their own architectural practices rather than be absorbed into large practices, an unusual and courageous course for young architects at the time.

Gerard Taylor
(b. 1955)
Student 1978–81
Habitat, Croydon, 1995

Catrina Beevor
(b. 1958)
Student 1980–82
Concrete Cottage, Cambridgeshire, Beevor Mull Architects, 1995

Michael Tonkin
(b. 1960)
Student 1984–86
Hugo House, Hong Kong, 1997

Andrew Gollifer
(b. 1960)
Student 1985–87
National Glass Centre, Sunderland, Gollifer Associates, 1998

Stephen Bates
(b. 1964)
Student 1987–89
The Wharf Public House, Walsall, W. Midlands, Sergisson Bates, 1997

Stuart Forbes
(b. 1963)
Student 1986–89
Millennium Dome, co-ordinating team leader for Richard Rogers Partnership, 1999

INTERIORS

Mark Guard
(b. 1952)
Student 1979–82
Apartment, Paris,
Mark Guard Architects, 1994

Nick Coombe
(b. 1958)
Student 1981–83
Barbican Duplex, London, Stickland
Coombe, 1998

Ken Mackay
(b. 1959)
Student 1981–83
York Central, London,
Harper Mackay, 1997

Alex de Rijke
(b. 1961)
Student 1984–86 Staff 1995–96
Gymnasium, City of London, de Rijke
Marsh Morgan, 1997

Mark Dytham and Astrid Klein
(b. 1964 and b. 1962)
Students 1986–88
Workstation for Idee, Tokyo, Klein
Dytham Architecture, 1996

Philip Gumuchdjian
(b. 1958)
Student 1986–88, Staff 1997–98
Think-tank for David Puttnam, 1998

Michael Jones
(b. 1965)
Student 1988–90
Law Library, Law Faculty, Cambridge
University, project architect for
Foster and Partners, 1995

James Gowan
(b. 1923)
Staff 1983–90
Royal College of Art shop, 1997

Derek Walker
(b. 1933)
Professor 1985–90
Kowloon Park, Hong Kong, 1987

90s ARCHITECTURE &

David Adjaye
(b. 1966)
Student 1991–93
Tutor 1998–present
*Lunch, Exmouth Market, London,
Adjaye and Russell, 1998*

Sadie Morgan
(b. 1969)
Student 1991–93
*Floating House project, de Rijke
Marsh Morgan, 1997*

One legacy of Derek Walker's professorship was the division of Architecture and Interior Design into two separate courses running in parallel, a programme that was continued under Theo Crosby. When Dinah Casson took over as Course Director in 1993, she brought the two together by creating a core course – Architecture and Interior Design.

Nigel Coates's appointment as Professor in 1995 radically changed the direction of the course. Renowned as the *enfant terrible* of British architecture, but well-respected as a teacher at the Architectural Association, Coates brought to the course a vitality and spirit that has made it one of the most notable and distinctive architectural courses in the world. Central to his strategy has been the introduction of the system of architectural design studios, each specializing in a different urban architectural condition, both seen and unseen, and headed by some of the rising stars of the profession.

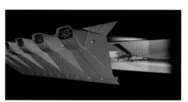

Robin Clark
(b. 1972)
Student 1994–96
*'Whale Projection Unit', Digital
Playground, Play Zone, Millennium
Dome, Project leader for Land, 1999*

Sarah Harkins
(b. 1968)
Student 1994–96
*Art Bar, Royal College of Art (with
Robin Clark), 1996*

Sally Mackereth
(b. 1966)
Staff 1995–99
*'Infinite Dining', Polygon Bar and
Grill, London, Wells Mackereth, 1996*

Liza Fior
(b. 1962)
Tutor 1998–present
*Southwark Street project, London,
Muf, 1998*

INTERIORS

Edward Barber and Jay Osgerby
(b. 1969, b. 1969)
Students 1992–94
*Soho Brewing Company, London,
Barber Osgerby Associates, 1998*

Diana Cochrane and Alex Mowat
(b. 1968, b. 1970)
Students 1993–95
*Skyscape, Greenwich,
Urban Salon, 1999*

Mark Garside
(b. 1969)
Student 1993–95
*Vexed Generation shop, London,
Lifeform, 1996*

Janek Schaefer
(b. 1970)
Student 1994–96
Tri-phonic turntable, 1997

Dinah Casson
(b. 1946)
Visiting Staff
Director 1993–95
*Sand and Light Zone, The Garden,
The Science Museum, London,
Casson Mann, 1995*

Clive Sall
(b. 1962)
Tutor 1996–present
*Office interior for advertizing agency
Kessels Kramer, Amsterdam,
FAT, 1998*

Fiona Raby
(b. 1964)
Student 1986–88
Tutor 1996–present
*Tuneable City project, Dunne and
Raby, 1997*

Theo Crosby
(1925–94)
Professor 1990–93
The Globe Theatre, London, 1997

Nigel Coates
(b. 1949)
Professor 1995–present
*National Centre for Popular Music,
Sheffield, Branson Coates
Architecture, 1999*

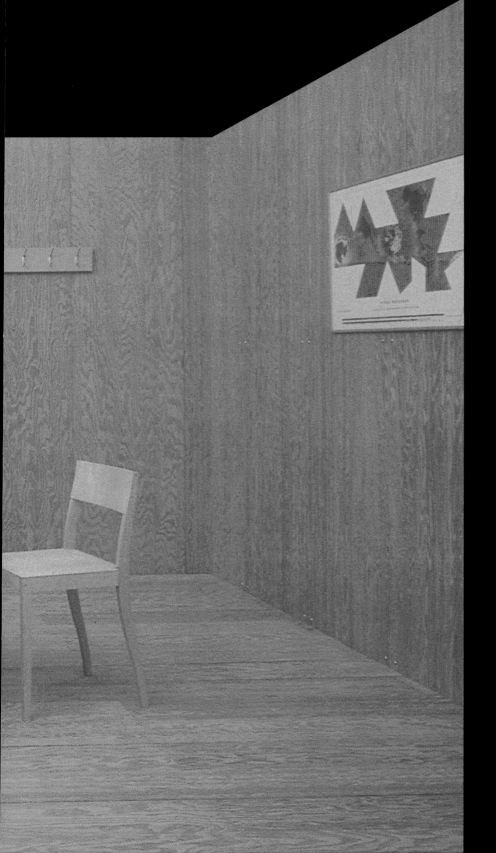

When Jasper Morrison presented an installation *New Items for the Home Part 1* for Designwerkstatt Berlin in 1988, he prepared the stage for what would become the new spirit of the 90s. In a bare room, with plain wooden floor and walls, he placed a couple of wooden chairs and a table. A simple wooden coat-rack was hung on the wall, and the contours of a bookcase and a door were drawn in outline. This room was a call-to-arms for design, a return to a back-to-basics approach, a questioning of the role of design and its place in the late twentieth century.

There was nothing 'new' in Morrison's designs – he had utilized existing forms and technologies, appropriated and recycled everyday objects and materials. But the application itself was startling in its simplicity and ingenuity, representing a breath of fresh air in an international design arena where design had become self-conscious, over-worked, and over-consumed.

In 1989 Morrison took the Milan Furniture Fair by storm, and by the early 90s he was working alongside fellow-RCA graduates James Irvine and Konstantin Grcic for a number of international design companies. Simplicity had become the watchword for a new global design language.

Jasper Morrison
New Items for the Home Part 1,
installation for Designwerkstatt
Berlin, 1988

INTERIORS

The new simplicity: design for the 90s

At the RCA the influence of these graduates fed a new generation of design students. Sebastian Bergne, Michael Marriott, Shin and Tomoko Azumi, Tord Boontje and Roberto Feo, among others, extended the ideas of their predecessors to develop simple, inventive designs that suited the contemporary mood. Using plain, unsophisticated materials such as pine and MDF, and borrowing from existing manufacturing processes and technologies, furniture and products were designed to be inexpensive, utilitarian and flexible. References to the ordinary and everyday were evident in the design – sometimes in the detail, or in the material used, or in the everyday behaviour and rituals the designs drew on. The idea was that the familiar element would introduce a spark of recognition, allowing for a personal attachment with the object.

Shin and Tomoko Azumi's wire chair was developed from the same material and process used to make shopping trolleys and hamster cages. Tord Boontje and Emma Woffenden's glass vessels were made from recycled wine bottles. Michael Marriott's *Furniture for People without Gardens* was a series of generic furniture shapes, pierced with holes into which could be placed rubber vases. This was a new kind of sustainability for the 90s. Objects would last longer because they were less reliant on fashion. Instead, they gained meaning through use and through their intrinsic

Michael Marriott
Furniture for People without Gardens, installation at 'Living Rooms',
Atlantis Gallery, London, 1998

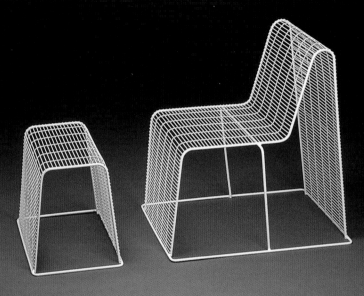

Shin and Tomoko Azumi
Wire Frame Chair, 1998

Tord Boontje and
Emma Woffenden
TranSglass recycled
glass vessels, 1997

70s VEHICLE DESIGN

Ten years after Misha Black's appointment in 1959 as Professor of Industrial Design (Engineering), the car industry was booming. But there was still no design course in the country offering a specialism in vehicle design. However, in 1967, the Ford Motor Company approached the RCA and offered to sponsor two bursaries to study automotive design. Peter Stevens and Dawson Sellar, whose work in the department was on cars rather than products, were selected. They were given almost free rein to choose visiting lecturers; they also built the first clay oven in the department for making vehicle prototypes. The course was given the title 'Advanced Studentship in Automotive Design' and it soon became a fully-fledged specialism within the Industrial Design programme. Throughout the 1970s, there was a steady growth in student numbers as Chrysler UK, Talbot and Rover followed Ford's example. These were boom years and sponsored bursaries guaranteed work in the supporting companies.

Dawson Sellar
(b. 1945)
Student 1965–69
Green Machine Street Sweeper, 1990

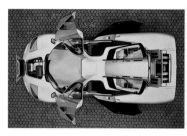

Peter Stevens
(b. 1943)
Student 1965–69
Staff 1972–87
Visiting Staff
McLaren F1, Model, 1995

Steve Ferrada
(b. 1947)
Student 1970–72
Mercedez-Benz F100 show car, 1990

Peter Birtwhistle
(b. 1951)
Student 1971–73
Audi Sport Quattro, 1983

Dick Powell
(b. 1951)
Student, 1973–76
Seymour Powell, Norton P55, prototype, 1988

Keith Helfet
(b. 1946)
Student 1975–77
Jaguar XJ220, 1991

Paul Gebbett
(b. 1945)
Student 1968–70
Ford Galaxy, Interior, 1998

John Hartnell
(b. 1946)
Student 1968–70
Ford Mercury MC4 show car, 1997

Graham Hull
(b. 1947)
Student 1969–71
Rolls Royce Silver Seraph, 1998

Martin Smith
(b. 1949)
Student 1971–73
Audi Quattro, 1982

Peter Horbury
(b. 1950)
Student 1972–74
Volvo S80, 1998

Richard Seymour
(b. 1953)
Graphic Design student, 1974–77
Visiting Professor, Architecture
and Design
Seymour Powell, Scorpion MZ, 1994

Gerry McGovern
(b. 1955)
Student 1976–77
MGF, 1995

Roland Sternmann
(b. 1954)
Student 1976–78
Mazda 323F, 1994

Ian Callum
(b. 1954)
Student 1977–79
Staff 1990–96
Aston Martin DB7, 1993

153

80s VEHICLE DESIGN

The 80s saw a steady rise in the numbers of students attending the course including those less reliant on sponsorship. Still under the banner of Industrial Design (Engineering), the 82/83 prospectus announced a new course title, the Automotive Design Unit, now with its own core staff and first director, Nigel Chapman. Many designers from the industry were invited to lecture, including Ken Greenley, who was working for General Motors, and ex-students Joachim Storz and Peter Stevens.

In the early years of the decade, the Unit largely focused on the technological aspects of vehicle design, offering an understanding of plastics technology, electronics, ergonomics and engineering workshop technology. The emphasis on technology was matched aesthetically, with car design veering towards the 'wedge-shape' in an attempt to look dynamic. This was evident in the Audi Quattro of 1982, designed by Martin Smith, a graduate of the course in 1973.

Pinky Lai
(b. 1951)
Student 1978–80
Porsche 911 Carrera Coupé, 1997

Peter Schreyer
(b. 1953)
Student 1979–80
Audi 80 Compact, Degree Show, 1980

Tony Hatter
(b. 1954)
Student 1979–81
Porsche 911, 1993

Adrian Griffiths
(b. 1959)
Student 1980–81
City car model, Degree Show, 1981

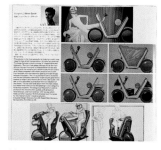

Murat Gunak
(b. 1957)
Student 1981–83
Yamaha motorcycle, Degree Show, 1982

David Wilkie
(b. 1958)
Student 1981–83
Model, Degree Show, 1983

Joachim Storz
(b. 1947)
Student 1979–80
Staff 1982–87
Ora, Degree Show, 1980

Christopher Bird
(b. 1956)
Student 1979–81
Model, Degree Show, 1981

Luciano D'Ambrosio
(b. 1957)
Student 1979–81
Bertone Bella show car, 1999

Erwin Himmel
(b. 1956)
Student 1980–82
Audi model, Degree Show, 1982

Roland Heiler
(b. 1958)
Student 1980–82
Porsche model, Degree Show, 1982

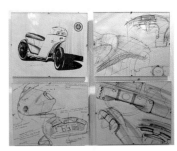

Martin Longmore
(b. 1958)
Student 1981–82
Study, Degree Show, 1982

Steve Murkett
(b. 1954)
Student 1981–83
Ford model, Degree Show, 1983

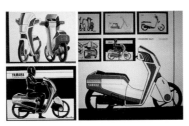

Howard Guy
(b. 1960)
Student 1981–83
Yamaha motorcycle,
Degree Show, 1982

Julian Thomson
(b. 1961)
Student 1982–84
Visiting Staff
Model, Degree Show, 1984

80s VEHICLE DESIGN

In 1986, the course reassessed its approach by devoting equal study time to design, technology and marketing, and it became the separate Department of Transport Design. With the departure of Nigel Chapman in 1988, the course was renamed Vehicle Design, and Ken Greenley became course director.

Student design work was beginning to show a sculptural tendency, as highlighted in Alex Padwa's model of 1987. The course developed a reputation for revolutionary 'concept work', as a stimulus to sponsoring companies, and like fashion, the annual degree shows became the catwalk of car design. Elements of these experimental designs might filter up into commercial vehicle design over a cycle of maybe five or ten years.

In 1989, the course was restructured again in a bid to attract a wider graduate intake. This was in response to the general view that automotive products were becoming too similar. As well as technology, the course now offered a new element, 'conceptual vehicle studies', with a particular emphasis on the fusion of art and industry.

Donato Coco
(b. 1954)
Student 1983–84
Citroen Xsara Picasso show car, 1998

Ulrich Lammel
(b. 1955)
Student 1983–84
Model, Degree Show, 1984

Mark Lloyd
(b. 1961)
Student 1984–86
Citroen Xanae, 1994

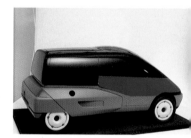

Pierre Terblanche
(b. 1956)
Student 1984–86
Model, Degree Show, 1986

Alex Padwa
(b. 1956)
Student 1985–87
Visiting Staff
Model, Degree Show, 1987

David Cutcliffe
(b. 1961)
Student 1986–88
Model, Degree Show, 1988

Richard Carter
(b. 1961)
Student 1983–85
Bentley Java show car
(with Graham Hull), 1994

Mark Adams
(b. 1961)
Student 1984–86
Model, Degree Show, 1986

Simon Cox
(b. 1959)
Student 1984–86
Isuzu Vehi-Cross, 1996

Michael Ani
(b. 1958)
Student 1985–87
IAD Venus, 1990

Matthias Kulla
(b. 1964)
Student 1985–87
Porsche Boxster, Interior, 1996

Anthony Lo
(b. 1964)
Student 1985–87
Model, Degree Show, 1987

Lester Allen
(b. 1954)
Staff 1987–present
Daihatsu show car, Tokyo, 1997

John Heffernan
(b. 1949)
Staff 1984–present
Aston Martin Vantage, 1992
(with Ken Greenley)

Ken Greenley
(b. 1944)
Staff 1981–95
Professor 1995–present
Bentley Continental, 1990
(with John Heffernan)

Sponsorship for the course was affected by the recession in the early 90s. However, student numbers were on the increase, and projects began to move away from the hi-tech concerns of the 80s towards more social consciousness. Environmental issues were explored, resulting in studies of urban vehicles, low-emission cars and 'micro' transport that used less road room. These concerns were evident in the work of Niels Loeb and Ivan Lampkin, who examined the implications of electric cars. The 90s also saw a diversification in types of transport – yachts, helicopters and motorcycles were all studied. Concept studies included Stefan Sielaff's sculptural form, the 'Induction Drive'.

Cultural concerns became increasingly important, and there was a strong interest in organic and biomorphic forms. Chris Svensson, who had a meteoric rise to fame from graduate to the Ford Ka launch of 1996, played with the language of organicism in his contributions to the vehicle. This also inspired Ford's 'New Edge' design philosophy, which led to an emphasis on roundedness in their vehicle design. The 'bio-design' approach also appeared in the curves of the 1998 London taxi, TXI, partly designed by course tutor Dale Harrow.

Martin Frost
(b. 1966)
Student 1988–90
Sports car, Degree Show, 1992

Aram Kasparian
(b. 1966)
Student 1988–90
MGX Model, Degree Show, 1995

Thomas Ingelnath
(b. 1964)
Student 1989–91
Volkswagen Noah show car, 1995

Niels Loeb
(b. 1966)
Student 1989–91
Model, Degree Show, 1991

Chris Svensson
(b. 1965)
Student 1990–92
Ford Ka, 1996

Giles Taylor
(b. 1968)
Student 1990–92
Visiting Staff
*Ultra-lightweight Tensile fabric car,
Degree Show, 1992*

Ivan Lampkin
(b. 1967)
Student 1988–90
Pisa Electric City car,
Degree Show, 1990

Stefan Sielaff
(b. 1962)
Student 1988–90
Induction Drive, Degree Show, 1990

Geoff Gardiner
(b. 1966)
Student 1989–91
2-seater saloon, Degree Show, 1991

Peter Naumann
(b. 1961)
Student 1989–91
Helicopter, Degree Show, 1991

Marek Reichman
(b. 1966)
Student 1989–91
Visiting Staff
Future 1 volume saloon,
Degree Show, 1991

Julian Wiltshire
(b. 1965)
Student 1989–91
Sports car, Degree Show, 1991

David Woodhouse
(b. 1968)
Student 1990–92

Sotiris Kovos
(b. 1965)
Student 1991–93

Karl-Heinz Rothfuss
(b. 1965)
Student 1991–93

90s VEHICLE DESIGN

The shift in automotive form was accelerated by computer-aided design. In the past, designers had been nervous about designing abstract forms that would be complicated to produce. Now computer technology made it possible to analyse new forms and find solutions without having to build expensive prototypes. At the end of the 80s, the American company Evans and Sutherland offered the department the first computers designed specifically for the job. Two machines, worth approximately £500,000 each, were installed on the understanding that they could be demonstrated to the European market. Today, the software, known as Parametric Technology, enables students to design full prototypes on screen, prior to committing themselves to scale models of concept cars.

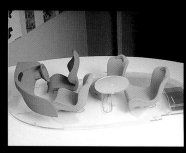

James Watkins
(b. 1968)
Student 1991–93
Interior, Degree Show, 1993

Mark Whiteley
(b. 1964)
Student 1991–93
45' jet-foil yacht, Degree Show, 1993

Stuart Jamieson
(b. 1971)
Student 1993–95
Mazda Tammuz, Degree Show, 1995

Adrian Morton
(b. 1970)
Student 1993–95
Yamaha motorcycle, Degree Show, 1995

Peter Wouda
(b. 1968)
Student 1994–96
Globe Surfer, Degree Show, 1996

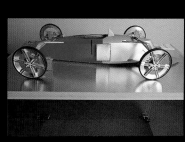

Stephane Janin
(b. 1973)
Student 1995–97
Blade, Degree Show, 1997

Steve Crijns
(b. 1968)
Student 1992–94
Lotus 28' sportsboat, 1998

Cesar Muntada
(b. 1967)
Student 1992–94
Harley-Davidson concept motorcycle,
Degree Show, 1994

Jon Dale
(b. 1970)
Student 1993–95
Opus 8 aircraft, Degree Show, 1995

Daniel Walker
(b. 1971)
Student 1993–95
Desert exploration vehicle,
Degree Show, 1995

Paul Wraith
(b. 1971)
Student 1994–96
Hyundai Euro 1 concept car,
interior, 1998

Eduardo Lana
(b. 1969)
Student 1994–96
VW interior study,
Degree Show, 1996

Matthew Hill
(b. 1972)
Student 1995–97
Model, Degree Show, 1997

Per Selvaag
(b. 1971)
Student 1995–97
Model, Degree Show, 1997

Dale Harrow
(b. 1960)
Staff 1989–present
TX1, London Taxis International, 1998
(with design team)

VEHICLE DESIGN

Gerry McGovern and the Rover Freelander

Winston Churchill with the 1948 model of the Land Rover

Gerry McGovern's early concept sketch of the Rover Freelander

The launch of the Rover Freelander in 1998 marked the fiftieth anniversary of the Land Rover. To make a radical design change to its characterful box shape took some courage. Gerry McGovern, a graduate from the Automotive Design Unit in 1977, had to work with the main factor that makes the Land Rover unique – its utilitarian pedigree.

Land Rover and the Rover Freelander have managed to keep their identity intact in the global market, retaining their feel of solidity, Englishness and the countryside. The appearance of the first Land Rover in 1948, in its trademark khaki green, was a direct response to the American Jeep, a generic vehicle. The Land

Rover's first advertizing campaign sold it as the 'Go anywhere vehicle' and its no-frills functionalism followed a military specification. Literally bolted together, it came with a removable cover, a flat fold-down windscreen, and three doors. Its functionalism, resembling a piece of agricultural machinery, made it a modernist's delight. It was taken on by the War Office and Winston Churchill, endorsed by the Queen, and soon became the vehicle of choice for farmers.

Based on a vehicle conceived as a workhorse, the Rover Freelander today has entered another realm: the recreation and leisure market. McGovern's Freelander constitutes a

radical shift in design from its predecessor. Like much product design of the 90s, the key words to describe it are desire and emotion allied to function.

At the College, McGovern was sponsored by Chrysler UK. Afterwards he went to work for the Chrysler Corporation in America, before settling at Austin Rover in Warwick. With car design, there is always a long period of gestation from initial drawings to final production. McGovern's early concept sketches for the Freelander give the vehicle an organic roundedness that was prevalent in RCA student work at the end of the 80s and the beginning of the 90s. Similarly, its early form

mirrors the urban grittiness of the vehicle designed for the 1994 US movie about the British cartoon hero, Judge Dredd, by 1992 RCA graduate, David Woodhouse. The peak of organicism in car styling was launched by Ford in 1996 with its cartoon-like Ka, with design contributions by 1992 RCA graduate, Chris Svensson. The curvilinear form has become a new aesthetic of car and product design.

McGovern's Freelander is a fusion of these stylistic traits, as well as a response to the design of Japanese 4x4s, but it still upholds an English reserve. The original hunting green colour is today called 'Epsom Green', in reference to the kind of setting where the Freelander is most at home.

Concept interior sketch of the Rover Freelander

ALISON BRITTON

'I was at the College from 1970 to 1973, and came from the Central School of Art. We had proper entrance exams in Ceramics – well, they were improper exams really; it was the first year Eduardo Paolozzi got his hands on them, and we had to do things like draw masks, pages and pages of facial expressions. One student walked out, but she still got in! And there were 3D tests, a modelling test, and we had to present a portfolio of drawings and photographs of ceramics. David Queensberry was the Professor, and the tutors were Hans Coper, Eduardo, Grahame Clarke, Martin Hunt and Sam Herman. It felt like there were about 11 of them in the room, all men with their feet on the table.

I found the course rather worryingly loose when I first arrived. I hadn't expected it to be a difficult transition. At the Central we had gone through every technique, it had been quite structured, and I left feeling very skilled. We didn't have much time to develop what we wanted to do with the skills, though. So there I was, pitched into a complete playpen where you could do anything, and I didn't know what to do. I really floundered. Everybody around me – like Carol McNicoll who'd come from a Fine Art course – seemed to be getting straight on with what they'd been doing before, developing their ideas. But I wanted to re-think and break with what I had been doing. It was something I'd grown out of; it was too tame and tight and pretty. I wanted to find something that was much more personal. But, what to do next? Eduardo's German assistant Artur helped me, when I was sent out with him to photograph architectural decoration, and I began a very circuitous route towards making things again – via photography, decoration and architecture. By the end of the course I was making pots again, and also tiles. I hate the word "vessels" with a

DESIGN

passion, by the way: it sounds "let's be a little more poetic about this" to me, which annoys me. I much prefer "container" or "pot".

So I had a pretty terrible first year, feeling guilty that I had this opportunity and wasn't taking it up. To be honest, the "pastoral" side wasn't strong with that gang of blokes. We certainly weren't spoon-fed! But if you badly weren't getting on with it, they'd start to look worried and stand round your desk in droves.

Carol McNicoll was in my year, and I became very friendly with her; and Jacqui Poncelet who was in the year above. Liz Fritsch had finished, but she was still around. It was friendly, and we supported each other; the staff were terrific, too, but you had to learn how to get something from them. I found an awful lot in Hans Coper. He came in once a week but was beginning to get ill; the journey was getting more difficult for him. I'd look forward so much to that day – he was a wonderful tutor – but it was a year before I discovered that.

The course was very, very good for me – anguishing but good: growing up, getting away from the girlish and "nice" work I'd done before, and starting again – by trying to be funny in a way: the tiles I did were quite cartoony. I already knew Quentin Blake, so I developed strong links with the Illustration Department, and that may have been another reason why the drawing bit of my work developed – drawing on tiles with pen and manganese. Memorable advice? Well, I can remember David Queensberry saying to me, "the trouble with art, Alison, is that you have to be so awfully good at it" – implying, I supposed, that I would never be good enough. But he gave me a lot, not in an overt teaching way, but in an encouragement and interest sort of way. With Hans Coper, there were no nuggety

ALISON BRITTON

sentences, but it was like a gentle drift towards helping you to find out what you wanted and who you were: a subtle dialogue and long, sensitive conversations which would always lead you somewhere useful.

I wrote my Humanities essay on the overlap between art and decoration, and I asked for external supervision which led me on to one stunning tutorial with Ernst Gombrich. He was writing *A Sense of Order* and he lent me the notes of an initial lecture series. A lot of what I was reading was nineteenth-century stuff – Dresser, Lewis Day and others – and I got a prize for the essay. What I was really worrying about was exactly where I fitted in. I didn't really want to be a dyed-in-the-wool craftsperson or a designer. It was suggested at one stage that I team up with someone in interior design, but I couldn't develop it because it was all hypothetical, because the work wasn't in front of me. I tried to design peppermint green tiles, or was it lime green? But it's all got to be on the table for me.

Some Ceramics students got quite involved in the Union while I was there, and we had a bit of sitting-in and stuff. I remember anxious debates about feminism, because we were reading *The Female Eunuch*, which was putting words around things we had felt but never articulated. But the Student Union view was, "we can't deal with that now, it will have to come afterwards." Class first, then gender. And that was annoying. I realized afterwards, about my education, that something subconsciously was preventing me from going into Fine Art, and that something was gender. I might have gone into sculpture if it had looked more welcoming. If the student bar was going to be smashed to pieces – which it was quite often in those days – it would always either be sculptors or printmakers. Some of those lads got really plastered, and violent. Which may have made it a less easy area to go into at that time. The girls that did, like Alison Wilding, looked heroic.

When we left, it didn't feel nearly so difficult as it does to students leaving now. Carol and I thought we'd share somewhere, and we gaily said, "Well, if it doesn't work we'll get a job." It seemed so straightforward. We had a studio in the 401 group workshop in Wandsworth, where some College people were already working. Because it was like a little commune in a way – 20 people – we got to see how each other worked and also to see that there was something new in the air and interconnections. I'd sold quite well at my show, which was mostly tiles and a green baize table with about ten objects on it, all handbuilt and drawn on. But I realized that tile commissions and trying to make people happy wasn't quite satisfying or three-dimensional enough. The Crafts Council was just coming into being, and we were the people they looked at first. We were lucky.

The students as they leave now are much more clued up than we were. And they work a lot harder, too. It's a completely different place – more teaching, more engagement, more projects, less time and space. What the College did for me, was to give me a chance to start again. And it changed me in a way that I was really pleased with. A lot of the people I met and got to like then are still my friends now. That's over 25 years, isn't it?'

PRE-WAR CERAMICS

Following the First World War, two figures dominated the rise of studio-pottery: Bernard Leach and William Staite Murray. Leach was a functional potter whose work in wheel-thrown stoneware combined forms and glazes derived from the Far East. Leach considered that, by example, his attitudes and his high standard of work might percolate through to influence industry. Murray was equally inspired by the Far East, but whereas Leach harked back to an idealized pre-industrial life, Murray wanted his ceramics to have contemporary relevance. Murray considered himself first and foremost an artist, and believed that studio potters should be considered as serious artists and not simply craftspeople.

Murray's appointment as Instructor in Pottery at the College in 1925 exacerbated an existing tension between himself and Leach. The principal, William Rothenstein, offered the post to Murray, but later suggested that both potters jointly run the course. Murray realized that the arrangement would not work and demanded that Rothenstein choose between them. Ultimately Murray was hired, but not without Leach feeling slighted by the whole affair.

Reginald Wells
(1877–1951)
Student c. 1890
Jar, 1910–14

Charles Vyse
(1882–1971)
Student 1905–10
Bowl, c. 1930

Charlotte Epton
(1902–70)
Student 1921–25
Jar and cover, c. 1930

Sylvia Fox-Strangways
(c. 1900–c. 1975)
Student 1922–24
Tiles, 1926

Heber Mathews
(c. 1907–59)
Student 1927–31
Bowl, c. 1940

George Cox
(1884–c. 1933)
Student 1908
Vase, 1913

Dora Lunn
(1881–c. 1955)
Student 1908
Dish, 1916–28

Dora Billington
(1890–1968)
Student 1912–17
Staff 1915–25
Coffeepot, sugar-basin and cups and saucers, c. 1950

Norah Braden
(b. 1901)
Student 1921–25
Jar and cover, c. 1935

Constance Dunn
(unknown)
Student 1924–28
Vase, c. 1935

James Dring
(1910–1985)
Student 1927–30
Plate, 1947

Reginald Marlow
(unknown)
Student 1927–30
Vase, 1962

James Walford
(b. 1913)
Student 1931–32
Vase, 1954

Sam Haile
(1909–48)
Student 1931–35
Jug, 1948

Philip Wadsworth
(b. 1910)
Student 1931–36
Jar, 1939

PRE-WAR CERAMICS

Murray's teaching was to be immensely important to the development of studio pottery.

Notable graduates to benefit from his teaching included James Dring, Constance Dunn, Reginald Marlow, Vera Moss, Margaret Rey and Philip Wadsworth. Rey's work is characteristic of the Murray school: large, heavily thrown stoneware vases with abstract painting in greys and browns. Perhaps the most distinguished of Murray's pupils, however, were Sam Haile, Henry Hammond, Heber Mathews and Robert Washington. Mathews' most successful work encapsulates Murray's aesthetic in its purest sense, exploring form virtually to the exclusion of decoration, and Washington's vessels have slender forms with thick lips and heavy feet.

Amongst the London venues to exhibit studio pottery during the 20s and 30s were Lefevre Gallery, Brygos Gallery, Paterson Gallery and The Little Gallery. Norah Braden exhibited with other contemporary potters such as Michael Cardew, Charles Vyse and Murray. In 1938 the Brygos Gallery held an exhibition to showcase the work of Murray's pupils, including Braden, Haile and Rey.

Margaret Rey
(b. 1911)
Student 1932–35
Vase, 1937

Vera Moss
(unknown)
Student 1932–36
Bowls, 1933

Henry Hammond
(1914–89)
Student 1934–38
Jugs, 1949–50

Gwilym Thomas
(unknown)
Student 1935–38
Coffeepot, 1939

Sue Parkinson
(b. 1925)
Student 1945–49
Figures (with David Parkinson), 1954

Paul Barron
(1917–83)
Student 1946–49
Bowl, c. 1950

DESIGN

Marianne de Trey
(b. 1913)
Student 1932–36
Bowl, 1949–50

Steven Sykes
(b. 1914)
Student 1933–36
Dish, 1950

Robert Washington
(1913–97)
Student 1933–37
Vase, 1988

Helen Pincombe
(b. 1908)
Student 1937–40
Staff c. 1940–48
Bowl, c. 1960

Pamela Tacon
(b. 1916)
Student 1938–40, 1942–47
Jug, 1939

Ray Marshall
(1913–86)
Student c. 1946
*Vase with handles and
bottle vase, 1960*

Peter O'Malley
(b. 1917)
Student 1947–50
Staff 1953–69
Vase, 1958

Rosemary Wren
(b. 1922)
Student 1947–50
Vase, 1957

William Staite Murray
(1881–1962)
Staff 1925
Chief Instructor 1926–39
Vase, c. 1930

CERAMICS
Canvas-free Artists

William Staite Murray
Wheel of Life, 1937

DESIGN

William Staite Murray
Vase, c. 1935

In 1930, Herbert Read wrote
enthusiastically of William Staite
Murray's teaching in an article
entitled 'Art and Decoration' in
The Listener:
'Some experiments recently
conducted at the Royal College of
Art School of Pottery under the
direction of Mr. W. Staite Murray
are interesting as revelations of
the possibilities that lie before
canvas-free artists.'
In one sentence Read had
summed up Murray's
overriding belief that
ceramics was as valid
an art form as
painting or
sculpture. Murray
taught at the
College from 1925
to 1939 and his
unique approach
was informed by
Oriental mysticism
and the notion that
the Zen Master
teaches by
demonstrating rather
than by speaking.
Murray often spoke of
'feeling judgement' and
saw throwing as a
procreative symbol. His pots

173

CERAMICS

anvas-free Artists

Henry Hammond. Vase, 1939

Heber Mathews. Vase, 1958

were often enormous in size, and he would leave the marks of the throwing pieces as expressive features, but always turned the feet after throwing. Many works were left undecorated, covered only in rich glazes of greys and browns. Having been introduced by Bernard Leach, Murray learnt a great deal of craft technique from the Japanese potter Shoji Hamada and succeeded in significantly advancing techniques in kilns and glazes.

The first artist-craftsman to have identified himself with the Fine Art world, Murray remained very involved with the avant-garde. He was friends

Fraser Hamilton (a collaborator) and Wyndham Lewis, and the artist Ben Nicholson. Murray also knew Henry Moore and during the 20s and 30s regularly exhibited work alongside fine artists in spaces such as Lefevre Gallery and Beaux Arts Gallery.

Students who were particularly influenced by Murray's ideas included Sam Haile, Heber Mathews, Henry Hammond and Robert Washington. All four had initially studied painting at the College, but later transferred to Murray's class. In contrast to Hans Coper's later encouragement of individuality, Murray's distinct style

Murray's gift to Hammond was the style of his brushwork, and the latter's absolute control of the art of brush decoration is the defining feature of his work. Haile was an innovative potter both in terms of the forms and the decoration of his work. Like Murray's work, his pieces embodied contemporary concerns in painting and sculpture, and he saw his work in ceramics as an extension of his activities as an artist. Haile produced large and very powerful stoneware vessels, in addition to tall, unusually shaped pieces which echo Murray's style. Washington similarly used the technique of iron-painted decoration in a freely brushed style, although to less effect than Haile.

Mathews saw pottery as a non-representational medium of expression in which to explore ideas relating to texture, substance and surface. He was to have an enormous influence upon Coper who later became his student at Woolwich Polytechnic School of Art. Murray wrote in Mathews' memorial pamphlet of 1959 that he was one of '... the few students who sensed the inner meaning of potting, and who saw that pots, when infused with vitality, could be an articulating art.'

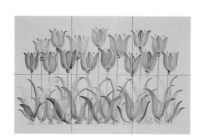

Tarquin Cole
(b. 1933)
Student 1956–59
Tile panel, 1983

Michael Harris
(1933–94)
Student 1957–60
Staff 1962–67
Seascape, c. 1985

Professor Robert Baker, Head of the Ceramics School from 1948 to 1959, had little time for studio pottery. The policy of training students for design in the industry was continued by Professor David Queensberry, who succeeded Baker in 1959. By the mid-60s, however, the emphasis began to shift towards one-offs, spearheaded by Queensberry's appointment of Hans Coper and the sculptor Eduardo Paolozzi. There was a movement away from the throwing or casting of utilitarian domestic ware. Coper was to have a profound influence, fostering a respect for the integrity of the vessel and an understanding of inside and outside form, which was particularly inspirational to Mo Jupp.

Stained glass had been studied at the College during the 50s. However, it was not until 1967, when the American Sam Herman was appointed to introduce and establish new techniques in glass blowing, that students got a real chance to work with hot glass themselves. Herman's influence produced a 'new wave' of graduates who became studio-glass artists, including Dillon Clarke, Annette Meech and Pauline Solven.

James Kirkwood
(1943–95)
Student 1965–68
Teapot, bowl and cup, 1968

Pauline Solven
(b. 1943)
Student 1965–68
Carafe and glasses, 1968

Dillon Clarke
(b. 1946)
Student 1967–70
Rose Poppy bowl, 1986

Gary Standige
(b. 1946)
Student 1967–70
Jar and lid, 1980

James Campbell
(b. 1942)
Student 1960–64
Stoneware shapes, 1964

Mo Jupp
(b. 1938)
Student 1964–67
Helmets, 1972

John Cook
(b. 1942)
Student 1965–68
Free-blown bottles, 1968

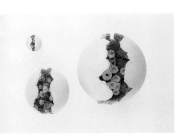

Mary Keepax
(b. 1945)
Student 1966–69
Untitled, 1969

Poh Chap Yeap
(b. 1927)
Student 1967–68
Dish, 1981

Val Barry
(b. 1937)
Student 1967–70
Vase, 1981

Geoffrey Swindell
(b. 1945)
Student 1967–70
Pots, 1970

Robert Baker
(1910–92)
Professor 1948–59
Evesham pattern, 1961

David Queensberry
(b. 1929)
Professor 1959–83
Cut crystal, 1963

The 70s heralded a more intellectual approach to 'craft' within the College and a re-definition of craft skills. Industry had benefited from the work of applied art students, but the 70s counterculture produced a climate of experimentation, and a 'new wave' of creative talent emerged. Professor David Queensberry considered his hiring of Hans Coper as Tutor in Ceramics between 1966 and 1975 to have been 'the most important thing that I have done in twenty years' work at the College.' Coper's emphasis on individuality, and a rejection of tradition inspired a new generation of graduating students including Alison Britton, Jacqueline Poncelet, Glenys Barton and Elizabeth Fritsch. The 'new ceramics' were primarily non-utilitarian but still made reference to functional vessel forms. The move towards the expressive and an exploration of the grey area between function and ornament can be seen in the work of Britton, Carol McNicoll and Richard Slee.

By the mid-70s, the orientation of the Department was clear. Many graduating students set up their own workshops, often with the support of the rejuvenated Crafts Council, which aimed to promote the 'artist-craftsman'.

Elizabeth Fritsch
(b. 1940)
Student 1968–70
Jar from Tlon, 1984

Paul Astbury
(b. 1945)
Student 1968–71
Ceramic forms, 1974

Jacqueline Poncelet
(b. 1947)
Student 1969–72
Bowls, 1972

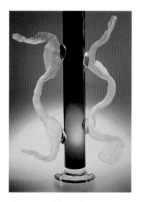

Annette Meech
(b. 1948)
Student 1970–72
Tower Lights, 1987

Jane Bruce
(b. 1947)
Student 1971–73
Vessel, 1982

Antony Bennett
(b. 1949)
Student 1971–74
Cop, 1973

Peter Aldridge
(b. 1947)
Student 1968–71
Staff 1972–78
Untitled, 1971

Glenys Barton
(b. 1944)
Student 1969–71
Plaque, 1981

Jill Crowley
(b. 1946)
Student 1969–72
Hollow Man, 1978

Alison Britton
(b. 1948)
Student 1970–73
Staff 1984–present
'Bird' jug, 1978

Carol McNicoll
(b. 1943)
Student 1970–73
Bowl, 1983

Clifford Rainey
(b. 1948)
Student 1971–73
Staff 1977–85
Untitled, 1973

David Grant
(b. 1948)
Student 1971–74
Vase, 1985

Ingeborg Strobl
(b. 1949)
Student 1972–74
Untitled, 1974

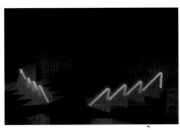

Steven Newell
(b. 1948)
Student 1972–74
Untitled, 1974

The 1970s proved to be pioneering times for glassmaking. Sam Herman, Tutor in Glass from 1968 to 1974, brought from America a certain freedom of expression. His fascination with glassblowing was facilitated by Dominick Labino's invention of the small studio furnace in the early 1960s. Herman established the first independent production workshop in London, known as the Glasshouse, which energized studio glass practice for a new generation of RCA students to come. Graduates who became involved with the space included Annette Meech, Steven Newell and Christopher Williams. Martin Hunt was responsible for developments in glass at the College from 1976 to 1986. He was also involved in the key international 'Hot Glass Symposium' of 1976. His work in architectural glass in the 1980s was influential. Lindsay Ball, Diane Radford and Clifford Rainey went on to create important monumental glasswork.

Nicholas Homoky
(b. 1950)
Student 1973–76
Bowls, 1976

Robin Levien
(b. 1952)
Student 1973–76
Vase, 1976

Martin Smith
(b. 1950)
Student 1975–77
Staff 1989–present
Form on Plinth, 1977

Lindsey Ball
(b. 1952)
Student 1975–78
Perfume bottle and holder, 1978

Maureen Robinson
(b. 1956)
Student 1978–80
Cocktail shaker and glasses, 1980

Martin Hunt
(b. 1942)
Student 1963–66
Staff 1968–86
Ashtrays and vases for Habitat, 1971

David Scott
(b. 1950)
Student 1973–76
Landscape, 1976

Jane Osborn-Smith
(b. 1952)
Student 1974–77
Untitled, 1977

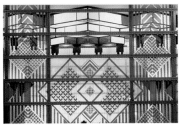

Diane Radford
(b. 1943)
Student 1975–77
Architectural glass, 1978

Julia Wood
(b. 1953)
Student 1975–78
Untitled, 1978

Christopher Williams
(b. 1949)
Student 1976–78
Cut vase, 1995

Charlie Meaker
(b. 1946)
Student 1977–79
Vase, 1979

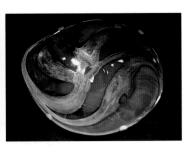

Sam Herman
(b. 1936)
Staff 1968–74
Glass form, c. 1970

Hans Coper
(1920–1981)
Staff 1966–75
Vase, 1958

Eduardo Paolozzi
(b. 1924)
Staff and Visiting Staff 1968–89
Portrait of Matta, 1978

THE NEW CERAMICS

The outer limits of function

Elizabeth Fritsch
Dart Three, 1984

Elizabeth Fritsch
Optical Pot, c. 1980
This work illustrates Fritsch's interest in manipulating the vessel
form by flattening its shape and using perspectival constructions.

Bernard Leach's belief that there can be no beauty without utility has had an enduring influence on British ceramics in the twentieth century. By the 70s, however, a new generation of makers began to question the area between function and ornament. Spearheading this change were a number of female ceramicists who graduated from the RCA between 1970 and 1973, most notably Glenys Barton, Alison Britton, Jill Crowley, Elizabeth Fritsch, Carol McNicoll and Jacqueline Poncelet. In breaking with British tradition, these makers often appear as a group, although their individual practices are very different. In *The Maker's Eye* catalogue of 1981 Britton commented: 'I would say that this group is concerned with the outer limits of function, where function, or an idea of a possible function, is crucial, but is just one ingredient in the final presence of the object, and is not its only motivation.'

In addition to their tutors, such as Hans Coper, Britton, Fritsch and Poncelet benefited from the influence of American ceramicists of the 50s, particularly Peter Voulkos, and

THE NEW CERAMICS

The outer limits of function

Jacqueline Poncelet
Form, 1981
The open 'boat' shape is characteristic of Poncelet's work during
the early 80s. Here she incorporates the edges into the overall
pattern by using colour, illustrating her interest in blurring the
boundaries between inside and outside.

Alison Britton
Pair of Jugs, 1978
Highlighting Britton's interest in a
multiplicity of viewpoints, the images
are painted so that they read like a book.

American abstract painters of the 50s
and 60s. Voulkos's work highlighted
the sculptural and abstract possibilities
of the medium of clay, and American
abstraction opened the way for the
adoption of the gestural mark. During
the late 60s and early 70s, craft was
marginalized in Britain, receiving little
critical attention, and it is not
surprising that applied art students
at the College sought to align
themselves with Fine Art.

Fritsch was the first of the 'new
ceramicists' to graduate in 1970,
although she was originally rejected
when she applied in 1966. David
Queensberry accepted her to the
Department the following year due
to 'a most unusual sensitivity'. Coper
prompted her interest in painting pots
which led to her experimenting with
geometrical patterns and colour. Her
intention was to combine form and
pattern, and she drew upon her
background in music (she had
studied at the Royal Academy of
Music) and her intellectual leaning
towards mathematics.

184

DESIGN

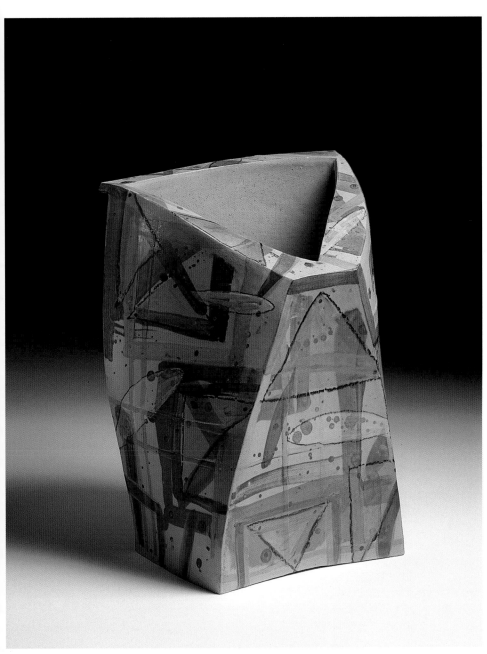

Alison Britton
Vase, 1981
Here Britton's move to abstraction can be seen in painted
decoration which is bold, expressive and gestural. The interior of
the pot is emphasized by the shadows cast by the angled edges.

While at the RCA and for a short period after graduating, Britton produced ceramics with a figurative content, as seen in her tiles. However, by the early 80s, Britton had moved on to 'containers' and the decoration applied to these works became abstract rather than pictorial. Informing this change was an interest in modern painting and architecture. In her early pots she broke away from the conventional round shape of the wheel-thrown pot and, through slab building, was able to develop a freer association between form and decoration. Britton's interest in asymmetry and surface decoration then deepened.

Poncelet was similarly concerned with the form of the vessel, but began to move much more towards ceramic sculpture. Her early pots were made of fine bone china but, by the mid-80s, she was exhibiting work as sculpture in contemporary art galleries. With angular and geometrical shapes and bold decoration, these large sculptural works broke away from the convention of a single base support. Together, the graduating students of the 70s expanded the boundaries of ceramics well beyond the traditional definition of 'craft'.

80s CERAMICS & GLASS

During this decade, the disciplines and facilities of Ceramics and Glass at the College were amalgamated into the same studios. Whereas the previous decade had seen the rise of the 'artist-craftsperson', the 80s paved the way for the emergence of the 'designer-craftsperson'. The latter category encapsulated the skills and interests of the emerging generation as a renewed interest in the commercial sector grew in response to a demand for interesting design at affordable prices. The resulting move from studios to 'workshops' enabled the production of both prototypes and original works. This decade also saw the rise of an eclecticism in applied ceramics through the use of historical styles and techniques. Philip Eglin's figurative ceramics, which draw upon eighteenth-century tradition, were a good example of this. In 1985 David Hamilton took over from David Queensberry as Professor of Ceramics.

Developments in Ceramics were paralleled by those in Glass – by the mid-1980s the College prospectus noted that the Glass specialism was involved in the 'fast-growing international arena of contemporary art-glass'. New techniques and technical developments in this decade saw a move away from glassblowing,

Arlon Bayliss
(b. 1957)
Student 1978–81
Pod, 1986

Jane Macdonald
(b. 1955)
Student 1978–81
Untitled, 1981

Fiona Salazar
(b. 1949)
Student 1979–82
Pot, 1982

Deborah Fladgate
(b. 1957)
Student 1980–82
Glass, 1982

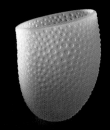

Ulrike Umlauf
(b. 1953)
Student 1980–83
Vase, 1983

Anne Smyth
(b. 1958)
Student 1981–83
Untitled, 1983

ian Stair
1955)
udent 1978–81
itled, 1981

Liz Lowe
(b. 1956)
Student 1979–81
Basket, 1981

Magdalene Odundo
(b. 1950)
Student 1979–82
Pot, 1982

ian Blanthorn
1957)
udent 1980–83
wl, 1982

Jennifer Lee
(b. 1956)
Student 1980–83
Pot, 1983

Anne Turner
(b. 1958)
Student 1980–83
Untitled, 1983

Sasha Ward
(b. 1959)
Student 1983–84
Rosey Garden, 1985

Anna Dickinson
(b. 1961)
Student 1983–85
Vase, 1985

and the facilitating of larger-scale works, such as the glass panel for Lime Street Station, Liverpool, created by Lindsay Ball, Diane Radford and Clifford Rainey. Keith Cummings who became Tutor in Glass in the mid-80s, promoted the making of kiln-formed glass.

In 1986, the international conference 'Glass in the Environment', which involved the RCA, the Crafts Council and the Royal Institute of British Architects, acknowledged the growing possibilities of work in glass. Gradually, a more solid infrastructure for the collecting and selling of glass was growing in Britain, seen in the establishment of the Victoria and Albert Museum's Glass Collection and the continued work of the Contemporary Applied Arts gallery. The sculptural and decorative possibilities of glass were explored in relation to architecture and architectural form, as illustrated in the work of Brian Blanthorn, Diana Hobson and Rachael Woodman. The work of current artists reveals a diversity of expression, ranging from Steve Newell's visual narratives to Keith Cummings' use of natural form.

Rosa N-D Quy
(b. 1960)
Student 1983–86
A Man Called Horse, 1986

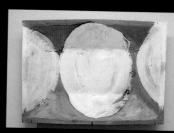

Ken Eastman
(b. 1960)
Student 1984–87
Dish, 1987

Paula Slater
(b. 1964)

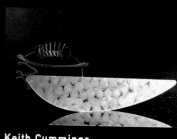

Keith Cummings
(b. 1940)

DESIGN

Stephen Dixon
(b. 1957)
Student 1983–86
Untitled, 1986

Philip Eglin
(b. 1959)
Student 1983–86
Reclining Nude, 1986

Kate Malone
(b. 1959)
Student 1983–86
Vase, 1986

Karen Densham
(b. 1960)
Student 1985–87
Dish, 1987

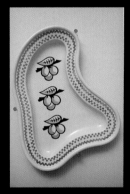

Richard Slee
(b. 1946)
Student 1986–88
Dish, 1988

Gwen Heeney
(b. 1952)
Student 1987–89
Untitled, 1989

Janice Tchalenko
(b. 1942)
Staff 1981–96
Bowl, 1985

James Roddis
(b. 1949)
Staff 1985–93
Still Vessel VI, 1991

David Hamilton
(b. 1940)
Staff 1974–84
Professor 1984–present
Euston Underground Station, 1988

90s CERAMICS & GLASS

With the refurbishment and re-equipping of the Ceramics and Glass studios and workshops in the early 90s, a level of integration far surpassing that of previous decades has been achieved, and this melting-pot atmosphere is revealed in the diversity of students' work. Within the structure of the course, the individual histories of both the ceramics and glass disciplines are acknowledged, in addition to the exploration of issues relevant to both subjects. The decade has seen an increase in the use of computers as a creative tool for the ceramic designer, and the introduction of CAD/CAM facilities to the Ceramics and Glass course.

A number of exhibitions of contemporary work held at the Victoria and Albert Museum throughout the 90s indicates that recent ceramics graduates and current practitioners seem apprehensive of function, being motivated more by a gallery approach than a desire to produce functional ware or design for industrial production. A lack of confidence in British industry can perhaps explain this. In addition, ceramics currently benefits from a cross-fertilization with painting and sculpture, and the ceramic avant-garde now receives greater critical appreciation

Lawson Oyekan
(b. 1961)
Student 1988–90
Untitled, 1990

Teleri Jones
(b. 1964)
Student 1989–91
Bottle and stopper with two double vases, 1991

Ben Dunington
(b. 1966)
Student 1991–93
Staff 1994–present
Tall vases, 1993

Steve Harrison
(b. 1967)
Student 1991–93
Salt-glazed jugs, 1993

Sue Pryke
(b. 1966)
Student 1992–94
Kitchenware, 1994

Dai Rees
(b. 1961)
Student 1992–94
Blue and green should never be seen . . . , 1994

DESIGN

Keiko Mukaide
(b. 1954)
Student 1989–91
Metamorphosis, 1996

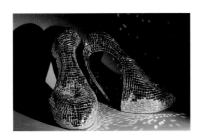

Rebecca Newnham
(b. 1967)
Student 1989–91
Mosaic stilettos, 1991

Jackie Sneade
(b. 1958)
Student 1989–91
Dichroic table light, 1991

Hadrian Pigott
(b. 1961)
Student 1991–93
Freezeframe, 1993

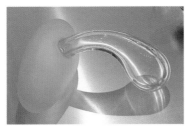

Emma Woffenden
(b. 1962)
Student 1991–93
Eyeless, 1993

Jane Cox
(b. 1962)
Student 1992–94
Large server, 1994

Rupert Blamire
(b. 1972)
Student 1993–95
Urns and bowl (detail), 1995

Neil Brownsword
(b. 1970)
Student 1993–95
Four Months, 1995

Martin Moore
(b. 1967)
Student 1993–95
Teapot – These Boots, 1995

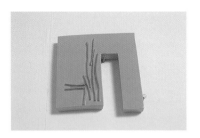

Nick Rena
(b. 1963)
Student 1993–95
Blue-grass, 1995

Bruno Romanelli
(b. 1968)
Student 1993–95
On the Edge II, 1995

than in the past. Cross-overs with other disciplines have led Hadrian Pigott to achieve success within the art world, and enabled Dai Rees to diversify into fashion. The history of ceramics is appropriated in the figurative work of Martin Moore, which caricatures the conventions of Staffordshire figures.

Significant advances have been made in glass practice, considering that this is only the third decade in the history of the studio glass 'movement' (although this movement has never been cohesive and encompasses many individual and diverse styles and techniques). Reflecting these advances, the 1992 College prospectus states:

'Upon graduation, a student may become a professional maker, a designer for the glass or ceramic industry, a decorator of industrial ware or a creator of architectural decoration. In a lifetime's career each one of us might work in several or all of these.'

Claire Twomey
(b. 1968)
Student 1994–96
Dark Spaces, 1996

Marianne Buss
(b. 1967)
Student 1995–97
'Trails' bowl, 1997

Peter Aldridge
(b. 1947)
Student 1968–71
Staff 1972–96
Portals of Illusion, 1993

Alison Britton
(b. 1948)
Student 1970–73
Staff 1984–present
'Light Double' pot, 1998

Felicity Aylieff
(b. 1954)
Student 1993–96
Water vessel, 1996

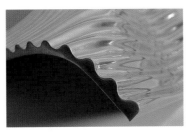

Janine Clements
(b. 1970)
Student 1994–96
Evocation of Presence I–IV, 1995

Mary Jo Doherty
(b. 1971)
Student 1994–96
Free and Easy, 1996

David Field
(b. 1965)
Student 1996–98
Just arrived but time to go, 1998

Hsueh Chun Liao
(b. 1969)
Student 1996–98
Silence, 1998

Shaun Wells
(b. 1968)
Student 1996–98
Ruptured Square, 1998

Simon Moore
(b. 1959)
Visiting Staff
Visiting Professor
Conical leaf vase, 1998

Martin Smith
(b. 1950)
Student 1975–77
Staff 1989–present
Untitled, 1992

Elizabeth Swinburne
(b. 1957)
Staff 1997–present
Chain, n.d.

Martin Travers joined the College to oversee work in stained glass in 1925 and taught Lawrence Lee who later became a partner in his studio. Lee then succeeded Martin Travers as head of the new and independent School of Stained Glass in 1948. A comprehensive exhibition of students' work was shown at the Royal Society of British Artists in 1950 which led to a new generation of students attracting a great deal of attention. In particular, the work of Lawrence Lee and students Keith New and Geoffrey Clarke was favoured by architect Basil Spence, and the three were awarded the prestigious commission to design windows for the nave of the new Coventry Cathedral – the earlier cathedral had been destroyed by enemy bombs in 1940. The old mural studio, which joined the RCA to the Victoria and Albert Museum, was made available for Lee, Clarke and New to create ten seventy-foot windows based on 'man's progress from birth to death and from death to resurrection and transfiguration'.

Geoffrey Clarke
(b. 1924)
Student 1948–52
Nave Window, Coventry Cathedral, with Lee and New, 1956

Keith New
(b. 1926)
Student 1948–52
Nave Window, Coventry Cathedral, with Clarke and Lee, 1956

Brian Milne
(b. 1933)
Student 1958–62
For the British Section of Italia Exhibition, 1961

Pauline Boty
(1938–66)
Student 1959–62
Landscape, 1960

Timothy Lewis
(b. 1940)
Student 1962–65
Glass appliqué, 1964

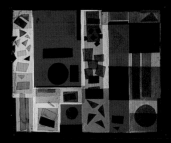

Rita Wild
(b. 1940)
Student 1962–65
Glass appliqué, 1965

Jane Gray
(b. 1931)
Student 1952–55
Glass panel, 1982

Antony Hollaway
(b. 1928)
Student 1953–57
St George's Window, c. 1977

Ken Baynes
(b. 1934)
Student 1957–60
Student work, 1959

Ray Bradley
(b. 1938)
Student 1959–62
*Main Chapel Window, Bar Hill
Church, Cambridge, c. 1970*

Michael Coles
(b. 1940)
Student 1961–64
Glass panel, 1964

Joseph Nuttgens
(b. 1941)
Student 1961–64
Crucifixion, 1964

Diana Taylor
(b. 1942)
Student 1963–67
Degree Show, 1967

Martin Travers
(1886–1948)
Staff 1924–48
*North Chapel Window of St Stephen's
Church, Portsmouth, c. 1924*

Lawrence Lee
(b. 1909)
Student 1944–48
Staff 1948–68
*Nave Window (detail), Coventry
Cathedral, with Clarke and New, 1956.*

Brian Asquith
(b. 1930)
Student 1947–51
Trophy, 1979

Eric Clements
(b. 1925)
Student 1949–52
Tea service for Mappin and Webb, 1964

Britain witnessed a surprisingly swift renaissance in silversmithing in the post-war years, considering the debilitating effects of the Second World War on the silver industry. The Worshipful Company of Goldsmiths encouraged a revival in the patronage of craftsmiths by civic and corporate bodies, boosting the market during the 50s and 60s and allowing greater artistic freedom to makers.

Silversmiths Gerald Benney, David Mellor and Robert Welch were part of the 50s generation of RCA graduates who successfully combined their roles as artist-craftsmen with their equally influential roles as industrial designers. The inclination to design for mass production was due in part to the high price of silver, which made it difficult for professional silversmiths to survive, but also to the Scandinavian design influence which introduced stainless steel as a viable alternative to silver. In addition, there was a demand for affordable, well-designed household products. During the 50s, the Scandinavians led the way in developments in silversmithing, introducing a simple, modernist aesthetic. In Britain, although these ideals were readily adopted, the pre-war tradition of producing decorative work in silver

Robert Welch
(b. 1929)
Student 1952–55
Coffeepot, 1973

John Donald
(b. 1928)
Student 1952–56
Badge of Office for Sheriff of City of London, 1973

Keith Tyssen
(b. 1934)
Student 1957–60
Altar cross and candlesticks, 1964

Gerald Whiles
(b. 1935)
Student 1957–60
Tea caddy, 1960

196

EWELLERY DESIGN

Jack Stapley
(b. 1925)
Student 1949–52
Rose bowl, 1953

David Mellor
(b. 1930)
Student 1950–54
Candelabrum, 1958

Gerald Benney
(b. 1930)
Student 1951–54
Professor 1974–83
Chalice, 1957

Stephen Maer
(b. 1933)
Student 1954–56
Ring, 1973

Brian Wood
(b. 1932)
Student 1955–58
Necklace, 1958

Keith Redfern
(b. 1935)
Student 1956–61
Trophy, 1973

Stuart Devlin
(b. 1931)
Student 1958–60
Coffeepots, 1959

Tony Laws
(b. 1935)
Student 1958–61
Cigarette box, 1970–71

Ronald Stevens
(b. 1936)
Student 1958–61
Water jug, 1973

Andrew Bray
(b. 1938)
Student 1960–63
Punch ladle, 1962

Anthony Elson
(b. 1935)
Student 1960–63
Teapot, 1963

(incorporating allegorical and heraldic motifs) was equally dominant.

The Festival of Britain in 1951 and the Coronation of Queen Elizabeth II in 1953 were key opportunities for commissioning commemorative silver and recognizing the talent of British silversmiths. Robert Goodden, who became Professor of Silversmithing and Jewellery in 1948, played a leading role in the Lion and Unicorn Pavilion, and his tea service in parcel-gilt silver is typical of this phase. Gerald Benney, who became Professor of Silversmithing and Jewellery in 1974, was commissioned to make work for Coventry Cathedral in 1958 and for Leicester University. The Goldsmith's Hall began to commission and collect work by emerging silversmiths and purchased Stuart Devlin's coffee service while he was a student. With its sleek, minimal form (achieved by using heat-resistant nylon for the bases, which meant that he did not have to include handles in the design), his work moved away from figurative decoration and was inspired by Benney's technical innovations in surface texturing.

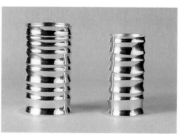

Ian Beech
(b. 1941)
Student 1962–65
Pair of vases, 1965

David Frost
(b. 1939)
Student 1962–65
Bowl, 1965

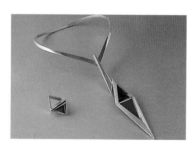

Dorothy Hogg
(b. 1945)
Student 1967–70
Necklace, pendant and ring, 1968

David Courts
(b. 1945)
Student 1968–71
Necklace, 1969

EWELLERY DESIGN

Laurence Sparey
(b. 1939)
Student 1960–63
Sunglasses, 1984

Ian Rodger
(b. 1938)
Student 1961–64
Teapot, 1964

Robin Beresford
(b. 1938)
Student 1961–64
Pair of candlesticks, 1964

Jacqueline Mina
(b. 1942)
Student 1962–65
Staff 1985–86
Ring, 1980

Roger Millar
(b. 1942)
Student 1963–66
Teapot, 1965

Malcolm Appleby
(b. 1946)
Student 1966–68
Chess pawns, 1973

Hector Miller
(b. 1945)
Student 1968–71
Honey dish, 1969

Michael Milligan
(b. 1944)
Student 1968–71
Flower necklace and ring, 1983

Robert Goodden
(b. 1909)
Professor 1948–74
Tea service, Festival of Britain, (made by Leslie Durbin), 1951

Under the leadership of Robert Goodden, the Department of Silversmithing and Jewellery was intensely skill orientated. The main aim of the course was 'the art and craft of gold and silversmithing', in addition to related work in other materials. Students produced a variety of objects, ranging from tea sets and cutlery to home ornaments and jewellery. The late 60s and 70s saw the rise of the artist-craftsperson, in which traditional concepts and forms of metalwork and jewellery were re-defined, and ideas were prioritized over the inherent value of materials.

Characteristic of the mid-70s was an interest in using unorthodox, non-precious metals and materials, such as paper, glass, wood and plastic, and in experimenting with colour, for example in Eric Spiller's work. Industrially developed materials, such as titanium, also found favour with RCA students, as seen in the jewellery of Edward de Large, Ann Marie Shillito and James Ward. Esther Knobel produced original jewellery using anodized aluminium and coloured titanium, which was refreshingly inexpensive, and was part of a general move to make jewellery more accessible.

Ann Marie Shillito
(b. 1947)
Student 1968–71
Belt, 1971

Patti Clarke
(b. 1948)
Student 1969–72
Ring, 1971

Eric Spiller
(b. 1946)
Student 1969–72
Bracelet, 1972

Edward de Large
(b. 1949)
Student 1972–75
Necklace, c. 1975

Kevin Coates
(b. 1950)
Student 1973–76
Visiting Staff
'Golden Fleece' brooch, 1976

Diana Hobson
(b. 1943)
Student 1973–76
Toothpick and case, 1976

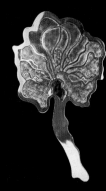

Robert Marsden
(b. 1947)
Student 1969–72
Box, 1971

Celia Over
(b. 1946)
Student 1969–72
Mirror, 1972

Michael Rowe
(b. 1948)
Student 1969–72
Staff 1978–present
Double inkwell, 1971

Roger Morris
(b. 1946)
Student 1972–75
Bracelet, 1975

Ros Conway
(b. 1951)
Student 1973–75
Triangular-winged brooches, 1979

Fotini Kafiri
(unknown)
Student 1973–75
Ring, 1975

Michael Lloyd
(b. 1950)
Student 1973–76
Bowl, 1976

Martin Page
(b. 1952)
Student 1973–76
Box, 1976

Robert Birch
(b. 1947)
Student 1974–77
Bowl, 1977

Kevin Coates, who later became a visiting tutor, created brooches which he called 'objects for contemplation'.

Although a number of galleries had supported modern jewellery in the late 60s, it was the opening of Electrum Gallery in 1971 which provided the first space devoted solely to exhibiting the 'new trends' in jewellery. Like graduates in Ceramics and Glass, studio jewellers emerging from the RCA were given a great deal of support from the Crafts Council. Tutors Wendy Ramshaw and David Watkins were highly innovative and influential in the 70s, both sharing an interest in new materials and in the relationship between function and ornament.

Towards the end of the 70s, it was clear that a new inventiveness was emerging from the RCA. It was now accepted that makers could use jewellery as a means of personal expression. The Department also witnessed a certain intellectualization of craft practice, as exemplified in the student metalwork of Michael Rowe.

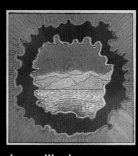

James Ward
(b. 1949)
Student 1974–77
Titanium pendant, 1977

Esther Knobel
(b. 1949)
Student 1975–77
Bracelet, 1978

Robert Legg
(b. 1946)
Student 1976–79
Hand mirror, 1979

Reema Pachachi
(b. 1951)
Student 1976–79
Accessories, 1979

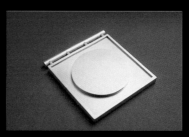

Gordon Burnett
(b. 1951)
Student 1977–80
Folding clock (closed), 1980

Ray Stebbins
(b. 1942)
Student 1978–80
Spherical box, 1980

JEWELLERY

Tom Dobbie
(b. 1953)
Student 1975–78
Bracelet, 1978

Alistair McCallum
(b. 1953)
Student 1975–78
Pill boxes, 1978

Clive Burr
(b. 1953)
Student 1976–79
Ebony and silver chopsticks, 1979

Valerie Robertson
(b. 1953)
Student 1976–79
Hat pins, 1979

Jane Short
(b. 1954)
Student 1976–79
Tea caddy, 1979

Nick Aikman
(b. 1955)
Student 1977–80
Stainless steel tube, 1978

Philip Popham
(b. 1919)
Student 1946–50
Staff 1950–83
Senior Common Room condiments set, c. 1960

Gerald Benney
(b. 1930)
Student 1951–54
Professor 1974–83
Court wine cup, 1981

Bakri Yehia
(1925–82)
Student 1951–55
Staff 1967–76
Gavel, 1954

In 1984, David Watkins took over as Professor, and, in response to the diversification of activities, the Department's name was changed to Goldsmithing, Silversmithing, Metalwork and Jewellery.

During the mid-80s, as part of a College rebuilding programme, the facilities were reorganized and rationalized. David Watkins and Michael Rowe initiated a pilot scheme for a Small Metal Production Unit which was fully developed by the late 80s. This scheme aimed both to provide students with the design, production, marketing and management skills essential to produce batch jewellery and metalwork articles, and to foster fruitful collaboration with commerce. The craft-based jewellery and silversmithing studios remained integral. By 1985 the RCA prospectus was able to state that:

'Metalwork ... may include the designing or making of artefacts in any suitable material or in combination with other metals. Jewellery may include fine, fashion or non-precious wearable objects. Silversmithing and Goldsmithing may be practised with an emphasis placed on imagination and originality.'

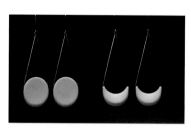

Elisabeth Holder
(b. 1950)
Student 1978–80
Staff 1985–88
Earrings, 1980

Richard Fox
(b. 1954)
Student 1978–81
Cruet set, 1981

Leonard Smith
(b. 1956)
Student 1979–82
Brooch, 1982

Marianne Forrest
(b. 1957)
Student 1980–83
Clock, 1983

Debra Allman
(b. 1960)
Student 1983–86
'Element Pins: Fire, Water, Earth, Air', 1986

Alex Brogden
(b. 1954)
Student 1983–86
Menorah, 1987

JEWELLERY DESIGN

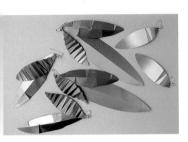

Clarissa Mitchell
(b. 1950)
Student 1978–81
Earrings, 1981

Cynthia Cousens
(b. 1956)
Student 1979–82
Ridged brooch, 1988

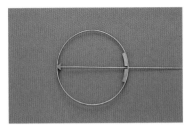

Trevor Jennings
(b. 1955)
Student 1979–82
Brooch, 1982

Rod Kelly
(b. 1956)
Student 1980–83
Honey pot and spoon, 1983

Julie Chamberlain
(b. 1958)
Student 1981–84
Bowl, 1984

Jane Adam
(b. 1954)
Student 1982–85
Necklace, 1985

Tom McEwan
(b. 1959)
Student 1983–86
Necklace, 1986

Amanda Bright
(b. 1962)
Student 1984–87
Etched steel form, 1987

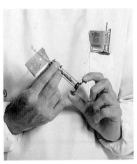

Hazel Jones
(b. 1962)
Student 1985–87
*'The Currant Bun Project.
A conceptual device to extract
currants from buns', 1989*

Amanda Bright, Alex Brogden, Mike Savage and Simone ten Hompel became significant metalworkers, having benefited from the teaching of Michael Rowe and his seminal research into the colouring and texturing of base metals. In addition to the use of such materials as iron, steel, aluminium and copper as viable alternatives to silver, the mid- to late 80s saw the rise of computers in the design process, seen, for example, in Daniel Spring's development of CAD/CAM generated bowls.

The enthusiastic use of non-precious materials continued, as seen in the work of Daniel Spring, Maria Wong and Hazel Jones, amongst others. Like students in Ceramics and Glass in the 70s, this decade's generation embraced a wide range of influences and moved between the realms of both craft and art.

The boom years of the 80s and the rise of disposable incomes provided a better support structure for independent craftspeople or 'designer-makers'. The increasing interest in individual work was aided by a growing infrastructure of galleries and shops.

Michael Savage
(b. 1962)
Student 1985–87
Spiral form, 1987

Mike Abbott
(b. 1963)
Student 1986–88
Brooch, 1988

Malcolm Betts
(b. 1964)
Student 1987–89
Rings, 1989

Sophie Harley
(b. 1965)
Student 1987–89
Brooch and earrings, 1989

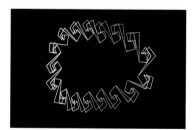

Esther Ward
(b. 1964)
Student 1988–90
Neckpiece, 1990

Katy Hackney
(b. 1967)
Student 1989–91
Multistorey brooch, 1991

JEWELLERY DESIGN

Zsuzsanna Morrison
(b. 1964)
Student 1986–88
Reversible-sided brooch, 1987

Daniel Spring
(b. 1964)
Student 1986–88
Bowl, 1987

Maria Wong
(b. 1962)
Student 1986–88
Earrings, 1988

Mah Rana
(b. 1964)
Student 1987–89
'His 'n' Hers' ring, 1996

Simone ten Hompel
(b. 1960)
Student 1987–89
Bottle, 1989

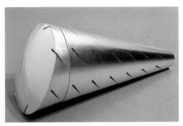

Rebecca de Quin
(b. 1958)
Student 1988–90
Visiting Staff
Cone-shaped container, 1990

Maria Hanson
(b. 1967)
Student 1989–91
Triangle neckpiece (detail), 1991

Michael Rowe
(b. 1948)
Student 1969–72
Staff 1978–present
Cylindrical vessel, 1985

David Watkins
(b. 1940)
Professor 1984–present
Voyager, 1985

Diversity characterizes metalwork and jewellery of the 90s. The previous decade, which freed precious metals from a historically perceived elitism, laid the foundations for the enriched metalworking practice of this period. A greater degree of eclecticism can be seen in contemporary work produced by RCA graduates – the natural is combined with the artificial, the everyday with the exceptional. Chris Knight's work surprises the viewer with combinations of contrasting materials such as silver and cork, and Adele Tipler has used electro-forming to create headpieces which operate within the worlds of art and craft, millinery and metalwork. Others have explored issues of gender and society.

Key to the Department is the merging of the practices of goldsmithing, silversmithing, metalwork and jewellery, and as a result it is often difficult to categorize work, as students move freely between materials and their function. Emma Hauldren's work, for example, often serves a dual role as functional object and urban body jewellery. Such cross-overs between function and form, the use of non-precious metals, experimentation in production methods, and the mixing of precious and non-precious metals make this a

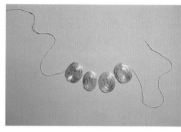

Andreas Fabian
(b. 1957)
Student 1989–91
Knife, fork and spoon, 1991

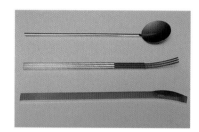

Elizabeth Callinicos
(b. 1966)
Student 1990–92
Necklace, 1992

Nedda El-Asmar
(b. 1968)
Student 1991–93
Condom holder, 1993

Ian Ferguson
(b. 1945)
Student 1991–93
*Mokume Gane, research
samples, 1993*

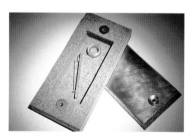

Gavin Fraser-Williams
(b. 1966)
Student 1992–94
*Brooch and ring in felt
jewellery box, 1994*

Emma Hauldren
(b. 1967)
Student 1992–94
Drinking flasks, 1994

EWELLERY DESIGN

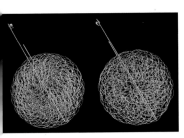

Giovanni Corvaja
(b. 1971)
Student 1990–92
Earrings, 1992

Chris Knight
(b. 1964)
Student 1990–92
Spiked bowl, 1992

Lucien Taylor
(b. 1967)
Student 1990–92
Cutlery, 1992

Dawn Gulyas
(b. 1963)
Student 1991–93
Bangle, 1993

Adele Tipler
(b. 1970)
Student 1991–93
'Golden Curls', 1993

Christoph Zellweger
(b. 1962)
Student 1991–93
Brooches, 1993

Antje Illner
(b. 1965)
Student 1992–94
Staff 1998–present
Necklace, 1994

Catherine Martin
(b. 1949)
Student 1992–94
Bracelet, 1994

Nicole Stoeber
(b. 1969)
Student 1992–94
Ring, 1994

stimulating time. Wendy Ramshaw, as Visiting Professor, and David Watkins, as Professor, have been extremely influential to the new generation of makers. As one of the leading British jewellers, Ramshaw has imaginatively pursued the use of precious metals, while Watkins has pioneered the use of acrylics and other synthetic materials in his work.

Most graduating students go on to establish their own workshops, designing and producing work for national and international exhibition and sale. Some become designers for the industry. The RCA prospectus, however, highlights the current emphasis of the Department:

'Whilst the course encourages a practical understanding and respect for the priorities and needs of existing industry and an appreciation of the wider cultural values of its subject area, central to its philosophy is the sustaining of that individually directed contemplation, discovery and development which characterizes the postgraduate experience of this discipline.'

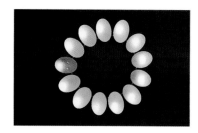

Castello Hansen
(b. 1965)
Student 1993–95
Untitled, 1995

Jo Thompson
(b. 1971)
Student 1993–95
Rings, 1995

David Clarke
(b. 1967)
Student 1995–97
'Strawberry' (detail), 1997

Claudia Langer
(b. 1973)
Student 1995–97
'A Memory ...', brooch, 1997

Claudia Westhaus
(b. 1964)
Student 1996–98
Untitled, 1998

Manuel Vilhena
(b. 1967)
Student 1993–94, 1997–98
Rings, 1998

EWELLERY DESIGN

Lara Bohinc
(b. 1972)
Student 1994–96
Necklace, 1996

Kate Wilkinson
(b. 1969)
Student 1994–96
Choker, 1996

Lin Cheung
(b. 1971)
Student 1995–97
Picnic tool, 1997

Amanda Mansell
(b. 1971)
Student 1995–97
Headpiece and necklace, 1997

Laura Potter
(b. 1971)
Student 1995–97
'Squeaky Clean', 1997

Richard Kirk
(b. 1962)
Student 1996–98
*'A Tryst', bowl with two serving
spoons, 1998*

Onno Boekhoudt
(b. 1944)
**Visiting Staff
Staff 1995–present**
Ring, n.d.

Wendy Ramshaw
(b. 1939)
**Visiting Professor
1996–present**
*White rings for 'Nude Lying in
White Bed', 1997*

Allan Scharff
(b. 1945)
**Visiting Professor
1996–present**
Vessel, 1993

JEWELLERY

Embracing the unexpected

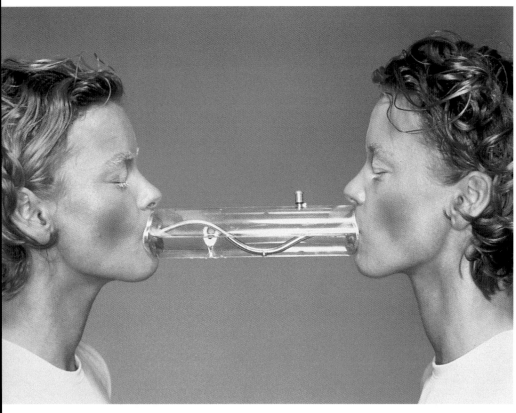

H2 Design, Double Mouth Flasks, 1994

H2 Design, Life Extension Pill Rings, 19[

Naomi Filmer, H2 Design and Christoph Zellweger reflect the experimentation and diversity of contemporary jewellery. At the end of the century, pluralism within the area makes it difficult to define any schools or movements. Instead, there is a wealth of creative energy emerging from designer-makers who are aware of tradition, but embrace the unexpected.

One aspect of current practice is a concern with manipulating the body and reassessing concepts of personal adornment. Filmer's primary interest lies in exploring the negative space in and around the body, and while at the RCA she produced *Toe Between Pieces* (1993). She views each object as being anonymous until it is activated by contact with the body, and often her work comments on the symbiotic relationship between people and technology. Drawing attention to the notion of the void, Filmer used LEDs to illuminate the mouths of models in Hussein Chalayan's 1994 catwalk show. Her work has since earned a high reputation in the fashion world.

The identical twins Emma and Jane Hauldren both studied Metalwork and Jewellery at the RCA, and since graduating in 1994 have worked as contemporary silversmiths under the name H2 Design. They draw inspiration from the 'millennial preoccupations of genetic engineering, environmental change, urban club culture and virtual reality', and share with Filmer an interest in technology. The resulting works, such as the *Life Extension Pill Rings* (1994) or *Double Mouth Flasks* (1994) blend fantasy with reality, science fiction with technological advances, and explore the boundary between Fine Art and adornment.

Christoph Zellweger, Chain, 1994

**Christoph Zellweger, Commodity
Chain-K22, 1997**

Environmental issues, society and
history are reflected in Zellweger's
work. He aims to create objects which
simultaneously allude to the past and
hint at the future, and often uses steel to
connote industrialization and modern
society. He echoes Filmer's sentiments in
not wanting to be tied to the traditions
of jewellery. Underpinning his work is a
concern with the effect that his pieces
have on the environment and society. In
Chain (1994), the combination of latex
and distressed steel suggests decay, yet
an allusion is made to the relationship
between technology and nature.

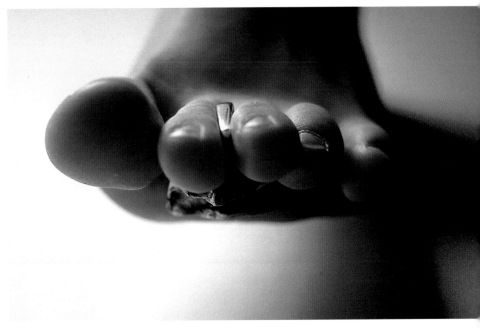

Naomi Filmer, Toe Between Pieces, 1993

PHILIP TREACY

I was at the College from 1988 until 1991. Alan Couldridge was a fantastic hat-maker, so he had an avid interest in developing a hat course, which didn't exist up until then. But I believe they were thinking of setting one up and so I was there at the beginning. And it changed my whole career. I had studied fashion design at the National College of Art in Dublin, but I'd made hats as a hobby in between. When I came to interview it was like a breath of fresh air. It was an incredibly grown-up environment for a College, and I showed hats at my interview – they knew as soon as I arrived that it was something I wanted to specialize in – but I was afraid to talk about them too much, because I thought maybe if I went on about the hats it might stop me getting onto the course. But it all worked out. For the first year I did the garment-related projects as well: the fashion environment became an added benefit, because I work all the time with fashion designers, so it was very important to understand how designers work and think. Alan looked after me, and from the end of my first year my tutor was Sheilagh Brown. Sheilagh was one of those tutors you come across only once in your career – somebody you can totally believe in: she was the type of person I would have jumped out of the window for, if she'd said that was the correct thing to do. There came a point when the tutors said, "Maybe you should do more fashion." Sheilagh Brown just took me aside and said, "You should make hats, because you're good at it and because few people are making hats."

Did my approach to hats seem revolutionary? Well, I love elegance and beauty, and hats relate to fashion in a more major way than people allowed for in the 60s and 70s; they underestimated and still underestimate what a hat can suggest. A hat can say so much more about fashion than a garment can. What I was most excited

214

DESIGN

about was having the opportunity to make interesting modern hats – that was my goal. I was the only student at the time, so there wasn't really a designated course for me – we did have outside tuition from various designers in the industry, but it was pretty loose – there was tuition one day a week and the rest of the time we were there to work. I had my own space. A tiny little room. And at the end of my first year, Isabella Blow introduced me to John Galliano, and he asked me if I'd be interested in making some hats with the lady who made his hats. So I persuaded Alan Couldridge to have Shirley come and teach for one day a week.

Motivation has never been a problem in my approach. I never really agreed with the students feeling "the world owed them a living". I think the most important thing for a student to realize in any educational establishment is that it's up to you – here's your chance – now you have an opportunity to do what you do, in the case of the RCA, in a fantastic environment. It just changed everything for me. At the end of my first year I made the hats for about eight different second-year students for their final show.

The most disconcerting thing about initially going to the RCA was the wealth and level of talent that surrounded you, whereas on other diploma or degree courses there's a number of students doing a course for the sake of doing a course. At the RCA, you are with a lot of extremely talented students, and the standard of what I considered to be good just rose and rose. It's a competitive world out there, – I'm not sure about other courses, but fashion courses tend to be competitive. It's the nature of the business, and when you graduate it gets worse! A lot of the students worked with other departments – I didn't, really, I had complete tunnel vision about

PHILIP TREACY

where I was going. I did love the history of art course with Madeleine Ginsberg, who was incredible, and some of my most memorable moments happened on her course. Some students would just say, "Oh, it's a distraction", but they were wrong.

One very interesting thing at the RCA was the good relationship we had with commercial outlets such as Harrods. So in my first year I was running a business through the College – through Harrods hat department – which was how my whole thing started, in addition to the Galliano arrangement. They asked me to create my own hats, which makes it exciting. It was a fantastic link for students to have, really reassuring. Until you start doing the business side of fashion yourself, you don't really learn how to do it properly. I had set out to make hats, not be a businessman. But I've had to develop business skills as a result.

The fashion show was held at the College in those days. While I was still at the RCA, the person who'd sponsored the hat course became my backer – I was incredibly naive about backing or anything like that – and he said to me, "When you finish, maybe we'll do something together." I didn't even think about it; I didn't think, "right". I just thought that what he was offering was what all this was about. He was a friend of Alan's. Straight from one to the other. It was easy – no, not easy, but it did just happen.

I think it's important to use every opportunity one is given, and at the RCA the opportunities I was given were incredible – the people I met, the lectures we had. I came from a very good course in Dublin, but a provincial fashion course – when I came to the RCA we would have Valentino and Armani come and lecture us – it made you have a totally different outlook. All the projects we did were very commercial, which I personally found quite difficult, but I didn't suffer from it.

When final exams came along, I remember the external examiner was Nicole Farhi, and she looked at me very blankly and said, "Why are you here?" "What do you mean, why am I here – I'm here because ..." So then the tutor called her aside and whispered in her ear. "Why are you here?" she said. Imagine. What she meant was, "This is a Fashion course – why's this person showing these hats?" It was a bit frightening I must say, but I've never been too deterred by that sort of thing.

When Sheilagh Brown said "make hats", in a way it was a risky piece of advice in the late 80s, but that's what I found so exciting. It was much more of a challenge to have an opportunity to change people's perception of hats and hat design and hat-making than it was to do something that everyone was used to. Did the hat thing come from Ireland, and looking at rows of hats in church? Well, they do cover their heads more there. But I think there's more of a hat consciousness here: hats are about Englishness – they're a part of the culture. I did grow up with a very religious, Catholic background, so hats and head covering was definitely a part of it, but it wasn't really something that made me want to make hats. I like hats because I like to make things, I like to work with my hands, and hats is one of the few areas where you get to make the actual piece yourself: with clothing, you design it, but you don't usually make it. The satisfaction of having produced something with your own hands – that's the prize, not the glory afterwards.

I'm always meeting RCA people – it's like a private club. There are people working all over the world who have been to the College: there's a huge professional network. And we were treated as young professionals, normal people, when we were there, not like students. It wasn't a tutor–student situation where everyone did their work because they were told to. Just by being there we were learning, everyone was intelligent enough to understand that.'

PRE-WAR TEXTILES

Barbara Hepworth
(1903–75)
Student 1921–24
Textile design, mid-1930s

Henry Moore
(1898–1986)
Student 1921–24
Staff 1924–31
Silk sample, Ascher, 1946

Textile design was included in the general design course, but from 1928 onwards craft classes were offered in 'embroidery, cotton printing by hand and weaving'. A textile unit had nominally existed since 1924, but was hampered through lack of equipment. After a fact-finding visit, Nikolaus Pevsner noted that the equipment was 'scanty and hardly suitable for instruction in industrial methods'. But the appointment of Reco Capey in 1925 changed the perception of textiles within the College, in particular the status of woodblock-printed cloth. Capey challenged the old Arts and Crafts philosophy, and encouraged the use of modernist motifs. As *The Studio* put it:

'One of the ablest of young men who have turned their attention to fabric designs is Mr. Reco Capey ... essentially modern in spirit and outlook.'

Such was Capey's international reputation that students such as Astrid Sampe travelled from as far afield as Scandinavia to join the programme before carrying the message back home. Paul Nash also tutored the students and designed patterns for the Footprints workshop and Cresta.

After failing her diploma in painting because her work was considered too

Astrid Sampe
(b. 1909)
Student 1931–32
Modular, 1954

Margaret Simeon
(b. 1910)
Student 1931–35
Furnishing fabric, c. 1940

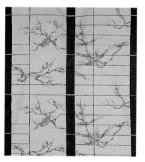

John Wright
(b. 1927)
Student 1946–51
Spring House, Hull Traders Ltd, 1959

Paul Nash
(1889–1946)
Staff 1922–25, 1938–39
Wild Cherry, textile design, c. 1920

DESIGN

Edward Bawden
(1903–89)
Student 1922–25
Staff 1930–40, 1948–53
Wallpaper, c.1939

Enid Marx
(1902–98)
Student 1922–25
Fabric moquette for London Underground, 1937

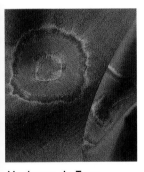

Marianne de Trey
(b.1913)
Student 1932–36
Square, 1935

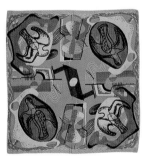

John Tunnard
(1900–71)
Student 1919–23
Bird and Stone, Ascher, 1947

Reco Capey
(1895–1961)
Student 1919–22
Staff 1925–53
Packaging for Yardley Cosmetics, 1936–38

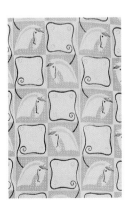

Lucienne Day
(b.1917)
Student 1937–40
Block-printed linen, 1938

abstract, Enid Marx was introduced by Nash to the Curwen Press to create decorative papers, and then to the Three Shields Gallery to see the work of textile designer-makers Barron & Larcher. Her resulting handblock-printed fabrics were exhibited with the modernist art of the period, and her work throughout the interwar years challenged the hierarchy of fine and applied arts. As the student magazine *Gallimaufry* noted in 1925:

'Among all the misses who flit with Art she alone woos it seriously; because she is the Cassandra who prophesies the doom of the old regime of design.'

Of the same generation, Barbara Hepworth and Henry Moore also turned their hands to textiles, Hepworth in particular with her constructivist fabrics for Mortons.

With the outbreak of war and the relocation of the RCA to Ambleside, textiles continued to be studied and practised, but in a converted barn. Sadly, very little remains of the wartime output as students could only keep their printed or woven fabrics in exchange for clothing coupons.

The first Professor of Textiles was Alan Walton from Glasgow University, who died before he could take up the post. He was replaced by James de Holden Stone in 1949, who introduced rigorous teaching methods – students progressed from calligraphic marks to vertical stripes, to horizontal, Bauhaus-style design.

Post-war reconstruction and the drive to recapture export markets directed the spotlight onto the training of textile designers. Writing in the February 1950 edition of *Textile Weekly*, Mr. Jacks, director of Messrs. R. Greg & Co, a firm of spinners, said that textile designers should possess:

' ... artistic ability, craftsmanship, a real appreciation of industry, willingness to become a partner in an exciting adventure, more than a passing acquaintance with the markets of the textile industry, and finally the ability to design at a price.'

His views, he added, stemmed from the fact that most fabrics produced for export were expensive, artisanal and produced in limited quantities.

The introduction of inexpensive roller-printed fabrics and mechanized screen prints created a new market for textiles that was championed by Roger

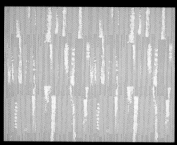

Audrey Levy
(b. 1928)
Student 1948–51 Visiting Staff
Visiting Professor 1990–present
Palladio 'Impasto' wallpaper design, 1957

Pat Albeck
(b. 1930)
Student 1950–53
Printed textile designs, 195

Shirley Craven
(b. 1934)
Student 1955–58
Shape, Hull Traders Ltd, 1964

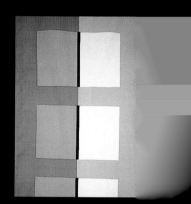

Doreen Dyall
(b. 1937)
Student 1955–58
Alternation, Heal's Fabrics L

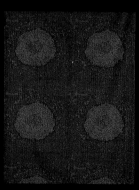

Fay Hillier
(b. 1936)
Student 1956–59
Corona, Heal's Fabrics Ltd, 1961

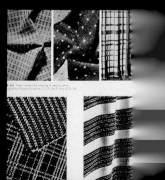

Margaret Leischner
(1907–70)
Head of Weaving 1948–6
Fabric designs, c. 1952

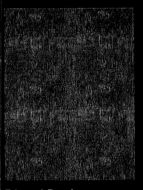

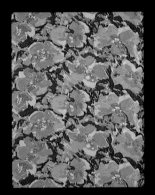

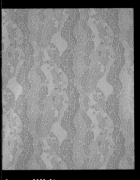

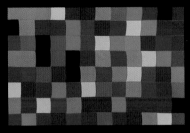

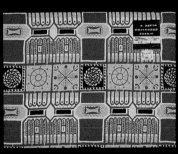

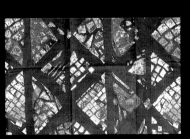

Anne White
(b. 1932)
Student 1952–55
Mosaic, Warner & Sons Ltd, 1986

Barbara Brown
(b. 1932)
Student 1953–56
Staff 1968–90
Shawl, 1981

Edward Pond
(b. 1929)
Student 1955–58
Cathedral, Bernard Wardle Ltd, 1962

Robert Dodd
(b. 1934)
Student 1956–59
Flora Bella, Heal's Fabrics Ltd, 1960

Roger Nicholson
(unknown)
Professor 1958–84
Range no. CP 445, David Whitehead Ltd, 1951

Humphrey Spender
(b. 1910)
Staff 1953–75
Minster, Edinburgh Weavers Ltd, 1958

The course adopted these industrial methods and began to turn out a group of confident graduates, highly favoured by the new Design Council. The promotion of much of their work indicated an acceptance of textiles and wallpapers as design-worthy objects in their own right, rather than as aspects of a wider scheme.

This new-found confidence inspired many graduates to start their own firms or go freelance. Dan Johnson, Industrial Officer of the Design Council, observed of their work:

'Some designers are so surprisingly versatile that they can work successfully for producers whose ideas of good design differ greatly from one another.'

This resistance to design dogma is attributable not only to the general lack of consensus of the time, but also to the teaching of the School.

221

60s TEXTILES

The prospectus for 1962/63 advertized facilities that included 'a greenhouse for the study of flowers and plants'. By 1966 the facilities extended to a dyeing laboratory and photographic processing rooms. The teaching of surface design was also expanded to include 'additional study in the design of knitted fabric, floor covering, wall covering and design for plastics and new materials.'

The possibilities of new materials and techniques became a focus at the RCA with the setting up of the Textile Design Research Unit in the mid-60s, led by John Foulds. Individual projects developed in collaboration with industrial companies and included the lamination of fabric for ICI fibres and the development of stitch-bonded, non-woven materials.

In the furnishings marketplace, textiles graduates had a string of critical and commercial successes. Firms producing ranges by ex-College students included Liberty, F. W. Grafton, Tootals, Cavendish, Hull Traders, Bernard Wardle and David Whitehead. Eventually the design direction within some of these firms came from the graduates as well – Shirley Craven at Hull Traders and Eddie Pond at Wardle's, for example.

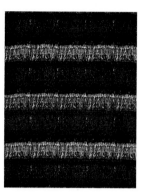

Nicola Wood
(b. 1936)
Student 1957–60
Vibration, Heal's Fabrics Ltd, 1962

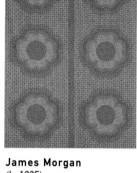

James Morgan
(b. 1935)
Student 1958–61
Petit Point, Heal's Fabrics Ltd, 1971

Janet Taylor
(b. 1936)
Student 1958–61
Degree Show, 1961

Peter Hall
(b. 1938)
Student 1959–62
Interlude, Textra Furnishings, 1970

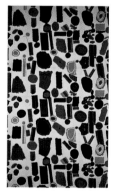

Zandra Rhodes
(b. 1940)
Student 1961–64
Medals, Heal's Fabrics Ltd, c. 1965

Michael Moon
(b. 1937)
Painting student 1962–63
Insulating Jacket, 1978

Natalie Gibson
(b. 1938)
Student 1958–61
Textile, 1980

James Park
(b. 1935)
Student 1958–61
Staff 1986–present
Hand-woven hooked rug, 1964

Pamela Kay
(b. 1939)
Student 1959–62
Before Harfleur, c. 1963–65

Howard Carter
(b. 1938)
Student 1960–63
Sunflower & Pansies, 1961–63

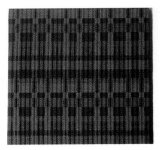

John Drummond
(unknown)
Tutor 1956–68
Sabines, Hull Traders Ltd, 1958

Marianne Straub
(1909–94)
Tutor 1968–74
*Fabric for London Underground,
John Holdsworth Ltd, 1974*

With the 60s emphasis on dress fabrics – and on textile design as the bedrock of the fashion industry – the Textiles Department responded by building into the syllabus 'visits to fashion houses and the execution of printed and woven fabrics for making up into clothes and for use as furnishing'. One of the first students to anticipate the swing away from furnishing fabrics was Zandra Rhodes:

'When I left the Royal College, it was fashionable to design furnishing fabrics; and, in fact, my degree print was bought by Heal's as a furnishing fabric. But it was during my second year at the Royal College that I became interested in the different discipline of dress fabrics. I was the first in the College's Textile School, for a long time, to turn away from furnishing fabrics to doing dress fabrics ... Furnishing fabrics tended to be large-scale, and in the 1960s frustrated would-be artists designed furnishing fabrics, painting such things as abstract landscapes.'

70s TEXTILES

The 'new crafts' of the 70s had an impact on the careers students that sought after graduation. Professor Roger Nicholson complained that 'the aim of most students is to become independent designers or producers rather than to be employed by an individual firm'. While print design for export entered a boom period, knit design established itself as a viable career destination for students: many small-scale knitting production workshops were set up with help from the Crafts Council.

Within the Research Unit, computer-aided textile design systems were installed in collaboration with Deryk Healey Associates. The Research Unit was one of the first places to use computers to originate patterns, which were then constructed from digital information by a knitting machine. Between 1974 and 1976, the Research Unit also embarked on an investigation into the possibilities of using shaping and moulding techniques in garment formation that included an associated photographic anthropometric study.

Such innovative projects, combined with the new emphasis on designer-craftspeople, led to much diversification and specialization.

Lesley Sunderland
(b. 1947)
Student 1969–71
Degree Show, 1971

Kay Cosserat
(b. 1948)
Student 1970–72
Degree Show, 1972

Ian Simpson
(b. 1952)
Student 1973–75
Degree Show, 1975

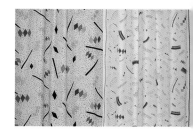

Val Furphy
(b. 1951)
Student 1974–76
Degree Show, 1976

Helen Yardley
(b. 1954)
Student 1976–78
Degree Show, 1978

Beryl Gibson
(b. 1954)
Student 1976–78
Degree Show, 1978

DESIGN

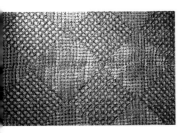

Philippa Watkins
(b. 1946)
Student 1971–73
Staff 1997–present
Degree Show, 1973

Diana Harrison
(b. 1950)
Student 1971–73
Degree Show, 1973

Mary Restieaux
(b. 1945)
Student 1972–74
Degree Show, 1974

Pam Hogg
(b. 1951)
Student 1974–76
Degree Show, 1976

Lindsay Taylor
(b. 1952)
Student 1974–76
Degree Show, 1976

Sally Jenkyn-Jones
(b. 1955)
Student 1976–78
Degree Show, 1978

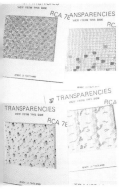

Hilary Scarlett
(b. 1954)
Student 1976–78
Degree Show, 1978

Graham Fowler
(b. 1956)
Student 1977–79
Degree Show, 1979

Sue Timney
(b. 1950)
Student 1977–79
Degree Show, 1979

80s TEXTILES

Roger Nicholson stated in 1980 that 'the main target in the School of Textiles ... has been to encourage better industrial liaison with the British Textile Industry'. Alexandra Buxton was commissioned to research possible areas of industrial collaboration at a time of decline in the manufacturing sector. Nicholson was succeeded in 1984 by Professor Bernard Nevill.

The shift towards wearable craft textiles, often in the form of a scarf or shawl, became an important growth area in this period, while cloth colourists such as Sally Greaves-Lord and Rushton Aust spearheaded site-specific commissions for interiors. Postmodernism infiltrated surface design at the RCA with a return to symbolic decoration and a tendency to use pattern in an explicit way.

The continuing financial support of the Sanderson Art in Industry Fund established the post of a part-time Industrial Liaison Tutor. In 1987, the textile studios were rebuilt to install a new range of computer systems: this inevitably involved the abandoning of some of the hand machinery acquired since the turn of the century.

Sally Freshwater
(b. 1956)
Student 1978–80
Degree Show, 1980

Rushton Aust
(b. 1958)
Student 1979–81
Degree Show, 1981

Brian Bolger
(b. 1959)
Student 1981–83
Degree Show, 1983

Lucy Sprigge
(b. 1960)
Student 1981–83
Degree Show, 1983

Patricia Needham
(b. 1961)
Student 1983–85
Degree Show, 1985

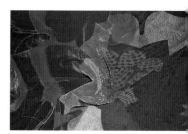

Neisha Crosland
(b. 1960)
Student 1984–86
Degree Show, 1986

Sally Greaves-Lord
(b. 1957)
Student 1980–82
Degree Show, 1982

Sian Tucker
(b. 1958)
Student 1980–82
Degree Show, 1982

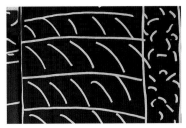

David Band
(b. 1959)
Student 1981–83
Degree Show, 1983

Carolyn Quartermaine
(b. 1959)
Student 1981–83
Degree Show, 1983

Paul Wearing
(b. 1959)
Student 1981–83
Degree Show, 1983

Cressida Bell
(b. 1959)
Student 1982–84
Degree Show, 1984

Carolyn Corben
(b. 1963)
Student 1987–89
Degree Show, 1989

Freddie Robins
(b. 1965)
Student 1987–89
Degree Show, 1989

Ingrid Tait
(b. 1962)
Student 1987–89
Degree Show, 1989

90s TEXTILES

With the arrival of John Miles as Professor in 1989, supported by James Park, the Fashion and Textiles courses were amalgamated for the first time since the Second World War. Research – especially into fabric technology and 'intelligent fabrics' – had become increasingly central to both.

The Textiles area now comprised printed textiles and constructed textiles, subdivided into woven, knitted and embroidered. This diversity has resulted in an unusual range of responses, including applications as diverse as installation, interior decoration and car design.

A particular focus has been the influence of Japanese designers, evident in student intake, making techniques and industry placements. Issey Miyake, when receiving an honorary doctorate, referred to the students on the amalgamated courses as 'a nourishment to the world'.

Paul Simmons
(b. 1967)
Student 1988–90
Timorous Beasties, 1990

Karina Holmes
(b. 1966)
Student 1990–92
Degree Show, 1992

Janet Stoyel
(b. 1949)
Student 1992–94
Degree Show, 1994

Vanessa Doyle
(b. 1971)
Student 1994–96
Degree Show, 1996

Ptolemy Mann
(b. 1972)
Student 1995–97
Degree Show, 1997

Kerry Rudgley
(b. 1973)
Embroidery student 1995–97
Degree Show, 1997

Sharon Ting
(unknown)
Student 1990–92
Degree Show, 1992

Donna Payne
(b. 1969)
Student 1991–93
Degree Show, 1993

Paul Stamper
(b. 1961)
Student 1992–94
Degree Show, 1994

Hiroshi Fukuda
(b. 1969)
Student 1994–96
Degree Show, 1996

Frances Geesin
(b. 1941)
Student 1990–95
Degree Show, 1995

Mayu Yoshikawa
(b. 1970)
Student 1994–96
Degree Show, 1996

Craig Wheatley
(b. 1973)
Student 1995–97
Degree Show, 1997

Jenny Wright
(b. 1973)
Student 1995–97
Degree Show, 1997

James Bullen
(b. 1966)
Student 1996–98
Degree Show, 1998

50s FASHION

The Fashion School at the RCA began in Summer 1948 with the appointment of Madge Garland, a former editor of *Vogue*.

Picture Post marked the event with an article that claimed, 'what once seemed a feminine priority is now dignified by university status ... London has just made history'. But London still looked to Paris for inspiration – Garland incorporated this into the curriculum in the form of reverential trips to the Paris fashion houses, where female students were expected to dress in hats and white gloves for the occasion. 'Paris, Kensington', wrote the press.

The Fashion School was based in a large period house in Ennismore Gardens, some way away from the other design studios. In 1956, Garland was succeeded by her senior assistant, Janey Ironside.

Ironside quickly established strong relationships with the British fashion press, and closer relationships with the industry. Thereafter, the School was seldom out of the papers, and the patronizing coverage of the early days made way for promotion.

Jean Matthew
(b. 1927)
Student 1948–49
Dress, 1949

Eileen Blackman
(b. 1927)
Student 1948–51
Dress, 1950

Sonia Townsend
(b. 1929)
Student 1950–53
Ski outfit, 1953

Mary Lenanton
(b. 1933)
Student 1951–54
Satin top, jersey pants, 1953

Donald Julian Robinson
(b. 1931)
Student 1952–55
White kid suit, 1958

Richard Lachlan
(b. 1933)
Student 1955–58
Dress, 1958

Kenneth Burgess
(b. 1928)
Student 1949–52
Beach suit, 1952

Joanne Brogden
(b. 1929)
Student 1950–53
Staff 1957–71
Professor 1971–89
Coat, 1952

Gina Fratini
(b. 1934)
Student 1950–53
Ensemble, 1970

David Watts
(b. 1929)
Student 1951–54
Outfit, 1952

Bernard Nevill
(b. 1930)
Student 1952–53
Professor of Textiles 1984–88
Ribbon Dress, 1974

Juliet Grime
(b. 1931)
Student 1952–55
Playsuit, 1955

David Sassoon
(b. 1932)
Student 1955–58
Evening dress, 1957

Bill Pashley
(b. 1934)
Student 1956–59
Evening dress, 1959

Sylvia Ayton
(b. 1937)
Student 1958–61
BEA Uniform, 1959

60s FASHION

Summer 1959 was when Mary Quant and Alexander Plunkett-Green decided to start selling a new and young style of dress at their shop Bazaar, on the King's Road. Like contemporaries at the College, such as Tuffin & Foale, they were typical of a new breed of young, creative professionals who were challenging the old guard, dressing a new generation of consumers and opening brightly coloured retail outlets.

Janey Ironside noted:

'The young people of today work; it is fashionable as well as in most cases necessary to work, and it is fashionable to be a designer or to take an interest in the arts, to paint, to design furniture.'

The Fashion School fed the new colour supplements, particularly when it experimented at annual fashion shows with the possibilities of dress design. In 1964, at the suggestion of Sir Hardy Amies, a Menswear section was added with support from Hepworth's. Graduating students were now expected to add a 'swinging' touch to the ranges of commercial fashion houses.

James Wedge
(b. 1937)
Student 1959–60
Waistcoat and breast jewellery, 1968

Lindsay Robertson
(b. 1934)
Student 1958–61
Outfit, 1960

Valerie Couldridge
(b. 1940)
Student 1960–63
Staff 1974–83
Water Work, 1963

Angela Sharp
(b. 1940)
Student 1960–63
Evening coat, 1963

Brian Godbold
(b. 1943)
Student 1963–65
Outfit, 1965

Brian Walsh
(b. 1941)
Student 1963–65
Menswear, 1965

Sally Tuffin
(b. 1938)
Student 1958–61
Childrenswear, 1961

Marion Foale
(b. 1939)
Student 1958–61
Outfit, 1961

Pauline Denyer
(b. 1940)
Student 1959–62
Dress, 1962

Janice Wainwright
(b. 1940)
Student 1961–64
Outfit, 1962

Christopher McDonnell
(b. 1940)
Student 1961–64
Outfit, 1964

Ossie Clark
(1942–96)
Student 1962–65
Culotte Dress, Degree Show, 1965

Bill Gibb
(1943–1988)
Student 1966–67
Outfit, 1966

John Hicks
(b. 1940)
Student 1965–68
Menswear, 1966

Anthony Price
(b. 1945)
Student 1965–68
Outfit, 1966

FASHION

Ossie Clark

'Ossie Clark, 23, final year student, RCA'
Photograph by David Bailey; model Chrissie Shrimpton, British Vogue, August 1965

**Printed silk culotte dress,
Degree Show, 1965**

**Silk gauze trousers and coat,
blouse with silver paillettes,
Degree Show, 1965**

The legacy of Ossie Clark as a fashion designer and flamboyant character encapsulates the growth and decay of Swinging London. The maturing of his designs – from sharp opticals to intoxicated patterns – parallels a scene that wished to burn ever brighter.

Raymond Ossie Clark entered the Fashion School of the RCA in 1961, a technically proficient pattern cutter from his training at Manchester College of Art. Under the guidance of Janey Ironside (who first asked the question 'Who is that boy who wiggles his bottom when he walks?'), Ossie immersed himself in ideas. Trawling through Portobello Market for vintage finds, or marvelling at Mme Vionnet's bias-cut dresses at the Victoria & Albert Museum, he was entranced by the glamour of the past.

Ossie met David Hockney through his flatmate Mo McDermott who was a life model for the artist. Hockney introduced Ossie to the brashness of Pop on a trip they took to America. The trip was to inspire his graduating collection of 1965 which captured the headlines with an evening coat whose collar was trimmed with battery-operated, flashing lightbulbs.

FASHION

Ossie Clark

His first commercial break came with a paper dress commissioned by Molly Parkin, then fashion editor of *Nova* magazine, which sealed his creative relationship with his wife Celia Birtwell. Birtwell designed printed fabrics exclusively for Clark, and the first – an Art Deco design directly inspired from Poiret – struck a wonderfully unlikely chord with the modernity of the shift garment.

Working as chief designer at Quorum on the King's Road before showing as a designer in his own right, Ossie Clark introduced a style of dress that developed the flat-chested and waistless androgyny of modern youth into a sexually confident romanticism following the contours of the body. Using fluid fabrics such as chiffon, marocain and crêpe de Chine, he cut the fabric on the bias so that his dresses emphasized shoulders, nipples and waist. Coupled with Birtwell's stylized floral designs, they defined a high point in ready-to-wear dress design utilizing printed textiles.

Lips dress for Quorum, 1966

**Crêpe fringe trouser suit
and silk two-piece for Quorum,
Nova magazine, 1969**

**Throwaway wedding dress,
Nova magazine, 1969**

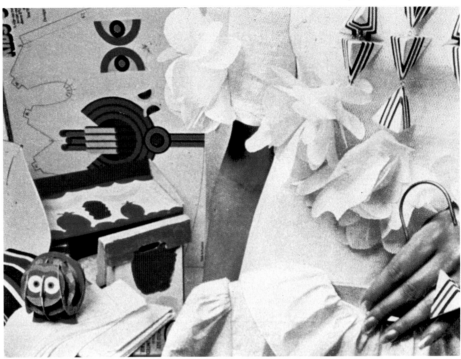

The perfect foil to this look was a jacket or coat made from diamond python skin, a material Ossie personally unearthed in a Dickensian leather warehouse by the Thames. Claiming 'they sprung to life and lay opened before me', Ossie Clark used the skins to make the zippered catsuits that were favoured by Mick Jagger among others.

His fashion shows were spectacular events where the stars in the audience shined as brightly as the lights on the catwalk. Suzy Menkes described one such show at the Royal Court Theatre in 1971 as 'the most extraordinary moment in the history of fashion.' The moment was shortlived, though, as Ossie faded from attention due to a cocktail of mismanagement, poor business sense and economic recession.

The posthumous publication of his diaries after his brutal murder in 1996 has re-established his reputation as a talented yet tainted figure of his generation; while Hockney's painting of Ossie and Celia in their Powis Terrace flat, *Mr and Mrs Clark and Percy*, has established itself as the most visited picture in the Tate Gallery.

70s FASHION

The beginning of the 70s was marked by Joanne Brogden's appointment as Professor of Fashion, and the introduction of the two- rather than the three-year course. The change led to a move away from open-ended creativity towards more directed study.

In the Annual Report for 1969/70, Brogden noted that graduates (as they now were) 'were very choosy about the jobs they took, some preferring to go into "boutique" work as opposed to that which could be termed industrial.' The decade was marked by the swift progress Brogden made in the professionalization of the course, and in establishing a closer relationship with industry. Projects sponsored by commercial concerns became a central element of the teaching, visits were regularly arranged to assess the needs of firms for RCA designers, and in turn, industry came to the College to source talent. In many ways, the Fashion course at this time was the most 'industrial' in the College.

David McIntyre
(b. 1948)
Student 1969–71
Degree Show, 1971

Lee Pring
(b. 1948)
Student 1969–71
Degree Show, 1971

Laurence Roberts
(b. 1947)
Student 1970–72
Menswear, 1972

Roy Peach
(b. 1950)
Student 1973–75
Degree Show, 1975

Ragence Lam
(b. 1951)
Student 1974–76

David Emanuel
(b. 1952)
Student 1975–77

Clare Dudley Hart
(b. 1948)
Student 1970–72
Degree Show, 1972

Bill Kadasis
(b. 1946)
Student 1970–72
Menswear, 1972

Stephen King
(b. 1948)
Student 1970–72
Menswear, 1972

Felicity Clegg
(b. 1952)
Student 1974–76
Degree Show, 1976

Sarah Dallas
(b. 1951)
Student 1974–76
Degree Show, 1976

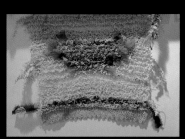

Liz Griffiths
(b. 1952)
Student 1974–76
Degree Show, 1976

Elizabeth Emanuel
(b. 1953)
Student 1975–77
*Wedding ensemble
(with David Emanuel), 1979*

Lynne Burstall
(b. 1954)
Student 1976–79
Degree Show, 1979

Anne Storey
(b. 1955)
Student 1976–79
Degree Show, 1979

80s FASHION

The Fashion School's networking with the industry, in the UK and overseas, reaped big dividends in the 1980s. Joanne Brogden wrote of how it was 'now easy to organize work study periods with French, German and Italian manufacturing companies for three-week periods or holiday periods.' Groomed for a global business, the students stretched themselves as far as they could. In 1983 alone, they worked in Switzerland, Scandinavia and Hong Kong, in addition to New Delhi, where they oversaw an RCA collection for Monsoon.

The Fashion School celebrated the 150th anniversary of the College by launching the RCA Wool Collection for winter 1987, in association with the International Wool Secretariat. Organized by tutor Anne Tyrrell as a professional selling collection designed by the students, it sold in Paris, Milan, New York and Tokyo.

All this was expensive and complex to run, and to raise extra resources the School abandoned the traditional format of the College fashion shows in favour of a glamorous, high-price gala event. At first this was held in the RCA galleries, and then off site.

Elaine Chaloner
(b. 1957)
Student 1979–81
Degree Show, 1981

Eric Bremner
(b. 1958)
Student 1982–83
Degree Show, 1983

Ian Griffiths
(b. 1961)
Student 1985–87
Outfit, 1987

Neil Barrett-Barber
(b. 1964)
Student 1986–88
Degree Show, 1988

Ann Hardiman
(b. 1965)
Student 1987–89
Degree Show, 1989

Charles Hunter
(b. 1962)
Student 1987–89
Degree Show, 1989

Nigel Luck
(b. 1959)
Student 1981–83
Degree Show, 1983

Karen Baker
(b. 1960)
Student 1982–84
Degree Show, 1984

Sara Sturgeon
(b. 1960)
Student 1982–84
Degree Show, 1984

Kevin Carrington
(b. 1965)
Student 1986–88
Degree Show, 1988

Judith Bremner
(b. 1964)
Student 1987–89
Degree Show, 1989

Sue Chowles
(b. 1966)
Student 1987–89
Degree Show, 1989

Sarah Jane Wilkinson
(b. 1964)
Student 1987–89
Degree Show, 1989

Peter Witham
(b. 1966)
Student 1987–89
Degree Show, 1989

Anne Tyrrell
(unknown)
Student 1957–60
Staff 1967–95
Visiting Professor
Outfit for John Marks, 1977

90s FASHION

Rector Jocelyn Stevens was close to the world of fashion journalism, and in 1989 he appointed John Miles, a textile designer, as Professor of the amalgamated School of Fashion and Textiles. The intention was to integrate the two disciplines to offer a flexible model of interdependency that could parallel working practices within the industry.

Miles inherited a range of fashion courses producing professional young designers who were snapped up by industry, increasingly overseas. He began to change this perception by stressing 'individuality as the key to the future'. This was reflected in the choice of students, the directions in which their work could mature and the emphasis placed on personal research.

The approach has produced a crop of successful 'own label' designers who have helped refocus the Fashion School. Building on this energy, Fashion and Textiles have separated again while retaining their close links. The end of the decade has also seen the appointment of Wendy Dagworthy (formerly the very successful head of fashion at Central St. Martin's) as Professor.

Harvey Bertram-Brown
(b. 1966)
Student 1988–90
Degree Show, 1990

John Crummay
(b. 1966)
Student 1988–90
Degree Show, 1990

Kait Bolongaro
(b. 1968)
Student 1990–92
Degree Show, 1992

Cathryn Avison
(b. 1969)
Student 1992–94
Degree Show, 1994

Jane Whitfield
(b. 1966)
Student 1992–94
Degree Show, 1994

Laura Watson
(b. 1967)
Student 1993–95
Degree Show, 1995

Andrew Fionda
(b. 1967)
Student 1988–90
Degree Show, 1990

Deborah Milner
(b. 1964)
Student 1988–90
Degree Show, 1990

Justin Oh
(b. 1963)
Student 1988–90
Degree Show, 1990

Julia Jentzsch
(b. 1964)
Student 1992–94
Degree Show, 1994

Brian Kirkby
(b. 1965)
Student 1992–94
Degree Show, 1994

Aisling Ludden
(b. 1967)
Student 1992–94
Degree Show, 1994

Roger Lee
(b. 1970)
Student 1994–96
Degree Show, 1996

Julien Macdonald
(b. 1971)
Student 1994–96
Degree Show, 1996

Nancy Tilbury
(b. 1972)
Student 1995–97
Degree Show, 1997

FASHION
The hidden designers

There are graduates of the Fashion School whose impact is not as visible as a name stitched into the back of a garment. Some call them 'the hidden designers', although this is to underestimate their importance. Their careers reflect well on the teaching they received at the College; they also serve to illustrate the diversity of the fashion business.

Since 1976, Brian Godbold has been responsible for promoting design as an integral part of the culture at Marks & Spencer. As design director of the company, he has had a big influence on the structure of the British fashion industry from a retail perspective. In particular, his use of well-known designers as consultants and the establishment of M&S sponsorship of The New Generation of Designers at London Fashion Week (an event with which he has been deeply involved) have won him much respect.

A student of the 60s, Godbold did not, in fact, graduate from the RCA. Instead, he managed to secure a professional design job in New York on the strength of his student portfolio. As there were three Brians in his year group at the College, Godbold had made a point of signing his fashion drawings 'Brian G' for identification. Fascinated by the shortened name at his interview, his

**Brian Godbold
Maxi coat for Wallis, 1968**

**Brian Godbold
Marks & Spencer outfit, Autumn 1994**

**Lynne Burstall
Oasis Store Identity, 1999**

employers christened Godbold's first collection 'Brian G at Jovi', an early example of the use of a designer name at middle-market level. His Professor, Janey Ironside, had allowed Godbold to return to the course, although by the start of the next academic year his collection had become a commercial success, and so he stayed in America.

The professionalism of graduating students in the 70s was underpinned by the ambassadorial role of Professor Joanne Brogden, who forged international links with industry. Keith Varty, a graduate of 1975, went on to form the highly successful design label Byblos, in partnership with Alan Cleaver (who graduated from Environmental Design in 1976). Varty was an excellent example of Brogden's influence – he was instantly snapped up to freelance for European fashion houses before starting a label that

FASHION
The hidden designers

Liz Griffiths
Missoni, Autumn/Winter 1977–78

Liz Griffiths
Missoni, Autumn/Winter 1978–79

became known for its mix of Anglo-Italian style rather than for the designers' names. He still remembers the anxiety that pervaded the College studios when it was time for the staff to appraise student projects.

Graduating in 1976, Liz Griffiths was one of the first designers to be courted by the Italian fashion houses: her designs – with a strong flair for fabrics – came to the attention of Ottavio and Rosita Missoni at the Degree Shows. Griffiths was inspired by her aunt Muriel Pemberton, who studied painting at the RCA in the 30s

**Jane Whitfield
Louis Vuitton, Winter 1999**

**Jane Whitfield
Louis Vuitton, Winter 1999**

**Keith Varty and Alan Cleaver
Byblos, 1998**

and then went on to found the Department of Dress at the Central School of Arts and Crafts. Under Griffiths' influence, Missoni's experimental approach to knitwear construction and colouring took a new craft-based direction. She has remained with the company ever since.

Lynne Burstall's talent as design director for Oasis and more recently Coast, was decisively shaped by her education at the RCA. She cites learning to see a project through from start to finish as fundamental to her ability to communicate product-based design across the whole retail experience. She believes her understanding of how a total look is formulated can be traced back to company visits and an emphasis on collaborative projects with practitioners from other fields while at the RCA. Graduating in 1979, Burstall was impressed by the School's strong work ethic and principles.

Jane Whitfield is a freelance designer, who was taught in the Professor John Miles era. She went on to work for Gianfranco Ferre in Italy and, more recently, to assist Marc Jacobs in the setting up of a *prêt-à-porter* range for Louis Vuitton. Her work for Louis Vuitton involved streamlining industrial methods for designing bags: instead of a three-year cycle, high-end collections were produced in just six months. Whitfield recalls that a lot of her professional attitudes were gained from her RCA course.

MILLINERY

Millinery has been offered at the RCA as an option within the Fashion Womenswear Course since the late 80s, and as such has only been studied by very few students.

But from the beginning of the Fashion School in 1948, millinery has been an integral element of the School's teaching; as integral as a hat was to the appearance of Madge Garland, first Professor of Fashion, and to her students. At that time, and throughout the 50s and 60s, hats were designed and considered not in isolation, but in relation to the figure and to dress as a whole.

More recently, the creation of a specialist option within the course has nurtured the craft and produced practitioners who have been responsible for the revival of millinery at a couture level, and a new attitude to the wearing of hats. Spearheaded by the work of Philip Treacy, much has been made of the transformative qualities of headwear. Especially important has been the work of milliner Dai Rees, who originally trained at the RCA in Ceramics.

Peter Shepherd
(b. 1925)
Student 1947–50
Hat, 1949

Graham Smith
(b. 1938)
Student 1957–58
Fitting a hat, 1958

Philip Treacy
(b. 1966)
Student 1988–90
Degree Show, 1990

Rachel Drage
(b. 1968)
Student 1990–92
Degree Show, 1992

Ian Bennett
(b. 1971)
Student 1994–96
Degree Show, 1996

Pip Hackett
(b. 1963)
Student 1994–96
The Devil is a Woman, 1995

James Wedge
(b. 1937)
Student 1959–60
Staff 1975–78
Cowboy hat for Foale and Tuffin, 1966
(Image 'Young Idea', British Vogue)

Alan Couldridge
(b. 1939)
Student 1960–63
Staff 1972–92
Illustration for RCA Cookbook, 1987

Roger Nelson
(b. 1937)
Student 1960–63
Lurex hat and suit, 1963

Dai Rees
(b. 1961)
Ceramics student 1992–94
Pampilion autumn/winter, 1998

Jo Gordon
(b. 1967)
Student 1993–95
Forest, 1997

Flora McLean
(b. 1971)
Student 1993–95
Degree Show, 1995

Scott Wilson
(b. 1966)
Student 1994–96

Mayu Yoshikawa
(b. 1970)
Student 1994–97

Karen Scott
(b. 1970)
Student 1996–98

FASHION

Philip Treacy

On applying to the College to study Fashion Design, Philip Treacy wrote:

'Since I have a special interest in millinery, and have had no formal training in this field apart from two short periods at Stephen Jones, I would like to achieve international standards within this field.'

In the space of just ten years, Treacy has elevated the craft of millinery to the point where he now sets, rather than achieves, international standards.

Treacy has brought together progressive designs and British traditions. He was the first fashion student to benefit from the millinery course sponsored by the entrepreneur and chairman of the British Hat Guild, Bill Horsman. To celebrate the start of the course in 1988, Harrods invited him to design a range for the British social season. From this establishment starting-point, Treacy began a journey through modernism to his own brand of postmodernism.

On graduating from the RCA in 1991 with a catwalk collection of hats that received a standing ovation, he opened his showroom in Belgravia with financial backing from Horsman and mass-market hat manufacturers, W. Wright & Son Ltd. In the first year of trading he launched a ready-to-wear line, and began to supply custom-made hats to couture houses for their collections, in the first instance to the House of Chanel.

Ship hat, 1995

egree Show, 1990

Hat Collection, Spring/Summer, 1995

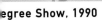
reen wind-blown hat, Autumn/Winter, 1999

These commissions soon built his reputation as a consummate craftsman. According to Karl Lagerfeld, his designs have a touch of madness about them – a reference to Lewis Carroll's Mad Hatter. The Hatter's hat had been appropriated by Treacy early on in his career.

His hats have often been described in sculptural or architectural terms, because of their purity of form and almost streamlined beauty. But Treacy's design process is rooted in drawing. When he states, 'You can tell if you draw it, if it's going to work or not,' he reveals that the supposedly extraneous elements of placing, pose, mood and gesture are actually embedded in the design, rather than added when the finished article is placed on the head.

INTRODUCTION

Walter Crane was sufficiently impressed by the work of some of the students of the new RCA to use it as illustrative material in his collection of essays *Ideals In Art* (1905), and other polemics about the Arts and Crafts philosophy. But these were students of 'Design' and 'Modelling'. At this time, there were still no specific courses in illustration, poster art or graphic design: the phrase 'graphic design' was to be coined in America in the mid-20s, and did not achieve common currency in Britain until some 20 years later.

A few students from the Crane era happened to specialize in these subjects after leaving the College: Harry Oakley designed posters for LNER, HMV and Bird's Custard; Sylvia Pankhurst, who hoped the RCA would teach her how to 'decorate halls where people would foregather in the movement to run the new world, and make banners for meetings and processions', decided at the end of her decorative painting course in 1906 to become the official artist of the Women's Social and Political Union, run by her mother.

The Birth of the Commercial Artist

As with Fine Art, the beginning of the William Rothenstein era coincided with a chemistry between students and staff – and a receptive market – which led to important new developments. The students were from the Painting and Design schools, and tutor Paul Nash called them 'an outbreak of talent': they included Eric Ravilious, Edward Bawden, Helen Binyon, Enid Marx and the painters Douglas Percy Bliss and Charles Tunnicliffe. Rothenstein's policy was to encourage fine artists and designers to mix in architecture and drawing classes as part of 'a general education through the arts'. Bliss recalled, however, that 'We used to say "designers do bad drawings and mount them beautifully. We do good drawings and don't bother about mounts". [Us painters] felt ourselves to be the Elect.'

Despite the traditional attitudes, these were the first students to make their names in the worlds of illustration and commercial art. They were preceded by John Gilroy who joined the 'Decorative Painting' course (as it was still called) in 1919 and missed a Prix de Rome by one vote in 1922. Gilroy produced illustrations for the RCA student magazine and, while still a student, designed a promotional leaflet commissioned by the Hydraulic Engineering Company. Shortly after leaving the College, he joined the agency S. H. Benson and, as one of their in-house designers, worked on the Guinness account for over 30 years. Pevsner was to observe in 1936 that much British design was less serious than its continental – and especially German – counterpart: Gilroy's menagerie of ostriches, toucans and seals for Guiness advertizing posters remain excellent proof.

By the mid-20s, the high spot of the design students' week was, however, 'Paul Nash day', when, as Helen Binyon was to recall, Nash would 'wear a bow tie and dark suit and look almost too smart for an artist. He would wander down the long room, looking carefully at what the students had to show him; he was witty and jokey.' He was particularly encouraging about watercolour painting, book illustration, wood-engraving and lino-cutting. And, together with his students, he rediscovered the work of Samuel Palmer and William Blake.

It was certainly imaginative of the Principal to appoint a well-known painter as 'a consultant to designers': Paul Nash was never, in fact, to teach the Fine Art students at the College. But then again, this was the era when Paul Nash produced his semi-abstract treatment, *The Rye Marshes*, which was attached to the sides of petrol lorries as they hurtled around the Home Counties, bearing the lithographed message, 'Everywhere You Go You Can Be Sure of Shell'. This was an era when 'art invaded commerce', and especially corporate advertizing, 'in no hole-and-corner way', (as Richard Guyatt was to observe) 'but with all the prestige of the avant garde.' Jack Beddington at Shell and Frank Pick at London Transport commissioned staff and ex-students of the College to create some of the most memorable interwar public images. For a brief period in the late 20s, there was even a 'poster design' option within the design course. Bawden designed a poster for the London Underground while still a student; Barnett Freedman did so after leaving, and later became an instructor himself in 1930.

The student generation which immediately succeeded these pioneering students, had a more demanding attitude towards the design programme, and a much stronger sense of political commitment. James Boswell contributed Grosz-inspired caricatures to *The Left Review* (of which he was art editor); Peggy Angus drew political cartoons for the women's page of *The Daily Worker*; and Percy Horton sold his portrait drawings in aid of the anti-Fascist course, while helping to found the Marxist group, Artists International, which later became the Artists International Association (AIA). In spring 1935, for the Silver Jubilee of King George V, while Eric Ravilious was supervising design students as they turned Ludgate Hill Bridge into a baroque arch, the late 20s graduates put up an AIA banner declaring '25 years of Hunger and War' across the Strand. Barnett Freedman, meanwhile, designed a special postage stamp for the occasion – the subject of a GPO documentary, *The King's Stamp*, the first film to be devoted to the design work of the College.

Post-war Transformations

When Robin Darwin introduced a major post-war exhibition of student work in 1950, he referred to the School of Graphic Design under Professor Richard Guyatt (with tutors Edward Bawden, Abram Games and John Nash) as one of the largest and most important in the College: 'It is a multi-purpose School', he went on, 'which aims to produce professional designers in commercial art, typography, lettering, bookbinding and – not least – illustration.' It had already come a long way since the reforms of two years before. Guyatt, who masterminded the transformation, rather touchingly was to recall: 'It was only after an article appeared in *The Times* rapping the College over the knuckles for the vulgarity of such a concept as "Publicity Design", that a serious quest for a name was made. With a sense of relief, but not much conviction, the name "Graphic Design" was chosen. No one was quite sure what it meant, but it had a purposeful ring to it …'.

He wrote this in a catalogue called *Graphics RCA*, published in 1963 to accompany a major touring exhibition celebrating 15 years' work in the School. Both were intended to show the results of the post-1948 emphasis on 'specialized, professionalized courses', and to promote them in France and Germany. Specialization was proving to be a spectacular success with several generations of ambitious, more mature students, who enjoyed the two-way traffic with the Painting School in the Exhibition Road studios. The show also demonstrated how the College itself was getting better and better at self-promotion. Critic Bryan Robertson has referred to 'the faintly old-fashioned smartness within the College Corporate Style which hovered halfway between Heal's and the old Faber and Faber house style when Barnett Freedman designed charming dust jackets for Walter de la Mare anthologies.' But there was nothing old-fashioned about the student work itself, which by now included Printmaking ('It is through the fine arts that the "useful" arts of design are invigorated' wrote Guyatt), Film and Television Design, the Lion and Unicorn Press, the student magazine *Ark* and photographic services.

Graphics RCA now looks like a comprehensive history of British communications design from 1948 to 1963: posters and illustrations by David Gentleman, Michael Foreman and Brian Tattersfield; book covers, advertisements and bus streamers by Alan Fletcher; a cookery strip by Len Deighton; the set for BBC television's *Quatermass and the Pit* by Cliff Hatts; Bernard Lodge's titles for *Z Cars*; a still from Ridley Scott's student film *Boy on a Bicycle*; or the covers of *Ark* magazine 1–33.

Mark Boxer (by then editor of *The Sunday Times* colour section) contrasted the pallid early days of *Ark*, when 'page after page was devoted to wet English romanticism and Betjemanesque collections of old trains', with *Ark* issues from the late 50s onwards when 'the concern has been for images and patterns of life today': photographic covers featuring Brigitte Bardot and bottles of Coca Cola, celebrations of New York streetlife, a link-up with the concerns of the Independent Group at the ICA and 'an end to latter-day Victorianism'. This contrast has recently been called 'the early development of a postmodern sensibility': Pop Art/Pop Graphics; Uptown Pop/Downtown Pop; grainy blow-ups/the origins of the colour supplements. Boxer continued: 'Often wilful, sometimes seriously naive, this is at its best one of the most hopeful performances on the English visual scene.' Some pages of *Ark* 22 had been printed in invisible lettering on brown wrapping paper and dayglo ink on cellophane – about which Robin Darwin commented, 'The more generally unintelligible *Ark* becomes both in matter and presentation, the better it sells.' Eventually, *Ark* would go down in the 70s with a review of the RCA drag-queen contest which began with the words: 'Life is decomposing in front of our eyes … the first to be corrupted are bound to be the artists, because they are the ones who are aware and will accept first.'

As Darwin wrote in his Foreword to *Graphics RCA*, the School had become a focus for – and a way of getting into focus – the entire College. This 'early … postmodern sensibility' coexisted comfortably with the old school approach of most of the staff: Edward Bawden was still a tutor, Printmaking was settled within the Graphics area, and the conviction was in the air that 'easel-painting-was-good-for-you' and that 'the-rest-would-follow-of-course'. Tutors, such as Bobby Gill, who had experience of 'Madison Avenue' were especially influential. However, it is as well to remember that many of these images emerged from a social world where Gordon Russell, of the Design Council, could – in his occasional moments of doubt – be reassured that all was well with the world when he received through the post the pink wine list, illustrated by tutor in Printmaking Edward Ardizzone, of the RCA's Senior Common Room.

Graphic Arts in the 90s

Later in the 60s, the umbrella School of Graphic Arts evolved into a series of free-standing departments: Illustration, Film and Television, Graphic Design, Photography and Printmaking. Under the gentle guidance of Quentin Blake, who became head of Illustration in 1978 after many years' involvement, this small face-to-face department produced a succession of influential illustrators including Dan Fern (who succeeded Blake in 1986), Nicola Bayley, Su Huntley, Ian Pollock and Russell Mills. A branch called Natural History Illustration, under John Norris Wood (a graduate from the Len Deighton era), began to specialize in drawing and studying the natural world – increasingly with an ecological emphasis. Film and Television, which started life as a design unit and continued to offer a lively specialism in 'film design', added animation to its portfolio and came to focus on production, direction and cinematography. Graphic Design developed an important research unit in the 70s under Herbert Spencer, examining 'the readability of print'. Photography under Professor John Hedgecoe combined commercial work (photojournalism and advertizing) with a documentary tradition, before playing a key role in the rise of the artist-photographer of the 80s: eventually and inevitably, the course moved into the School of Fine Art, as did Printmaking. The Guyatt philosophy of 'Fine Arts inspiring the applied arts' now happened in less literal, more complex and convergent ways than it had in the 60s.

All have come to terms over the last 15 years with the implications of digital design, and with what used to be known as 'the new technologies'. Walter Benjamin's famous essay on 'the work of art in the age of mechanical reproducibility' has been revisited and reworked from a variety of new visual perspectives. The *Graphics RCA* generations may have established the basic structure, but the teaching – and the relationship with the ecstasy of communication, with which young designers have grown up, and which they take for granted – have changed beyond all recognition. Graphic Design now touches, at its outer edges, industrial design in the post-black-box era, the presentation of performance, three-dimensional image-making and installation work, as well as digital versions of the more traditional skills. The borderlines between illustration, photographic image and text are constantly shifting. As photography pushes the frontiers of digital manipulation, the old chemical processes begin to occupy similar artistic ground to the old printmaking processes. Graphics and Illustration are converging again, under Dan Fern, while a freestanding Animation course combines traditional modelmaking with multimedia.

Meanwhile graduates have successfully created spaces for themselves (often as teams) in and around the 'cultural industries'. Walter Benjamin was one of the first to coin this phrase, in the 30s, only he intended it as a pejorative: now the phrase describes one of the fastest growing sectors of the economy today.

RIDLEY SCOTT

'I was at West Hartlepool College of Art for four years – intermediate for the first two years, then I started to specialize for one year in painting. I realized that I would never make a painter – I was constantly told I would never make a painter, and there were these huge arguments about "But these are illustrations, boy, these aren't paintings – right?" And I couldn't fathom what that meant, so I decided to go for graphic design which gave me a much more specific creative target and also a broader canvas, because out of graphics would be photography, and already I was thinking, "How do I get into film?". And so I went for the RCA in graphic design and I got in, starting autumn 1958 and finishing in 1961. It was a time when "television and film design" and photography were just beginning to happen, and America was becoming a big influence.

On the course, I was never one to kick against the traces. I was so grateful and so amazed to be there because the competition to get into the RCA then was like getting a place on a moon-landing, as I'm sure it is now. So I conformed to the system and realized very quickly that as soon as we were given a "task", 85 per cent of the students in my year – let's say there were 40 – would empty the room. So there was me, on my own, sitting in the corner at my desk for the next three and a half to four weeks preparing my task, and I thought, "Wait a minute, there's going to be an interplay of ideas here – that's surely what's going to happen", and of course it didn't. I was trying to find my feet in London, because I didn't know anybody and for the most part it was southern England, and it was just me at a desk. And the shock was when the students would come in and put their presentations up on the boards around the room in the form of small exhibitions.

COMMUNICATIONS

All of them were covered, so I didn't know who did what. Eventually the master would come in – whoever it happened to be – and say, "this row" and all the covers came off, and I gawped at the level of professionalism. And it was a wake-up call. I really think the most value was how much of a wake-up call it was: the level of professionalism around me, and above all things the level of competition. In some ways, it was a good thing to be left to your own devices. I remember one of the tasks was about the Festival of Britain, another was to think of a scheme for IBM. With the race to get in, you are so experienced and practised after four years in a provincial art school, that by the time you arrive, what can a member of staff really say? It has to be all about encouragement and evolution, if the person is clearly skilled already.

By the second year I was beginning to leak into the Photography Department whenever I could, and it was quite difficult getting into it, so you had to spend a bit of time chatting everybody up, to allow you to go into that darkroom. The most valuable thing I did was to buy a camera and start on a real photographic vigil, so I was out every weekend, all weekend, taking pictures. Then the big trick was getting into the dark-room to do serious blocks of time. I loved photography. I was already thinking, "I've no idea how to get into film, but I think I can." I've still got the shots I took, which I put into my final year exhibition, funnily enough, and actually they were, and are, pretty bloody good.

I was influenced at College by George Haslam, who ran Television and Film Design. There was no film instruction in those days, but I liked George as a teacher and I loved his passion for his job. He was a practising designer in a very successful

RIDLEY SCOTT

television show, made at Teddington Lock studio. And George would give us scripts, and then we would flick through them and come back with a solution for a piece of set design and models if we wanted to. I was doing graphic design, but by then I was already into the Television Department as well, which was a one-year course. In that there was a steel wardrobe, inside of which was a wind-up clockwork camera and an instruction book and a light meter and, if we had to use it, we had to sign out for the camera – but we had to show George a script first. And that's finally how I got to have a shot at making a little movie. With *Boy on a Bicycle*, I may have been the first-ever student to submit a film for the Diploma examination. I managed to have, for £65, a 16mm film which ran half an hour, had a mix and had title on. It's about a kid who takes a day off school, and I introduced my brother Tony to film-making with it, by ruining his summer when he was a kid. He's six years younger than I am. I had no idea that the process of making a film was so painstakingly slow, particularly when there's just you and the actor who is also the chief bottle-washer and equipment carrier. But you never forget that process. My dad was in the film as well, in the sequence on the beach.

What I liked in the mix at the College, which I think left its stamp, was in that corridor where there was the tea wagon at 11 o'clock and again in the afternoon. There would be the engravers coming out smelling of paint and turpentine, there would be the painters wandering around and smoking in the corner, so there was always a bohemian, Fine Art atmosphere – that was the real meat and potatoes of the Exhibition Road environment. The odd men out were the graphic designers – and I think the mix was very interesting.

With the earlier generation of people teaching graphic design, there could have been big collisions, but there weren't. Richard Guyatt was a very genial man and a lot of the staff had been war artists. Herbert Spencer was very approachable, though he, too, was of another generation. So an American character like Bob Gill coming in with button-down shirts, thick crêpe soles, tight black suits, and talking in this incredibly sleek, New York, advertizing, Madison Avenue way, was incredibly attractive.

I got a travelling scholarship, so after leaving I went to the United States for nearly a year and then ended up working with a film-maker. Cliff Hatts of the BBC had come to my final exhibition – there were a lot of connections between the RCA and the BBC at the time. I went to see Dick Leven with Cliff Hatts who basically said, "There's a job here for you." I said, "Well, I'm going to New York." I'd never been, of course. Mecca. And they said, "We'll keep the job open for you," and they did.

But it was at College that I learned to write visual music. Definitely. I use it every day now. I do my own storyboards every day. It's like writing music. Because I find I can pre-visualize better. You stick a piece of paper in a typewriter and start and it just comes out. I think the creative process of art school is so organic, in every direction, because suddenly you discover music, you read different things. The healthy thing is meeting all these different kinds of people. When I went to the RCA, my world really opened up, whereas I think in the provinces the art school – whilst it was passion, it was wonderful – was more insular. The RCA suddenly was the big arena, there was a lot of competition, a lot of motherfuckers kicking around, who all knew exactly what they were doing, so it was like major league. And I'd go back home sweating. Oh, my God! It forced the pace. And that's where I discovered there's always a solution. It depends on how long you're prepared to fiddle with the canvas, and scrape it out, or start again. I was hopeless academically at school and I woke up when I went to art school.'

EARLY CALLIGRAPHY

Edward Johnston did not consider calligraphy a profession, more a study and practice of religious devotion. He was single-handedly responsible for rediscovering the principles on which formal writing had been developed. Through experimentation he found that the nature and form of a letter was determined by the nature and form of the pen. Seemingly simple observations, such as the size of strokes being determined not by pressure but by direction, led to a knowledge of materials and their correct preparation that made Johnston a master of his craft. This understanding became the basis for his teaching initially at the London County Council Central School of Arts and Crafts, and from 1901 at the RCA where he developed a lifetime association. At the Central School, he taught specialists; at the College he taught all design students.

Johnston was one of the first practitioner-teachers to give regular master classes, teaching by demonstration using chalk on a blackboard. As he stated at the time: 'I have a very big room, with a great black board worked by pulleys, and a platform with a railing, where I stand or sit and look down on the 17 embryo scribes sitting below.'

Edward Johnston
(1872–1944)
Staff 1901–39
Preface to Writing, Illuminating & Lettering, 1909

Anna Simons
(1871–1951)
Student c.1904
Woher Sind Wir Geboren by Goethe, n.d.

Thomas W. Swindlehurst
(1900–65)
Student 1924–27
Arms of the Borough of the West Riding of Yorkshire, 1961

Irene Wellington
(1904–84)
Student 1925–28
Staff 1928–30
Rule Britannia, 1944

Dorothy Mahoney
(1902–84)
Student 1924–28
Staff 1936–53
Lakeland Flower Tapestry, 1971

William M. Gardner
(b. 1914)
Student 1935–39
Unfinished Song of Sandy the Shepherd, 1955

COMMUNICATIONS

Mervyn C. Oliver
(1886–1958)
Student 1911–1916
Lycidas, by John Milton, 1907

Madelyn Walker
(unknown)
Student
Dream Children, by Charles Lamb, 1924

William R. Daizell
(b. 1910)
Student 1930–34
Example of lettering, 1997

Margery Raisbeck
(b. 1910)
Student 1932–34
Staff 1934–35
Freedom of the City of Lincoln conferred on Lord Tennyson, 1964

Marie Angel
(b. 1923)
Student 1945–48
A New Bestiary, 1964

John Woodcock
(b. 1924)
Student
Alpha and Omega, 1968

His need for everything to be honest and functional led to the dilapidated cane of the classroom wicker chairs being used, at Johnston's insistence, as the springs of pens to hold the ink. Such was the enthusiasm of the students that the chairs had to be quickly replaced with all-wooden ones.

His pupils were to perpetuate his influence: Anna Simons, unable to study in Prussia as a woman, studied under Johnston and went on to lead her field in Germany; Irene Wellington became Johnston's natural successor, making inscriptions at his behest towards the end of his life; Dorothy Mahoney, who had been Johnston's assistant, continued the teaching of calligraphy at the RCA after his death. While teaching at the College, Johnston developed the famous typeface for the London Underground.

GRAPHIC DESIGN

Design for travel: 30s posters

Commercial poster art of the 30s heralded a professionalism in the visual identity of companies in an age before graphic design. This form of advertizing came to be seen as having a value that went beyond commercial function, and was found in spaces that belonged neither to art, nor industry.

Publicity managers such as Frank Pick at London Underground and Jack Beddington at Shell were keen to shape company image through the use of artistic images and elegant typography that conveyed a notion of travel and adventure. Commissioning established practitioners such as Edward Johnston and Paul Nash, who both taught at the RCA, while also taking a gamble with their then-unknown pupils, they developed the medium with avant-garde endeavour to new heights of popularity.

Rather than problem-solving, the artists were invited to express themselves through the frame of company advertizing. The integration of image and type was often left unconsidered; in the case of London Underground the responsibility for lettering the posters was left to the printers.

The alphabet designed for the Underground by Edward Johnston in 1916.

ABCDEFGHIJKL
MNOPQRSTUV
WXYZ abcdefgh
ijklmnopqrstuvw
xyz (&£.,:;'!?-*"")
1234567890

Edward Johnston
Alphabet designed for the London Underground, 1916

Edward Bawden
Hyde Park,
London Underground, 1925

sworth
London Underground, 1936

GRAPHIC DESIGN

Design for travel: 30s posters

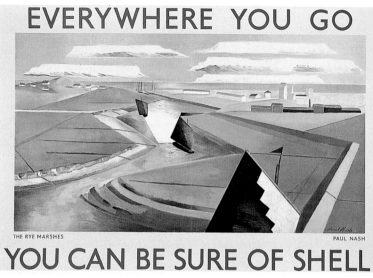

Paul Nash
The Rye Marshes, Shell, 1932

Focusing on metropolitan attractions or the British countryside, the posters made familiar terrain unfamiliar through the guise of modernity. The persistent use of a bold, centrally placed feature invited the eye to meander around the composition, the effect being to encourage exploration of the London Underground's recently opened stations, or of the highways and byways of Britain. The Underground used posters; Shell preferred 'lorry bills' attached to the sides of petrol-can delivery trucks.

At the same time, the work of John (James) Gilroy for Guinness created campaigns using humour and characterization to endear consumers to the charms of Irish stout. His posters were an early example of the fleeting and charming advertized image, its message eventually understood through the persistence of the style. Gilroy's association with Guinness was to last for over thirty years, from 1925 to 1960. The walls, hoardings and lorries of the era were to be christened, in true inter-war style, 'the people's art gallery'.

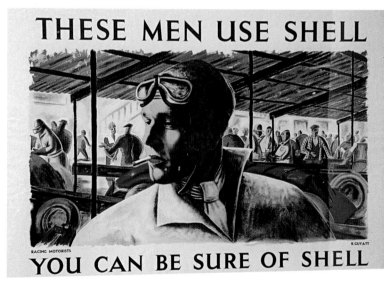

Richard Guyatt
These Men Use Shell, 1936

James Gilroy
Keep Smiling, 1936

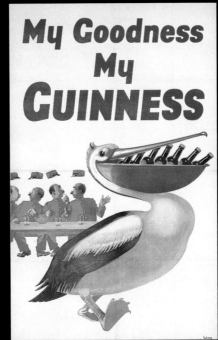

James Gilroy
My Goodness my Guinness –
Pelican, 1936

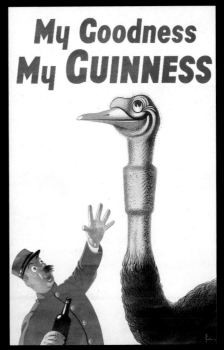

James Gilroy
My Goodness my Guinness –
Ostrich, 1936

50s GRAPHIC DESIGN

In 1948 Professor Richard Guyatt established the School of Graphic Design. The aim of the School was 'to produce professional designers who combine in their work the highest aesthetic standards of design with professional standards of technique'. Originally it was planned to call the School 'Typography and Publicity Design', but this was deemed too vulgar. Within the new School there were to be three departments: Commercial Design, Illustration and Printmaking.

The Commercial Design course primarily focused on advertizing media, such as press advertizements, leaflets, book jackets and posters. A mentor for many students in these early days was course tutor Abram Games, who had successfully designed the corporate identity for the Festival of Britain in 1951. A sense of national identity brought about an 'Englishness' in design, and the post-war years saw graphics reverting to neo-Victorian typefaces. RCA staff and students designed the Lion and Unicorn Pavilion for the Festival. This was followed by the Lion and Unicorn Press at the RCA in 1953, which produced a number of limited-edition books for subscribers each year, and emphasized 'experimental features'.

Geoffrey Ireland
(b. 1923)
Student 1948–51
Staff 1953–68
RCA poster, 1948

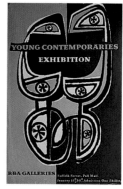

Derek Cousins
(b. 1928)
Student 1950–53
Young Contemporaries Exhibition poster, 1953

Alan Fletcher
(b. 1931)
Student 1953–56
Poster for IBM's Paris headquarters, 1960

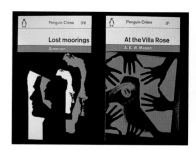

Romek Marber
(b. 1925)
Student 1953–56
Penguin book jackets, 1961–63

F.H.K. Henrion
(1914–90)
Staff 1953–56
Visiting Staff
Harper's Bazaar, cover, 1943

Herbert Spencer
(b. 1924)
Senior Research Fellow,
Readability of Print Unit 1966–68
Staff 1976–78 Professor 1978–84
Typographica 7, 1963

COMMUNICATIONS

David Gentleman
(b. 1930)
Student 1950–53
*Coronation Year Exhibition
poster, 1953*

Raymond Hawkey
(b. 1930)
Student 1950–53
*'Evolution', pop-up book, Michael
Joseph Publications, 1986*

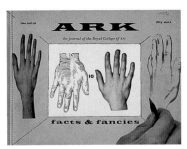

Len Deighton
(b. 1929)
Student 1952–55
Visiting Staff
Ark 10, cover, 1954

Anthony Bisley
(b. 1934)
Student 1955–59
*Edge of the City, poster for the RCA
Film Society, 1958*

Philip Smythe
(b. 1933)
Student 1955–58
Furniture Exhibition, poster, 1958

Abram Games
(1914–96)
Visiting Staff 1946–48
Staff 1948–53
*Emblem for the Festival of
Britain, 1948*

Berthold Wolpe
(1905–89)
Visiting Staff
Staff 1967–75
Faber & Faber cover, 1955

Edward Wright
(1912–88)
Staff 1956–59
*'This is Tomorrow', section with Theo
Crosby, Germano Facetti and William
Turnbull, 1956*

Richard Guyatt
(b. 1914)
Professor 1948–78
*Rank Xerox Identity,
with Ian Jenkins, 1978*

60s GRAPHIC DESIGN

The 60s were heady years for graphic design at the College. The student-run magazine *Ark* provided an encouraging platform for radical and abrasive experiments in design. The latter years of the 50s had seen the rise of photography as a College discipline, and *Ark* began to revolutionize its applications. These took their lead from American pop culture, celebrating ephemeral elements such as the comic strip – much to the annoyance of Guyatt and Darwin. Pop aesthetics and a familiarity with layout design saw many graphic design graduates take on the role of art editors on emerging Sunday colour supplements and consumer magazines. Rodney Springett, a graduate of 1967, was quickly snapped up by *Queen*.

In 1965, the Commercial Design course was renamed Communication Design which allowed for a growing diversity of media under the one title. In the same year Jock Kinneir took over as tutor: with Margaret Calvert, who was to become a member of staff in 1966, he had recently completed a radical redesign of Britain's road sign system, which is still in use today.

Ridley Scott
(b. 1937)
Student 1958–61
Poster for SKF, 1961

Barry Bates
(b. 1935)
Student 1959–62
'Loving Tea', student project, 1962

Neville Malkin
(b. 1938)
Student 1960–63
Advertisements for Bass, 1963

Stephen Abis
(b. 1943)
Student 1961–64
British Paintings from the Paris Biennale, poster, 1963

Gerhard Dumbar
(b. 1940)
Student 1963–66
Professor 1985–87
Holland Festival logotype identity, Studio Dumbar, 1986

Rodney Springett
(b. 1944)
Student 1964–67
Visiting Staff
Cover of Queen, 1967

Brain Tattersfield
(b. 1936)
Student 1959–62
*Packaging for Giorgio Armani
Swimwear, Minale Tattersfield &
Partners, c. 1985*

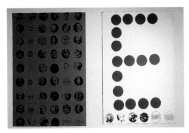

Michael Foreman
(b. 1938)
Student 1960–63
Staff 1968–69
*Meet the New President, poster,
RCA, c. 1960*

Brian Haynes
(b. 1939)
Student 1960–63
*'La Notte' and 'History of Nothing',
posters, RCA, 1963*

Thelma Roscoe
(b. 1940)
Student 1961–64
Visiting Staff
*'Graphics RCA' Exhibition,
poster, 1963*

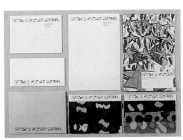

Richard Doust
(b. 1940)
Student 1962–65
Visiting Staff
Staff 1986–present
Stationery, 1965

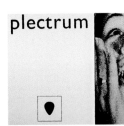

Stephen Hiett
(b. 1940)
Student 1962–65
Ark 36, 1964

Roger Dean
(b. 1944)
Furniture student 1965–68
*'Relayer', Yes album cover,
Atlantic, 1974*

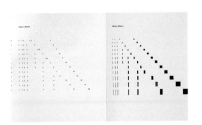

Anthony Froshaug
(1920–84)
Staff 1961–64
Typographic Norms, RCA, 1964

**Jock Kinneir and Margaret
Calvert**
(1917–94, b. 1936)
Head of Department 1965–68
Staff 1966–present,
Head of Department 1987–1990
British road sign system, 1963

GRAPHIC DESIGN

Ark and the rise of postmodernism

Ark was a journal edited and produced by students. It was initiated by Jack Stafford in 1950, a student in the School of Woods, Metals and Plastics. Its aim, he said, was to explore 'the elusive but necessary relationships between the arts and social context'. While it never followed an editorial line, it did provide students with a prominent outlet for their work.

Ark was produced within the newly established Graphic Arts School headed by Richard Guyatt. In its early years the journal – like the course – had a distinct bias towards Fine Art. The first issue was designed by Geoffrey Ireland and, graphically, *Ark* tended towards an 'Englishness' mirrored in the 'New Elizabethan Age' of the Coronation era.

However, *Ark* also revealed an aesthetic tension within Graphic Design: between on the one hand neo-Victoriana and a fascination with folk art, Victorian type-faces, woodblocks and line engravings; and on the other, modernist graphic design and an interest in the mass media. Alan Fletcher, student in 1955, recalls that the staff used to 'lock up the sanserif type', while Raymond Hawkey, student and art editor of *Ark* 5–7, rebelled against the status quo of graphic design at the College by including photography in *Ark* 5

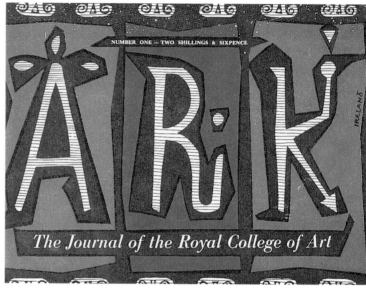

The launch issue of Ark, designed by Geoffrey Ireland, October 1950

Ark 7, 1953
This was the first cover to utilize a photograph, much to the disappointment of the staff.

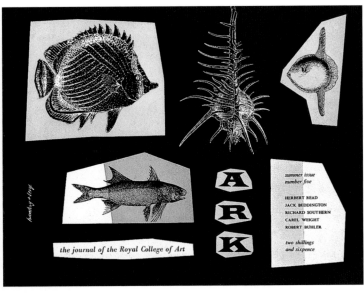

Ark 5, 1952
This issue was the first to include photography. The collaged cover was designed by Raymond Hawkey.

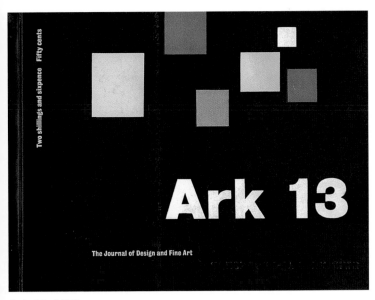

Ark 13, 1955
Designer Alan Fletcher introduced a modernist typeface for this issue, a radical shift from decorative type.

Ark celebrated icons of popular culture, such as Coca Cola (Ark 20, top) and Brigitte Bardot (Ark 25, above)

GRAPHIC DESIGN

Ark and the rise of postmodernism

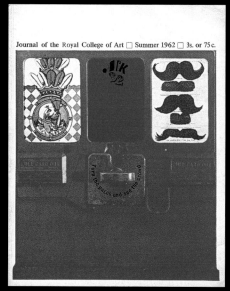

Ark 32, 1962
Cover of the seminal Pop Art issue
designed by Brian Haynes.

Do-It-Yourself Pop Art 'Kit of Images' for Ark 32 by Brian Haynes, 1962

(Summer 1952) and on the cover of *Ark* 7 (March 1953).

Len Deighton continued the use of photography in *Ark* 10 (Hawkey went on to design Deighton's spy thriller *The Ipcress File*) and caused another wave of disapproval from the establishment with his inclusion of a 'Hopalong Cassidy' comic strip. Deighton's appetite for American pop culture had been stimulated by a trip to New York during his summer vacation. He later observed that 'the [College] staff were living in the 1930s, referring to Paris as the centre of painting, while the students were living in the 1950s who knew New York was the new centre'.

In 1955 Alan Fletcher introduced a modernist typeface on the cover of *Ark* 13, a stark contrast from previous issues. This shift was inspired by Fletcher's former tutors at the Central School of Art, Anthony Froshaug and Edward Wright, who both began to teach at the RCA shortly afterwards. Roger Coleman, editor of *Ark* 18–20, in *Ark* 19 (Spring 1957) introduced the reader to hip cultural activists, the Independent Group, and launched a fruitful relationship with the College.

While images of pop culture continued to appear in *Ark*, the Summer 1962 issue, *Ark* 32, became the seminal issue which featured a wonderful pull-out section, a Pop Art 'Kit of Images'. This was art editor Brian Haynes' celebration of the work

of what were then seen as British Pop artists Derek Boshier, Peter Phillips, Peter Blake and David Hockney. Of these heady years Len Deighton was to recall that 'the tatty mess of 1951 became the exciting mess of the "swinging sixties".'

From the mid-60s onwards, *Ark*'s graphic design became visually seamless and very slick, which in turn created a blueprint for the Sunday colour supplements. *Ark* continued until 1972, was revived in 1976 and then finally laid to rest in 1978: yet *Ark*'s graphic styles were to have a huge impact on the British media, transforming advertizing, illustration, newspapers, magazines and, to some extent, the moving image as well.

**Pop Art 'Kit of Images' insert
for Ark 32 by Peter Blake, 1962**

70s GRAPHIC DESIGN

Darrell Ireland
(b. 1948)
Student 1968–71
Xmas Card, 1991

Brian Delaney
(b. 1948)
Student 1969–72
Ark 48, 1971

Towards the end of the 60s, Kinneir relinquished his role as tutor, and there remained a gap until 1972 when Lou Klein took up the position. In 1975, the College discussed adding another unit called Graphic Information, and by 1976 this had been implemented by former Research Fellow in the Readability of Print, Herbert Spencer. This new unit offered courses in the computer-aided graphic design, computer typesetting, photo-composition and information setting that was a precursor of the Macintosh-led desktop publishing of the 80s.

By the end of the decade, many former students had set up internationally renowned graphic design companies (Pentagram, Minale Tattersfield & Partners, Delaney & Ireland Co). In turn, this led to greater links between the RCA course and professional practice.

After a period of dormancy, *Ark* was rekindled in 1976 for two years before it finally became history.

David Freeman
(b. 1949)
Student 1970–73
Staff 1973
'Britain in the 30s', RCA, 1973

Susan Huntley
(b. 1949)
Student 1970–73
'Bring on the Night', Sting poster, 1988

Ian Delaney
(b. 1953)
Student 1975–78
Corporate Identity for Heal's, with Minale Tattersfield & Partners, c. 1980

Gary Rowland
(b. 1954)
Student 1976–79
Marks & Spencer logotype, 1986–89

Raymond Gregory
(b. 1946)
Student 1969–72
Poster, Fencing Club, RCA, 1971

Ronald van der Meer
(b. 1945)
Student 1969–72
Visiting Staff
Ark 50, 1972

Jelle van der Toorn
(b. 1946)
Student 1969–72
Ark 47, layout and artwork, 1970

Paul Leith
(b. 1946)
Student 1970–73
Wine label, 1988

Nicholas Wurr
(1950–1993)
Student 1973–76
Staff 1990–93
'Fetch', Silver D&AD Award, 1977

Liz McQuiston
(b. 1952)
Student 1974–77
Visiting Staff
Ark 52, 1976

George Hardy
(unknown)
Visiting Staff
*'Wish You Were Here', Pink Floyd
album cover, 1975*

Ken Garland
(b. 1929)
Visiting Staff 1977–87
Galt Toys logo, 1961

Lou Klein
(b. 1932)
Staff 1969–75
Professor 1973–75
*Book covers for Time Life;
logotypes, c. 1975*

80s GRAPHIC DESIGN

The most important influence on the teaching of graphic design in the 80s was the advent of the Macintosh computer. The digital revolution allowed a new freedom in the processes of graphic design and paved the way for a fresh graphic language. Gert Dumbar's arrival at the College in the mid-80s was also a key influence. The controversial Dutch graphic designer told students to 'think with your heart', encouraging them to break free of prescribed rules and conditions to express their own personality in their work.

This combination of new technology and experimental creativity meant that graduating students were armed with a new confidence. Empowered by their computers, they were able to set up studios on their own, or in groups of two or three, and to deliver large volumes of high-quality work, competing successfully with well-established design companies. A generation of RCA-trained graphic designers ignited the language of graphic design, subverting the old visual codes to create distinctive and highly individual work.

Moira Bogue
(b. 1960)
Student 1982–84
*Cover of i-D magazine
February, 1986*

Dirk van Dooren
(b. 1959)
Student 1983–85
*Spread for Alberto Aspessi summer
collection catalogue, Tomato, 1998*

Sean Perkins
(b. 1963)
Student 1985–87
*Corporate identity for the RAC,
North, 1997*

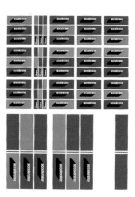

Richard Bonner-Morgan
(b. 1964)
Student 1986–88
Staff 1996–present
*Print work for 'Accelerator' exhibition,
Arnolfini Gallery, Bristol, 1998*

Jonathan Barnbrook
(b. 1966)
Student 1988–90
*'Delux' font from Virus
catalogue, 1997*

Martin Perrin
(b. 1965)
Student 1988–90
*Front cover for the brochure for
the American Foundation for
AIDS Research, 1997*

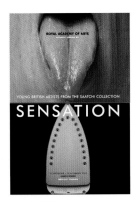

Andy Altmann
(b. 1962)
Student 1985–87
*Poster for 'Sensation' exhibition,
Royal Academy, London, Why Not
Associates, 1998*

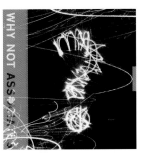

David Ellis
(b. 1962)
Student 1985–87
*Why Not Associates book cover, Why
Not Associates, 1998*

Phil Baines
(b. 1958)
Student 1985–87
Contribution to YAK magazine, 1987

Angus Hyland
(b. 1963)
Student 1986–88
*Cover for the Book of Revelation,
Pentagram, 1998*

Morag Myerscough
(b. 1963)
Student 1986–88
*Business card for Studio Myerscough,
Studio Myerscough, 1999*

Russell Warren-Fisher
(b. 1964)
**Student 1986–88,
Staff 1992**
*Poster for Ave Maria, Théâtre de
Complicité, 1991*

Peter Willberg
(b. 1962)
Student 1987–89
*you are here, cover for catalogue,
1997*

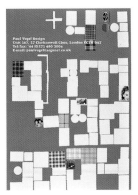

Paul Neale and Andy Stevens
(b. 1966, b. 1966)
Students 1988–90
*Poster and sticker set for Paul Vogel
Textile Design, Graphic Thought
Facility, 1998*

Gert Dumbar
(b. 1940)
**Student 1963–66
Visiting Staff
Professor 1985–87**
*House Style for PTT Nederland NV,
Studio Dumbar, late1980s*

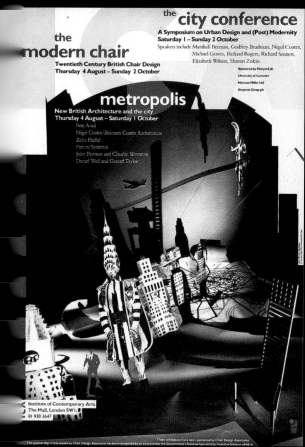

**Metropolis and the Modern Chair,
graphics and poster, ICA, 1988**

**Andrew Altmann
Poster for Yak magazine, RCA, 1993**

The day they put up their Degree how in 1987, Why Not Associates ndrew Altmann, David Ellis and Howard Greenhalgh began their professional career. Why Not were given the opportunity to redesign *Headlines*, a magazine for a US-based cosmetics company, Sebastian, in the same year. It was, however, fellow student John Newman, a former

their name after receiving a distinction for his thesis on Bob Gill. Newman had proposed that the 80s generation of graphic designers had a 'why not?' attitude, and the three designers were the perfect candidates. After their first commission, their accountant suggested they add 'Associates' to their name.

1984 had seen the last intake for

that by 1987 the gra Graphic Design had creating much excite Graphic Design stud with new materials a dimensional forms t modes of communic

For Andrew Altm student of the Centr Dutch designer Gert

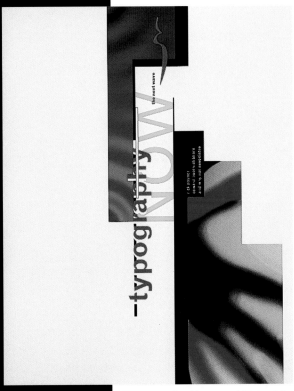

Typography Now, published by Edward Booth-Clibborn, 1991

Next Directory 5 (with Jonathan Barnbrook), 1988

The 'Holland' school of design, including Studio Dumbar, Total Design and Anton Beeke, in turn inspired Why Not Associates in their professional capacity. Recalling his tutorials with Professor Dumbar at the College, Altmann said, 'he drank Geneva Gin and talked about women'.

As trained typographers, Why Not Associates had the skills to break the ground rules of type. Fellow student Jonathan Barnbrook introduced them to the Macintosh computer, and they soon accommodated this 'polite revolution in graphic design'. In 1991, they were commissioned to design a new typeface for Midland Bank, using the software Fontographer and based on two existing typefaces, Perpetua and DIN. Why Not christened the new typeface 'Doddy', in homage to the comedian Ken Dodd.

Their big break came with the commission for *Next Directory* 5 in 1988 and, working with Barnbrook, they created the multi-textured feel that has become their signature. In the same year, Why Not's exhibition designs and poster for the Institute of Contemporary Art's 'Metropolis and the Modern Chair' exhibition attracted glowing reviews. Their book *Typography Now*, written by Visiting Professor Rick Poynor, was an unexpected success, attracting a very large and receptive market that many did not know existed.

90s GRAPHIC DESIGN

The 90s have seen a questioning of the computer in favour of traditional graphic design techniques. This process had already begun in the College during the tail-end of the previous decade, most notably in the work of Jonathan Barnbrook. Students returned to the traditions of hand-crafted typography through the techniques of letterpress, and sought to combine new technology with the old, creating innovation out of the collision of craft tradition with the computer.

Set up in 1992 and led by Alan Kitching, the letterpress course allowed students to become re-acquainted with the tactile qualities of paper and fresh ink, and encouraged the creative possibilities that could be gained from the awkwardness of the operation. The advantages of 'getting one's hands dirty' meant that students gained an understanding of the intricacies of type and the printing process, skills that the computer had all but eradicated. Slick computer-generated design was tempered with a more human, hand-made aesthetic to produce fresh, simple solutions to communication design.

Anthony Burrill
(b. 1969)
Student 1989–91
Man & Shape (no. 3), from Men & Shapes, Bless the Artist, 1999

Andy Johnson
(b. 1968)
Student 1990–92
Cover for Blueprint magazine, 1998

David Revell
(b. 1969)
Student 1992–94
Working model, 1996

Martin Carty and Ben Tibbs
(b. 1969, b. 1970)
Students 1993–95
Spread from Tactical Café mailer/book, Automatic, 1998

Jon Morgan and Mike Watson
(b. 1971, b. 1965)
Students 1993–95
Tea Leaf business card, Bump, 1999

Vera Daucher and Anna Subirós
(b. 1971, b. 1969)
Students 1994–96
Spread from RCA Summer Shows, (with Frank Stebbing), 1998

**Peter Miles, Damon Murray
and Stephen Sorrell**
(b. 1966, b. 1967, b. 1967)
Students 1990–92
*Image for Fuel Hype magazine,
Fuel, 1991*

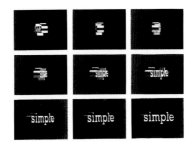

Paul Plowman
(b. 1966)
Student 1990–92
Logo animation for Simple, 1994

Jayne Alexander and Violetta Boxhill
(b. 1969, b. 1970)
Students 1992–94
*Poster for 'New Designers' exhibition,
Alexander Boxhill, 1997*

Jason Edwards and Tim Hutchinson
(b. 1971, b. 1969)
Students 1993–95
*Billboard for Multimedia Degree Show,
RCA, Bark, 1997*

Seonaid MacKay
(b. 1970)
Student 1993–95
Day, photographic installation, 1999

Huw Morgan
(b. 1971)
Student 1994–96
Tags for Jo Gordon Knitwear, 1998

Tony Cobb
(b. 1944)
Professor 1991–94
Visiting Staff
Reader's Digest World Atlas, 1998

Sophia Wood
(b. 1966)
Student 1994–96
*Crossing Borders, Urban Outfitters,
Fly, 1998*

Alan Kitching
(b. 1940)
Staff 1988–present
The Ring, letterpress print, 1998

GRAPHIC DESIGN

Jonathan Barnbrook

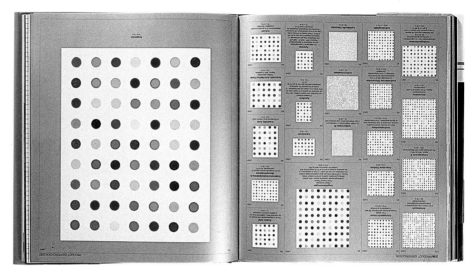

Since his graduation in 1990, Jonathan Barnbrook has attracted an international reputation as a graphic designer, font designer and art director. He has developed a visual language of dissent that has been employed in advertisements for the likes of Nike and Guinness: multinational corporations that are paradoxically the targets for his renegade agitprop typography.

His fonts have cynical names, such as Nixon, 'the typeface to tell lies in', and Drone, 'for text without content'. So, lucrative advertizing contracts support the Virus Foundry's critique of consumerism.

It was when Barnbrook was working on a never-to-be-seen commercial at Tony Kaye Films that he met Damien Hirst. This meeting led to him designing Hirst's first monograph.

The epically titled *I want to spend the rest of my life everywhere, with everyone, one to one, always, forever, now* was expected to take three months to complete but such was its visual complexity that it was delayed by over a year.

As a design for an artist's monograph, Barnbrook's work challenges many assumptions. The book is not linear but – rather like the periodic table mimicked on the cover – the content is grouped. It can be read in many different ways: with devices ranging from pop-up to peer-through, dipping-in becomes as rewarding as reading front to back.

The artist's statements hover in isolation as slogans. Themes are played out: images of sculptures cut in half are matched by pages cut in half, pages are turned, quotes become misfits. The numerous versions of Hirst's spot paintings are presented as biological permutations, as specimens rather than special things.

As Barnbrook said at the time: 'With most art books, you get large pictures on white pages and a piece of academic text which, unless you are writing a thesis, most people don't bother to read. We were trying to make an art book entertaining and a bit more populist.'

He was trying to take the directness of Young British Art and apply it to the way it is documented: the graphic design of pharmaceutical packaging – originally intended for clarity – becomes obscured by parody, multi-layering and self-promotion.

The collaborative exercise reached its logical conclusion in the graphic identity of Hirst and Marco Pierre White's restaurant Pharmacy. Such was the confusion of people entering the restaurant to collect their prescriptions that the British Medical Association was forced to intervene. So much for life imitating art.

I want to spend the rest of my
life everywhere, with everyone,
one to one, always, forever,
now, Damien Hirst, 1997

Wine menu, Pharmacy Restaurant, 1998

THIS IS

MASON

INCLUDED IN THE FONT ARE A NUMBER OF LIGATURES
EXPRESSING OFTEN USED COMPLETE WORDS, SUCH AS
'THE' AND 'TO'. A B C D E F G H I J K

L M N O P Q R S T U

V W X Y

Z

R

Mason, Virus Foundry, 1992/93

50s ILLUSTRATION

Following the 1948 reorganization under Richard Guyatt, several changes took place. In addition to commercial design, typography, lettering and bookbinding as taught subjects, there was illustration which was 'treated as a fine art as opposed to a commercial subject'. The reason for this was that the staff who taught it initially, did so from the Printmaking Department, which gave a very particular slant to the work produced.

Prospective students sat the entrance exam for the School of Painting and were then judged by the examining board for the School of Graphic Design. The small and specialized number of students applying led to the establishment of a Decorative Design Course in 1958 for both painters and designers. The inter-school course offered pattern work, decorative illustration, exhibition and mural design and was taught by Edward Bawden, veteran of the British decorative tradition, while book illustration was supported by the presence of Edward Ardizzone.

Both members of staff reflected in their own professional work the course's aim to produce artists as illustrators.

Sheila Robinson
(1925–88)
Student 1946–50
Staff 1964–80
About Britain, 1951

Philip Smith
(b. 1924)
Painting Student 1947–50
The Art of Byzantium Binding, 1963

Brian Keogh
(b. 1931)
Student 1951–54
The Compleat Imbiber, W&A Gilbey, 1963

John Sewell
(b. 1925)
Student 1951–54
Illustration, 1956

Don Foster
(b. 1932)
Student 1952–56
RCA Poster, 1958

Gaynor Chapman
(b. 1935)
Student 1955–58
Aesop's Fables, 1979

Dennis Bailey
(b. 1931)
Student 1950–53
RCA poster, 1952

Derek Cousins
(b. 1928)
Student 1950–53
The Merchant's Tale, Chaucer, Lion & Unicorn Press, 1960

David Gentleman
(b. 1930)
Student 1950–53
Illustration for Swiss Family Robinson, 1963

Len Deighton
(b. 1929)
Student 1952–55
Cook-Strip, The Observer, 1963

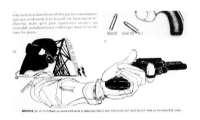

Rosalind Hoyte
(b. 1930)
Student 1952–55
Illustration for The Ipcress File, Evening Standard, 1962

Roy Morgan
(b. 1928)
Student 1952–55
Sir Gawain and the Green Knight, Lion & Unicorn Press, 1955

John Minton
(1917–57)
Painting Staff 1948–57
French Country Cooking, Elizabeth David, 1951

Edward Bawden
(1903–89)
Student 1922–25
Staff 1930–40, 1948–53
Barrow's Store Booklet, 1949

Edward Ardizzone
(1900–79)
Staff 1953–61
Senior Common Room, RCA, 1951

60s ILLUSTRATION

The expanded potential of print production in the consumer market of the 60s made illustration a lucrative prospect for recent graduates. By 1965, illustration had gained a degree of autonomy at the RCA by becoming one of three core specializations within Graphic Design (the other two being Printmaking and Communication Design). The prospectus offered a course 'based on drawing for reproduction' that hinted at the possibilities of new media.

The course was characterized by personal tuition that created strong bonds between staff and students. The work produced was a mix of commercial realities and hot-house experimentation.

In 1963 the College put together a major travelling exhibition called 'Graphics RCA'. John Brinkley wrote of the learning experience:

'Both parties are sustained by the knowledge that not only is their work needed, but that it can also bring genuine aesthetic enrichment to everyday life.'

The optimism placed in new-found markets became aligned with an exuberance in the work itself – bright colours, airbrushed realities and happy endings captured the moment.

Peter Woodcock
(b. 1939)
Student 1959–62
Poster for Mahogany, 1960

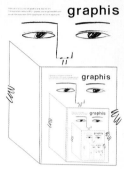

Wendy Coates-Smith
(b. 1940)
Student 1960–63
Graphis advertisement, 1963

John Riley
(b. 1938)
Student 1960–63
Wimbledon, 1963

Ron Sandford
(b. 1937)
Student 1960–63
Crisp Kippers, 1963–65

Adrian George
(b. 1944)
Student 1964–67
Royal Mail stamp, 1984

Diane Tippell
(b. 1944)
Student 1965–68
Wool, 1986

Michael Foreman
(b. 1938)
Student 1960–63
Pelican cover, 1963

Brian Haynes
(b. 1939)
Student 1960–63
Poster for Ark 32, 1962

Anne Morrow
(b. 1938)
Student 1960–63
Children's Book, 1986

Ken Sequin
(b. 1941)
Student 1960–64
RCA Jazz Society poster, 1963

Nigel Holmes
(b. 1942)
Student 1963–66
Degree Show, 1966

Philip Castle
(b. 1942)
Student 1964–67
Clockwork Orange film poster, 1971

Dan Fern
(b. 1945)
Student 1967–70
Staff 1974–86
Professor 1986–present
BBC Design Awards, 1987

Paul Hogarth
(b. 1917)
Staff 1964–71
Tower Hill, Bill and his mate 'working a flush', from London à la Mode, 1966

Quentin Blake
(b. 1932)
Staff 1965–76
Course Director 1976–87
Mr Magnolia, 1980

70s ILLUSTRATION

In the 70s, the Illustration Department disseminated its work in distinctive ways. There was a policy of small exhibitions for both staff and students, both inside the RCA and out. They ranged from an exhibition at the Royal Court Theatre made during rehearsals, to one on the theme of love and hate, with specially designed Valentine's cards for sale.

Student commissions, noted by the Head of Department, Quentin Blake, in his annual reports, included Penguin Books and *Jackanory* for BBC Television, while in 1977 the Department resumed printing informal publications, titled *Inklings*, illustrated and sometimes written by the students themselves.

This quaint appeal was actually at odds with a social and political dimension that began to enter student work. This personally expressive approach was matched by the rigorous expressionism of the Fine Art School and the quasi-art status illustration was now accorded in commercial galleries.

The influence of punk 'DIY' graphics revived collage as a medium and reintroduced typography as 'illustrational' when in slogan form.

Quay Brothers
(Stephen and Timothy Quay)
(b. 1947, b. 1947)
Students 1969–72
Institute Benjamenta, 1995

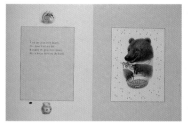

Nicola Bayley
(b. 1949)
Student 1971–74
I Eat my Peas with Honey, 'As I Was Going Up and Down', 1985

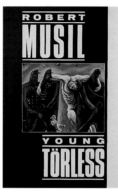

Robert Mason
(b. 1951)
Student 1973–76
Picador cover, 1988

Ian Pollock
(b. 1950)
Student 1973–76
Macbeth RSC poster, 1988

Russell Mills
(b. 1952)
Student 1974–77
Bell, Book, Candle: Trace Elements, c. 1980

Laura Knight
(b. 1954)
Student 1976–79
Sector, Annual Report, 1988

Susan Coe
(b. 1951)
Student 1971–74
New Scientist cover, 1988

Robin Harris
(b. 1949)
Student 1971–74
Signature magazine, 1988

Chloe Cheese
(b. 1952)
Student 1973–76
Poster for Seibu Department Store, 1985

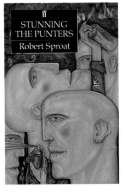

Janet Woolley
(b. 1952)
Student 1973–76
Faber and Faber cover, 1988

Anne Howeson
(b. 1952)
Student 1974–77
Tent Worms, c. 1981

Clare Jarrett
(b. 1952)
Student 1974–77
Illustration, 1988

Lawrence Mynott
(b. 1954)
Student 1976–79
Ark 54, cover, 1978

John Norris Wood
(b. 1930)
Staff 1971–present
The North-American Wood Turtle from Life, c. 1980

Brian Robb
(1913–79)
Staff 1961–66
Professor 1966–78
Celebrated Baron Munchhausen, 1947

ILLUSTRATION

Quentin Blake

For a large percentage of the British population under 30, Quentin Blake's illustrations were responsible for stimulating their first fantastical flights of the imagination.

Since the publication of his illustrations for the children's book *A Drink of Water* by John Yeoman in 1960, Quentin Blake's output as a book illustrator has exceeded 200 titles. His reputation has been built on his own picture storybooks and his collaborations with writers including Michael Rosen, Joan Aiken, Russell Hoban and, most famously, Roald Dahl. In Dahl, Blake found a writer whose compact narratives of absurdity, violence and wonder matched his own graphic technique.

With no formal art education, Sidcup-born Blake drew incessantly as a child, managing to have his drawings published in *Punch* while still at school. The idea of a child drawing for *Punch* is very characteristic of Blake as an illustrator – a mixture of the satirical and the nonsensical that is matched by the figures he admires: Ronald Searle, Edward Lear and Honoré Daumier.

His later commercial work for *Punch* and *The Spectator* led to him being invited by Brian Robb in 1965 to start teaching part-time on the newly separated Illustration course at the RCA. A course directorship for Blake followed from 1978 to 1986; since then, he has devoted himself full-time to illustration.

Dancing Frog, 1984

The Spectator Magazine, Spring Number, March 1961

The Twits, by Roald Dahl, 1980

Voyage to the Sun and the Moon, Cyrano de Bergerac, Folio Society, 1991

His technique is to draw the entire story very quickly, developing delightful nuances along the way. The results are then further developed through the use of scale, timing and mood, before being redrawn over a lightbox using pen and watercolour. This theatrical sense of direction is one of Blake's strengths; rather than appearing as a frozen filmic moment, his illustrations possess a concentrated sense of drama, while the shallow, tilted perspective (reminiscent of the stage) directly appeals to the reader's eye. The awe, trepidation and wonder found in the expressions of all his characters appeal equally strongly to the imaginations of his young readers.

80s ILLUSTRATION

By the 80s the Illustration Department had garnered an international reputation. In 1981 there were over 15 exhibitions by past and present students, and in 1987 seven international exhibitions took place in cities as diverse as New York, Colorado and Hong Kong. Students began to embrace international horizons, travelling widely and engaging in illustrative reportage.

Quentin Blake's influence continued to be felt. Each fresh intake of students was treated to a cliff-top assault course in Hastings followed by wine and chips at Blake's seaside home.

The appointment of Dan Fern as Professor in 1986 brought new perspectives: students learned the tradition of designing and making items such as trade union banners and Turkish paper marbling, and were given studio presentations by performance artists.

The work being produced by student illustrators was, according to Dan Fern, 'largely apolitical, noisy, urban, crowded and colourful, often executed on a large scale'. A big question was how this painterly approach would mesh with new technological developments.

Christopher Brown
(b. 1953)
Student 1977–80
Libra, 1988

Christopher Corr
(b. 1955)
Student 1977–80
Penguin covers, 1986

John England and Graham Elliott (Thunderjockeys)
(b. 1961, b. 1960)
Students 1983–86, 1985–87
Illustration, 1988

Richard Caldicott
(b. 1962)
Student 1984–87
Illustration, 1988

Marion Deuchars
(b. 1964)
Student 1987–89
Degree Show, 1989

Jason Ford
(b. 1965)
Student 1987–89
Degree Show, 1989

Carolyn Gowdy
(b. 1955)
Student 1977–80
The Blemyahs: End It Now!, c. 1984

Steven Appleby
(b. 1956)
Student 1981–84
Illustration, 1988

David Blamey
(b. 1961)
Student 1977–80
Staff 1989–present
Know became Tell, 1986

Geoffrey Grandfield
(b. 1961)
Student 1984–87
Picador cover, 1988

Andrew Kulman
(b. 1963)
Student 1985–87
Illustration, 1988

Simon Larbalestier
(b. 1962)
Student 1985–87
New Scientist cover, 1988

Lawrence Zeegen
(b. 1964)
Student 1987–89
Happy Head, 1989

Peter Brookes
(b. 1943)
Staff 1979–83
Radio Times cover, 1988

Linda Kitson
(b. 1945)
Staff 1979–83
Illustration, 1988

90s ILLUSTRATION

The donation of colour photocopying equipment by Canon at the start of the decade spawned the project 'Original Copies', which researched the creative use of photocopies. The results were exhibited in 1991 at the National Museum of Modern Art in Kyoto, with a parallel exhibition at the RCA.

However, in many ways this was an exception to the technological trend away from illustration. Commission-based work began to dry up due to the cult of the photographic image and a newly empowered breed of graphic designers who circumvented the need for illustrators.

In return, the Department of Illustration became more pro-active: the staff formed a self-motivated team of individuals who commissioned themselves and disseminated their work widely. Dan Fern confirmed this trend in an interview in 1997 for *Eye* magazine:

'The accent is on the development of an individual's talents and interests and obsessions to encourage a very strong personal aesthetic ... But to do that from a position of strength.'

Pui-Yee Lau
(b. 1948)
Student 1988–90
Degree Show, 1990

Christopher Draper
(b. 1965)
Student 1987–90
Degree Show, 1990

Peter Nencini
(b. 1968)
Student 1992–94
Michael, 1994

Graham Rounthwaite
(b. 1969)
Student 1992–94
Untitled, 1994

Aude Van Ryn
(b. 1970)
Student 1995–97
Degree Show, 1997

Claire Douglass
(b. 1962)
Student 1996–98
Degree Show, 1998

Bruce Ingman
(b. 1963)
Student 1988–90
Degree Show, 1990

Toby Morison
(b. 1965)
Student 1988–90
Hat Tree in the Fall, 1990

Sigune Hamann
(b. 1963)
Student 1990–93
Journeyman, set design, 1992

Sara Fanelli
(b. 1969)
Student 1993–95
Degree Show, 1995

Tatiana Karapanagioti
(b. 1971)
Student 1995–97
Degree Show, 1997

Reggie Pedro
(b. 1972)
Student 1995–97
The Household, 1997

Torsten Sachse
(b. 1962)
Student 1996–98
Degree Show, 1998

Andrzej Klimowski
(b. 1949)
Staff 1989–present
The Depository – A Dream Book, 1994

David Penney
(b. 1949)
Staff 1990–present
Island Records advertisement, 1980

70s–80s ANIMATION

During the 70s, before an animation course had been formalized, students had crossed over into animation work from other disciplines. Vera Neubauer began studying printmaking before creating short films using animation, that rejected the fluidity and perfectionism of mainstream approaches to the form. The Brothers Quay graduated in illustration, developing a surreal aesthetic in their work based on the lifelessness of puppet animation.

In the early 80s, animation was incorporated within the Film and Television School; it achieved departmental status in 1986. By the mid-80s, graduates were already producing extremely successful work, gaining world-wide recognition in festivals such as Annecy, Munich and Zagreb, in addition to selling (although the nature of the work was often far from commercial). Both Jonathan Hodgson and Susan Young made waves with their animations in the mid-80s. The later part of the decade saw a rise in students working in three dimensions, which reflected a tendency in the animation industry as a whole.

Vera Neubauer
(b. 1948)
Student 1968–72
Animation for Live Action, 1978

Quay Brothers
(Stephen and Timothy Quay)
(b. 1947, b. 1947)
Students 1969–72
Visiting Staff
Street of Crocodiles, 1986

William Latham
(b. 1961)
Student 1982–85
Biogenesis, 1993

Susan Young
(b. 1961)
Student 1982–85
Carnival, 1985

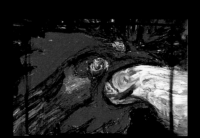

Karen Kelly
(b. 1966)
Student 1987–89

Sarah Kennedy
(b. 1965)
Student 1987–89

Phil Mulloy
(b. 1948)
Student 1970–73
The Possession, 1990

Emma Calder
(b. 1959)
Student 1980–83
Madam Potato, 1983

Jonathan Hodgson
(b. 1960)
Student 1982–85
Nightclub, 1985

Simon Pummell
(b. 1959)
Student 1983–86
Butcher's Hook, 1995

Andy Staveley
(b. 1962)
Student 1985–87
Strangers in Paradise, 1987

Jonathan Bairstow
(b. 1960)
Student 1986–88
Prophet and Loss, 1988

Petra Freeman
(b. 1964)
Student 1988–90

Bob Godfrey
(b. 1921)
Professor 1982–89

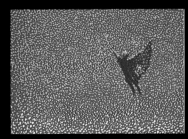

Richard Taylor
(b. 1929)
Staff 1986–89

90s ANIMATION

Professor Richard Taylor noted in 1991 that: 'animation embodies the purpose of the RCA, since it embraces both the fine and applied arts. Its capacity for imaginative expression is unlimited, but it remains an industrial product made for a specific purpose.'

The students graduating during this decade have benefited from a teaching environment which has placed an emphasis on producing artists, rather than solely training professionals, and has thus freed up the potential for creative expression.

The sponsorship of Channel 4 has encouraged and developed the growth of animated film nationally, and the series *Fourmations* has drawn heavily on RCA students' animation. In addition to building an appreciative audience, the Arts Council/Channel 4's 'Animate' scheme of commissioning work and providing grants has benefited emerging practitioners, such as Run Wrake and Stuart Hilton. Wrake's hard-edged graphic style is now well known in music papers and videos, including *NME* and *Howie B.* Hilton's uncompromisingly experimental work combines sound and abstract imagery, as seen in his student work *Wrong* (1991).

Andrew McEwan
(b. 1964)
Student 1988–90
Toxic, 1990

Run Wrake
(b. 1963)
Student 1988–90
Anyway, 1990

Sarah Cox
(b. 1966)
Student 1990–92
Reel to Reel, 1992

Ruth Lingford
(b. 1953)
Student 1990–92
Visiting Staff
Crumble, 1992

Brian Wood
(b. 1968)
Student 1992–94
Mr Jessop, 1994

Steven Harding-Hill
(b. 1969)
Student 1993–95
The Ticker Talks, 1995

Philip Hunt
(b. 1966)
Student 1988–91
Spotless Dominoes, 1991

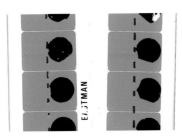

Stuart Hilton
(b. 1965)
Student 1989–91
Wrong, 1991

Debra Smith
(b. 1962)
Student 1989–91
Touch, 1991

John Parry
(b. 1965)
Student 1990–92
4 Something, 1992

An Vrombaut
(b. 1967)
Student 1990–92
Little Wolf, 1993

Anthony Hodgson
(b. 1969)
Student 1992–94
In the West Wing, 1994

Alan Smith
(b. 1967)
Student 1994–96
The Itch, 1996

Sam Morrison
(b. 1970)
Student 1995–97
Balls, 1997

Joan Ashworth
(b. 1959)
Professor 1994–present
Xmas on BBC 1, 1996

PRE-70s FILM & TV

Initial forays into film-making at the RCA began in a back room of the School of Graphic Design, where, in 1958, George Haslam introduced a course in 'Television and Film Design'. During the 40s and 50s Graphic Design students had begun to develop talents that were later used in the television and film industries. Cliff Hatts, for example, went on to become Head of Design at BBC TV. The trend for College students to enter the industry without previous training led to the establishing of the Department of Film and Television at the College in 1962.

Keith Lucas (an ex-RCA Painting student) became course director upon Haslam's sudden death, and gradually the emphasis began to shift from design to production. Although facilities were extremely modest at first, the course was structured to include a major project on film in the third year of study. Some of the earliest successful students from this period include the documentary maker Paul Watson (*The Family*), the director Tony Scott (*Top Gun*) and the set designer Anton Furst (*Full Metal Jacket, Batman*).

Richard MacDonald
(b. 1916)
Student 1938–39
Set designer, The Criminal, 1960

Cliff Hatts
(b. 1921)
Student 1946–49
Set designer, Quatermass and the Pit, 1959

Norman Vertigan
(b. 1935)
Student 1958–61
Director, Metamorphosis, 1961

Trevor Preston
(b. 1938)
Student 1960–63
The Temptress (detail), studies in head-dresses and make-up, 1963

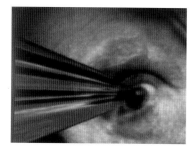

David Larcher
(b. 1942)
Student 1964–65
Granny's Is, 1989

Anton Furst
(1944–91)
Student 1964–68
Interior of adaptable auditorium, 1967

Peter Newington
(b. 1922)
Student 1947–49
Director, Monitor, BBC, 1958

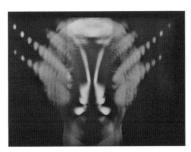

Bernard Lodge
(b. 1933)
Student 1956–59
Designer, Doctor Who titles, 1963

Ridley Scott
(b. 1937)
Student 1958–61
Visiting Professor
Director, Boy on a Bicycle, 1961

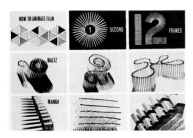

Melvyn Gill
(b. 1942)
Student 1961–64
*Film exploring animation
techniques, 1964*

Stuart Craig
(b. 1942)
Student 1963–66
Visiting Staff
*Production Designer,
The Mission, 1986*

Paul Watson
(b. 1942)
Student 1963–66
Director, The Family, 1974

Richard Loncraine
(b. 1946)
Student 1966–69
Director, Richard III, 1995

Patrick Uden
(b. 1946)
Student 1966–69
Patrick Uden, 1970

Albert Watson
(b. 1942)
Student 1966–69
Henry Rollins, 1996

FILM

Ridley Scott

COMMUNICATIONS

Ridley Scott, Blade Runner, 1982

Ridley Scott was educated as a painter at West Hartlepool College of Art in the mid-50s. He then studied at the RCA from 1958 to 1961. Although Scott joined as a Graphic Design student, he became intrigued by photography, and quickly realized that he wanted to pursue film. His arrival at the RCA coincided with the start of a 'Television and Design' course, taught by George Haslam, in which the 'role of photography as a design medium' was introduced. Although facilities were extremely basic, Scott wrote, directed and photographed the 16mm film *Boy on a Bicycle*, which starred his brother Anthony as a daydreaming truant bicycling through a northern town.

The course encouraged Scott to study design in an art environment, where crossovers were occurring between disciplines. Contemporaries of Scott's included David Hockney, Derek Boshier and Patrick Caulfield, at a time when Pop Art was exploding onto the British art scene. After graduating, Scott worked as a set designer for the BBC between 1961 and 1965, fostering his later commitment to close involvement with all aspects of set creation. Following the BBC, Scott directed television commercials for over ten years before

FILM

Ridley Scott

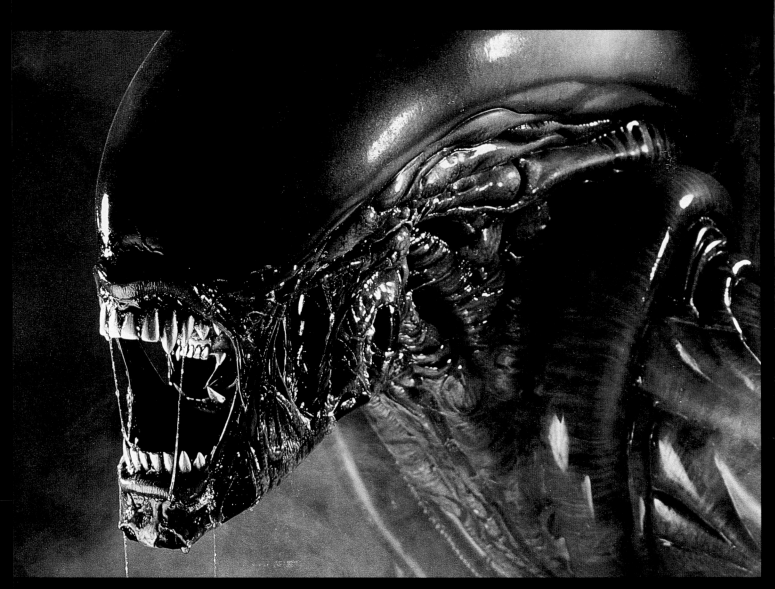

Ridley Scott, Alien, 1979

Ridley Scott, Thelma and Louise, 1990–91

directing his first feature film, *The Duellists*, in 1977.

The experience of working in advertizing proved invaluable to Scott, as it gave him an awareness of how to captivate the audience. The prioritizing of visual display and design is, in Scott's mind, the key to cinema, which he perceives primarily as a visual medium. Scott's second film, *Alien* (1979), won an Academy Award for its special effects, and the Swiss Surrealist Hans Rudi Giger's bio-mechanical alien life-form has become almost iconic. Both *Alien* and *Blade Runner* (1982) have been described as key examples of 'the designer as author'. *Blade Runner* has become a cult film for its alternative vision of a not-too-distant future. Set in 2019, Scott presents a densely

populated, pollution-filled city – a mixture of Los Angeles and Tokyo – in which a myriad of bars, noodle counters and massage parlours vie for attention. Hampton Fancher's initial drafts of the screenplay envisaged dramatic scenes centred in the interiors of buildings, but Scott was more interested in what lay 'outside'.

Fritz Lang's *Metropolis* (1926) provided useful reference material for Scott, particularly Lang's creation of a stratified city with the 'New Tower of Babel' as an omnipotent vantage point, echoed in the monolithic pyramid-like Tyrell Corporation building in *Blade Runner*. The second film of significance to Scott was William Cameron Menzies' *Things to Come*, which expounded a bright, modernist

futuristic Utopia. Scott reacted against this pristine cinematic vision of future cities, and aimed to create something more believable. Thus, he designed from the inside out: 'You wear your guts on the outside. That gives us a picture of a textured city.' Rather than deserted streets, Scott wanted visual noise, and he drew on his background as both an artist/designer and advertizer to create the unforgettable scenes in *Blade Runner*.

The combination of the atmosphere at the RCA, Scott's work with the BBC design department and an insight into advertizing inform the unusually visual approach that he takes to big-budget film making. Subsequent features have included *Legend*, *Black Rain*, *1492* and *Thelma and Louise*.

70s–80s FILM & TV

In 1972, Stuart Hood succeeded Keith Lucas as Professor when Lucas became Director of the British Film Institute. Under his Professorship, independent work was prioritized over forging links with industry. Consequently much experimental work emerged from the course at this time. The work produced reflected an interest in political and structural issues and semiotics. However, the course still embraced a wide range of approaches, from straightforward documentary through narrative to abstract film.

Although some important advances had been made in terms of equipment, the expense of film production, coupled with inflation, was proving problematic. Richard Guyatt, then Rector, was keen to see the Department return to the 'craft' of mainstream film. He set up a working party which recommended that an emphasis be placed on practical film, video and animation production.

Dick Ross was appointed as Professor in 1980 to tackle the funding issue and see through the development of the course, and it was his shift towards narrative cinema and film production that saw student films gaining recognition at international festivals through the 80s.

Tony Scott
(b. 1944)
Student 1967–70
Director, Top Gun, 1986

Mick Csáky
(b. 1945)
Student 1968–71
Director, Africa, 1983

Thaddeus O'Sullivan
(b. 1947)
Student 1972–75
Cameraman and director, Nothing Personal, 1995

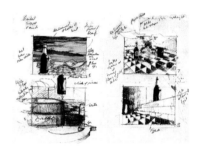

Jamie Leonard
(b. 1948)
Student 1974–77
Designer, 1977

Joy Perino
(b. 1960)
Student 1984–87
Director, This Life, BBC, 1996

Anna Campion
(b. 1952)
Student 1987–89
Director, Loaded, 1995

Peter Gidal
(b. 1946)
Student 1968–71
Staff 1974–82
Director, Close Up, 1983

Keith Griffiths
(b. 1947)
Student 1969–72
Producer, Deadpan, by Steve McQueen, 1997

Giles Foster
(b. 1948)
Student 1972–75
Visiting staff
Director, Coming Home, 1998

Sue Clayton
(b. 1953)
Student 1976–79
Director, Disappearance of Finbar, 1997

Bob Long
(b. 1952)
Student 1979–82
Executive producer, Video Diaries, BBC, 1990

Chris Newby
(b. 1957)
Student 1981–84
Director, Madagascar Skin, 1996

Peter Cattaneo
(b. 1964)
Student 1987–89
Director, The Full Monty, 1997

Carl Prechezer
(b. 1965)
Student 1987–89
Director, Blue Juice, 1995

Gavin Bocquet
(b. 1953)
Student 1975–78
Production designer, Star Wars: Episode 1 – The Phantom Menace, Interior of 'Naboo', 1999

90s FILM & TV

In 1989, for the first time in the history of film teaching and study at the RCA, a practising film maker for cinema was appointed to lead the course: Professor Christopher Miles. His aim was to 'equip students with a broad technical expertise but equally to encourage them to be experimental in the one time in their career that is devoid of the heavy arm of commercialization on their shoulders.'

An increase in the number of students interested in producing narrative drama, however, further highlighted existing funding difficulties within the school. By the mid-90s, the move towards a more vocational, specialized practice within the Department was becoming more apparent, with the introduction of seven distinct specializations: Cinematography, Design for TV and Film, Directing, Documentary, Editing, Production, and Sound Design. Documentary makers benefited from the specialized teaching of Elizabeth Wood and the BBC's continued support. Professional collaboration was encouraged in producing the BBC's documentary special *Seven Young Artists* and the documentary series *10 x 10*, from which a number of strong documentary makers have emerged.

Rajan Khosa
(b. 1961)
Student 1990–91
Director, Dance of The Wind, 1998

Henry Chancellor
(b. 1968)
Student 1991–93
Director, Oil on Canvas, BBC, 1997

Julian Court
(b. 1962)
Student 1993–95
Cameraman, Heart, 1999

Ben Hopkins
(b. 1969)
Student 1993–95
Director, National Achievement Day, 1995

Asif Kapadia
(b. 1972)
Student 1995–97
Director, The Sheep Thief, 1997

Stuart Mitchell
(b. 1967)
Student 1995–97
Director, Stood for this Massive, 1997

COMMUNICATIONS

Robert Letts
(b. 1959)
Student 1991–93
Director, Archie Gets a Clip, 1993

Charles Steel
(b. 1962)
Student 1991–93
Producer, Amy Foster, 1998

Kun Chang
(b. 1969)
Student 1993–95
Designer, Exterior Workshop, Concept Design for Lego Mindstorms/Lucasfilm Licensing: 'Droid Developer Kit', 1999

Claire Kilner
(b. 1964)
Student 1993–95
Director, The Secret, 1994

George Milton
(b. 1969)
Student 1993–95
Director, Appetite, 1997

Jamie Thraves
(b. 1969)
Student 1993–95
Director, The Hackney Downs, 1995

Billy O'Brien
(b. 1970)
Student 1995–97
Set designer, The Tail Of The Rat That Wrote, 1999

Christopher Miles
(b. 1939)
Professor 1989–92
Director, The Clandestine Marriage, 1998

Elizabeth Wood
(b. 1943)
Staff 1991–97
Director, The Future of Things Past, 1986

THE FUTURE

At the turn of the millennium, just about all the certainties of the Robin Darwin era have turned into uncertainties: the structure of the professions surrounding the RCA, a vastly expanded international system of art and design education, the technologies available to young artists and designers, the link with manufacturing where the story began: all are in a state of flux. As David Harvey has written in his remarkable book *The Condition of Postmodernity*: 'The relatively stable aesthetic of the era of ... modernism has given way to all the ferment, instability and fleeting qualities of a postmodern aesthetic that celebrates difference, ephemerality, spectacle, simulation, fashion and the commodification of cultural forms.' The defining features of the Darwin era – rigid specialization, an emphasis on short-termism, a stable notion of function, an obsession with the social status of the artist and designer, an educational model where fine art's role is to stimulate design, and a splendid isolation from other related institutions – these defining features are clearly no longer right for today. Instead, the emphasis must surely be on the meeting-points between disciplines – still in a pre-professional context, not as an adventure playground – on research and development and especially action research, on close partnerships with related institutions such as universities, galleries and museums. Graduates or, more likely, teams of graduates should be encouraged to create a niche around themselves rather than slotting into niches which are ready-made or well established.

Art and design graduates are in fact five times more likely than any other graduates to be self-employed, and, according to the College's latest statistics covering the five-year period from 1992 to 1926, on average 92.5 per cent of RCA alumni successfully find work, in the subjects they have studied, and at the right level. Put these two conclusions together, and you have new kinds of artists, craftspeople and designers managing to construct a world around themselves, in a very entrepreneurial and improvisatory way – a world where products and services seem to be blending together, and where in-house has become in-system, or to put it another way, wired into a complex mix of making, thinking, packaging, informing and distributing. In such a volatile setting, the key word has to be convergence.

Design itself has become more of a convergent activity, rather than the divergent activity of Victorian times (thinking versus doing), or the Arts and Crafts period (doing versus thinking) or the 50s and 60s (specialization, and the devil take the hindmost). Convergent at many different levels: between the present and the past, as history is reworked to supply a culture of quotations. Between Fine Art and design – traditionally at loggerheads – as both activities, with the applied arts in between, become in educational terms part of a seamless spectrum, and as the Fine Arts no longer have or need to be justified for their impact on design. Between technology and design, as on the one hand engineers and industrial designers begin to work more closely together, and on the other, as digital technology in studios and workshops means that for the first time in the history of art and design education, the technology available to students is similar to the technology they will be using in their professional lives. Between design and packaging, in the post-black box era. Between the applied arts and design, at the levels of batch-production and architectural detailing. Between the world inside the academy and the expanding world of the so-called creative industries, where many students have more direct contact on their courses with the worlds they aim to stimulate than ever before, and where the industries will increasingly use the RCA as a research resource because they want and need to be stimulated rather than served.

Perhaps above all, it is a convergence of the three main traditions which have made up the story of the last century and a half: the 'design as information' tradition of the Victorians, the 'doing is designing' tradition of the Arts and Crafts era and the expressive tradition of the post-war period. From the Victorian era of Christopher Dresser and Owen Jones – when the School was at the cutting edge of design thinking – comes a more thoughtful attitude towards design, design with attitude, and a new emphasis on research: the College as a think-tank for the creative industries, performing a similar role to the research and development wings of science and technology departments in universities. From the Arts and Crafts era comes a continued focus on a project-based, hands-on, practical approach, rather than on sitting in front of screens all the time or spending too much energy examining fundamentals: an approach where the punch-line remains a well-thought-out product or body of work. It is also a concern with sustainability and social developments. New technology, yes, plus a healthy cynicism about its capabilities. I don't see the future as an educational global village where all the students sit in their huts, in a latter-day version of a Victorian tableau called *And when did you last see your tutor?*. But digitalization has self-evidently had a profound effect on the processes of both art and design. From the post-war experiment comes a very post-Victorian, and indeed postmodernist emphasis on sensitivity, self-motivation and imagination, as well as a concern with having one's finger on the pulse of what's going on in the wider visual culture: art in a design environment and design in an art environment, but not in a literal, programmatic way. As John Ruskin put it back in the 1860s when he was criticizing the regime of Henry Cole and Mr Gradgrind, 'thus we may bring out the whole person'.

So maybe the Dodo isn't as extinct as it looks. And the Phoenix should look into the ashes even as it continues to regenerate itself and fly away from them. It could be that in time this convergence will itself become a model for higher education institutions in the future: a way of producing flexibly minded, self-reliant graduates who like practical results and who are being prepared for a very unpredictable world. Or maybe, like Robin Darwin in his lecture of 1954, I'm getting a little over-excited about the possibilities. But it is difficult not to, when looking back and reflecting on such a stimulating, varied and significant history of achievement. Most universities seek to understand the world: the RCA seeks to do that as well, in an inimitable way; the point, however, is to change it.

ACKNOWLEDGEMENTS

Richard Dennis and Magnus Dennis; Jan Murton and Dominic Sweeney, RCA Slide Library; Eugene Rae, RCA Archive; Stewart Drew, Photostore and Picture Library, Crafts Council; Nick Wise, Picture Library, Victoria and Albert Museum; Chantal Serhan, Prints and Drawings Department, British Museum; Guido Martini, Picture Library, Tate Gallery; Jane England, England & Co.; The Conway Library at the Courtauld Institute; Ray Galton; Alan Simpson; Chris Orr; Peter Kennard; Martin Smith; Michael Rowe; David Watkins; Amanda Mansell; Department of Goldsmithing, Silversmithing, Metalwork and Jewellery at the RCA; Al Rees, Research Fellow at the RCA; Moira Tait, Tim Miller, Jeremy Moorshead, Department of Animation at the RCA; Autocar; Richard Doust; Andy Altmann at Why Not Associates; Professor Ken Greenley; Dale Harrow; John Heffernan; Kate Trant; Shely Bryan; James Park; John Miles; Sarah Dallas; Audrey Levy; Brian Godbold at Marks and Spencer; Liz Griffiths at Missoni; Anne Tyrrell; Inge Cordsen; Mary Restieaux; Roy Peach; Ian Griffiths; Frances Pritchard at the Whitworth Art Gallery; Dai Rees and Simon Munro; Judith Clark at the Costume Gallery; Humphrey Spender; Jo Gordon; Pip Hackkett; Philip Treacy; Jane Whitfield at Louis Vuitton; Keith Varty and Alan Cleaver; Lynne Burstall at Oasis; Andrzej Klimowski; Rick Poynor; Quentin Blake; David Hockney; Ridley Scott; Alison Britton; James Dyson.

BIBLIOGRAPHY

For a much fuller bibliography of the history of the Royal College of Art, including primary documents, see Frayling, 1987. Listed below are outline books and items published or unearthed since 1987. For individual artists, designers or communicators, see monographs and catalogues devoted to them in the context of broader histories of British art, design and communications.

C. Ashwin: Art Education – documents and policies (London, 1975)

(ed.) Philip Dodd & Ian Christie: Spellbound (BFI/Hayward, 1996)

(ed.) Dan Fern: Breakthrough – twenty-five years of work by RCA illustrators (RCA, London, 1989)

(ed.) Boris Ford: The Cambridge Cultural History – vol 9, Modern Britain (CUP, 1992)

Christopher Frayling: The Royal College of Art – one hundred and fifty years of art and design (Barrie & Jenkins, London, 1987)

(ed.) Christopher Frayling and Claire Catterall: Design of the times (Richard Dennis, Somerset, 1996)

(ed.) Irena Goldscheider & Alena Zapletalova: Metalmorphosis, 1880-1998 (British Council, 1998)

(ed.) Paul Huxley: Exhibition Road – Painters at the Royal College of Art (Phaidon, London, 1988)

(ed.) Paul Huxley: The Royal College of Art Collection (RCA, London, 1988)

(ed.) Tim Mara and Silvie Turner: The Spirit of the Staircase – one hundred years of print publishing at the Royal College of Art (Victoria and Albert Museum, 1986)

Stuart Macdonald: The History and Philosophy of Art Education (London, 1970)

J. Minihan: The Nationalisation of Culture (London, 1977)

N. Pevsner: Academic of Art Past and Present (Rept. New York 1973)

Alex Seago: Burning the Box of Beautiful Things (Oxford University Press, Oxford, 1995)

(ed.) Keighley Snowden: International Drawing Congress 1908 (Office of the Congress, London, 1908)

Julie Summers: One hundred years of the Sculpture School at the Royal College of Art (Unpublished typescript, RCA, 1997)

Peter Webb: Portrait of David Hockney (Paladin, 1990)

CREDITS

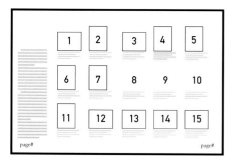

Picture credits: page number, followed by image number, unless stated otherwise

Copyright

Illustrations on these pages appear by kind permission of the following (in alphabetical order):

Courtesy Peter Aldridge page 192 (no. 11); © The Arts Council of England page 45, 95 (no. 4), 307 (no.3); © The Arts Council of England/Channel 4, "11th Floor" 1989/90 page 297 (no. 3); © The Arts Council of England/Scottish Arts Council page 64 (no. 11); © Austin Reed Group plc page 38; Autocar page 152 (no. 6), (no. 7), 153 (no. 5), (no. 9), (no. 14), (no. 15), 154 (no. 1), (no. 6), 156 (no. 1), (no. 6), 157 (no. 3), (no. 5), (no. 8), (no. 9), (no. 13), (no. 14), 158 (no. 6), 159 (no. 13), (no. 14), 161 (no. 9), (no. 15); © David Bailey page 234; BBC, 1959 page 300 (no. 2); © BBC, 1958 page 301 (no. 3); © BBC, 1996 page 306 (no. 11); © Quentin Blake page 287 (no. 15), 290 (both), 291 (both); Blue Dolphin Film & Video page 306 (no. 12); Booth-Clibborn Editions page 282 (both), 283 (top); © Alan Bowness, Hepworth Estate page 61 (right), page 63 (left); Ian Bourn courtesy Lux Distribution page 75 (no. 4); © British Architectural Library, RIBA, London page 141; British Architectural Library, RIBA, London page 195 (no. 14); © British

Motor Industry Heritage Trust/Rover Group page 162 (left); © British Museum page 88 (no. 2), (no. 11), 89 (no. 4), (no. 9), (no. 12), (no. 13), 90 (no. 6), (no. 11), 91 (no. 4), (no. 6), (no. 11), (no. 14); British Pathé courtesy England & Co Gallery, London page 32; Car Magazine, 1992 page 152 (no. 12); Casson Conder 1965/©Henk Snoek page 140 (top); Casson Conder 1965/©Shell Centre page 140 (bottom); Channel 4, 1995 page 297 (no. 8); Channel 4/Film Four page 306 (no. 6) Cinenova page 296 (no. 1); Clandestine Ltd page 309 (no. 14); Columbia Tristar Films (UK) page 309 (no. 4); courtesy Calum Colvin page 80, 81 (top), 82, 85 (no. 5); Courtauld Institute of Art page 58 (no. 1), (no. 2), (no. 7), (no. 12), 59 (no. 13), (no. 14); 64 (no. 1), (no. 6), (no. 7), 65 (no. 9), 67 (no. 13), (no. 14), 118 (no. 6), 224 (no. 2), Courtauld Institute of Art/© Cotton Board, Manchester page 65 (no. 9), Courtauld Institute of Art/© Gorhambury Collection, reproduced by permission of The Earl of Verulam page 65 (no. 4); Crafts Council page 134 (no. 11), 171 (no. 5), 175, 176 (no. 1), (no. 11), 177 (no. 9), 178 (no. 7), (no. 11), 181 (no. 9), 195 (no. 3), (no. 4), (no. 8), 196 (no. 1), (no. 6), (no. 7), 197 (no. 8), (no. 10), 199 (no. 3), (no. 10), 201 (no.8), (no. 9), 204 (no. 12), 212 (both), 213 (top left and top right), 218 (no. 7), 219 (no. 8), 221 (no. 4), 222 (no. 12); courtesy Keith Cummings page 186 (no. 12); courtesy Maria Csáky page 306 (no. 2); Dan Films Ltd page 307 (no. 10); Nina Danino courtesy Lux Distribution page 74 (no. 6); Richard Deacon courtesy Lux Distribution page 74 (no. 2); Catherine Elwes courtesy Lux Distribution page 75 (no. 8); Tony Emsley page 308 (no. 7); Enigma Productions, 1986, page 301 (no. 9); courtesy Anna Fox page 87 (no. 14); courtesy William M Gardner page 260 (no. 12); Nicholas Gentilli & Associates page 247; Judith Goddard courtesy Lux Distribution page 75 (no. 9); Bob Godfrey Films page 297 (no. 14); The Goldsmiths' Company page 197 (no. 3), 199 (no. 14); 1999 Granada Film page 308 (no. 5); Granada Film, 1974, page 301 (no. 10); Guild/Meyer Release courtesy Pathé Distribution page 301 (no. 13); David Hall courtesy Lux Distribution page 74 (no. 1); courtesy David Hamilton page 187 (no. 15); Hawkins and Brown page 115 (bottom); courtesy John Hedgecoe page 79 (no. 15); Henry Moore Foundation/© Michael Muller page 60 (top), 61 (top left), 62 (background), 63 (bottom right); Holburne Museum & Crafts Study Centre, Bath page 260 (no. 9) (no. 11) (no. 14), 261 (no. 3), (no. 10); Illuminations Films page 307 (no. 4); Judith Clark Costume Gallery, London page 249 (no. 8); courtesy Joan Kay and the Curwen Gallery page 96; Patrick Keiller courtesy Lux Distribution page 74 (no. 7); courtesy William Latham page 296 (no. 6); courtesy Michael Langford page 84 (no. 12); Steve Littman courtesy Lux Distribution page 75 (no. 10); London Transport Museum page 262 (both), 263; Bob Long/BBC page 307 (no. 9); Lucasfilm Ltd page 307 (no. 15), 309 (no. 5); Manchester City Art Gallery page 61 (right); Stuart Marshall courtesy Lux Distribution page 75 (no. 15); Kate Meynell courtesy Lux Distribution page 74 (no. 11); MGM courtesy The Ronald Grant Archive page 259; Pier Gallery, Stromness, Orkney page 60/61 (background); courtesy David Penney and Island Records (EMI) page 295 (no. 15); Keith Piper courtesy Lux Distribution page 75 (no. 13); Queensbury Hunt Levien, London page 177 (no. 15); Lisa Rhodes courtesy Lux Distribution page 75 (no. 3); courtesy Mary Robert page 84 (no. 7); Simon Robertshaw courtesy Lux Distribution page 75 (no. 14); John Rodgers/FSP page 307 (no. 5); The Ronald Grant Archive page 30, 31 (both), 33 (background and centre); © Ronald Searle, 1954, page 31; Royal College of Art Archives & Collection; Herbert Spencer/Typographic Magazine, cover and page 266 (no. 12); © Martin Smith page 193 (no. 14); © Sunday Times Magazine page 39 (top left); Mike Stubbs courtesy Lux Distribution page 74 (no. 12); John Tappenden courtesy Lux Distribution page 74 (no. 6) ; © Tate Gallery, London page 29 (no.13), 43 (no. 3), 58 (no. 11), 59 (no. 8), (no. 9), 63 (top), 66 (no. 1), 70 (no. 7), 95 (no. 3); Tate Gallery, London/© John Nash Trust page 27 (no. 13), 37 (no. 13); Tate Gallery, London/©Alan Bowness, Hepworth Estate page 63 (top); Tate Gallery, London/© Mrs D Mahoney page 28 (no. 12); Tate Gallery, London/© Keith Milow page 42 (no. 7); Tate Gallery, London/© Michael Moon page 41 (no. 13); Tate Gallery, London/© David Tremlett page 42 (no. 6); Tate Gallery, London/© Anthony Wishaw page 34 (no. 12); Richard Taylor page 297 (no. 15); courtesy Rt. Hon. The Lord Tennyson page 260 (no. 7); Twentieth Century Fox courtesy The Ronald Grant Archive page 248; Uden Associates page 301 (no. 14); Victoria and Albert Museum page 88 (no. 1), (no. 6), (no. 11), 89 (no. 3), (no. 5), (no. 15), 90 (no. 1), 92 (no. 1), (no. 6), 93 (no. 5), (no. 10), 118 (no. 7), 168 (no. 1), (no. 6), (no. 7), 169 (no. 3), (no. 5), (nos 9, 10, 13, 14, 15), 170 (nos 2, 6, 7, 11), 171 (no. 3), (no. 4), (nos 9, 10, 13, 14, 15), 172, 173, 174 (all), 176 (no. 12), 177 (no. 10), 178 (no. 1), 179 (no. 4), 181 (no. 14), 183, 184 (both), 185, 199 (no. 15), 223 (no. 14), 231 (no. 5), 265 (all); Warner Brothers courtesy The Ronald Grant Archive page 256/57 (all); ©Albert Watson page 301 (no. 15); courtesy Boyd Webb page 81 (bottom); courtesy Boyd Webb and Anthony D'Offay Gallery, London page 83 (both); Whitechapel Art Gallery page 64 (no. 2), (no. 12), page 65 (no. 10); The Whitworth Art Gallery, University of Manchester page 218 (no. 11), 219 (no. 9), 220 (nos 6, 7, 11), 221 (no. 3), (nos 8, 9, 13), 222 (no. 1), (no. 2), 223 (no. 8), (no. 13); Why Not Associates page 278 (both), 279 (both).

Many film and video works from RCA alumni are available from: Lux Distribution, The Lux Centre for film, video and digital arts, 2-4 Hoxton Square, London N1 6NU. Where no acknowledgement is given, the source is the Royal College of Art Archive or Collection.

Every effort has been made to acknowledge correctly and contact the source and copyright holder of each picture. The publisher apologises for any unintentional errors or omissions.

Photography Credits

Illustrations on these pages appear by kind permission of the following (in alphabetical order):

Alex Bailey page 301 (no. 13); 309 (no. 14); Richard Compton page 114 (all); David Churchill/Arcaid page 142 (no. 1); Mat Colishaw page 249 (no. 8); Magnus Dennis/Richard Dennis Gallery page 112 (no. 2), (no. 6), (no. 7), (no. 11), 113 (nos 3, 4, 5, 8, 9, 10, 13), 116 (no. 1), (no. 2), (no. 7), (no. 11), 117 (no. 4), (no. 5), (no. 9), 118 (no. 1), 119 (no. 10), 130 (no. 6), (no. 11), 131 (no. 3), (no. 13), 133 (no. 14), Richard Dennis page 112 (no. 1); Paul Rice/Richard Dennis page 168 (no. 2), (no. 11), (no. 12), 169 (no. 5), (no. 8), 170 (no. 1), (no. 12), 171 (no. 8); Richard Dennis Gallery page 176 (no. 1), 179 (no. 13), 196 (no. 2), 197 (no. 13); Robert Fairer page 251 (bottom); Jonathan Fisher page 307 (no. 15); Graham Gaunt page 147 (no. 15); Julian Hawkins page 127 (no. 4); Tim Hill page 187 (no. 13); courtesy Jay Jopling, London page 56/57; Andy Lane page 308 (no. 7); Liam Longman page 307 (no. 14); Keith Parry page 124 (no. 11); Louie Quayle page 280 (no. 7); Rocco Redondo page 277 (no. 4); Rocco Redondo and Photodisc page 277 (no. 3); Doc Rowe page 309 (no. 15); Phil Sayer page 164; Sham page 147 (no. 4); Lord Snowdon page 20, page 214.

Every effort has been made to acknowledge correctly and contact the source and copyright holder of each picture. The publisher apologises for any unintentional errors or omissions.

INDEX

319